Ethnic Ironies

Ethnic Ironies

Latino Politics in the 1992 Elections

EDITED BY
Rodolfo O. de la Garza
University of Texas at Austin
and Louis DeSipio
University of Illinois at Urbana-Champaign

WITH A FOREWORD BY
Bruce E. Cain

WestviewPress
A Division of HarperCollinsPublishers

*For Ileana, David, and Daniel, and
for Janet*

All rights reserved. Printed in the United States of America. No part of this publication may be reproduced or transmitted in any form or by any means, electronic or mechanical, including photocopy, recording, or any information storage and retrieval system, without permission in writing from the publisher.

Copyright © 1996 by Westview Press, Inc., A Division of HarperCollins Publishers, Inc.

Published in 1996 in the United States of America by Westview Press, Inc., 5500 Central Avenue, Boulder, Colorado 80301-2877, and in the United Kingdom by Westview Press, 12 Hid's Copse Road, Cumnor Hill, Oxford OX2 9JJ

A CIP catalog record for this book is available from the Library of Congress.
ISBN 0-8133-8910-0.—ISBN 0-8133-3012-2 (pbk.).

The paper used in this publication meets the requirements of the American National Standard for Permanence of Paper for Printed Library Materials Z39.48-1984.

10   9   8   7   6   5   4   3   2   1

Contents

List of Tables	vii
Foreword, Bruce E. Cain	ix

PART ONE
NATIONAL OVERVIEW — 1

1. Latinos and the 1992 Elections: A National Perspective,
   Rodolfo O. de la Garza and Louis DeSipio — 3

PART TWO
THE OLD RELIABLES: MEXICAN AMERICANS IN
SMALL WESTERN STATES — 51

2. Conventional Politics Under Unusual Circumstances:
   Latinos and the 1992 Election in New Mexico,
   F. Chris García — 53

3. An Essential Vote: Latinos and the 1992 Elections in Colorado,
   Rodney E. Hero — 75

4. Promise and Missed Opportunity: The 1992 Latino Vote
   in Arizona, *Manuel Avalos* — 95

PART THREE
THE MUST-WINS: KEY STATES WITH LARGE LONG-TERM
LATINO ELECTORATES — 111

5. Unrealized Expectations: Latinos and the 1992 Elections
   in Texas, *Valerie J. Martínez* — 113

6. Theory, Reality, and Perpetual Potential: Latinos in the 1992
   California Elections, *Fernando Guerra and Luis Ricardo Fraga* — 131

PART FOUR
THE NEW KIDS ON THE BLOCK: KEY STATES WITH NEW
AND POTENTIALLY INFLUENTIAL LATINO ELECTORATES 147

7   Leverage Without Influence: Illinois Latino Politics in 1992,
    Roberto Rey 149

8   The Conservative Enclave Revisited: Cuban Americans in
    Florida, *Dario Moreno and Christopher Warren* 169

9   Puerto Ricans in Postliberal New York: The 1992 Presidential
    Election, *Angelo Falcón* 185

About the Contributors 211
About the Book 213
Index 215

Tables

1.1	Latino Share of the 1992 Statewide Vote, Selected States	30
1.2	Latino Voter Turnout, by State, 1988 and 1992	31
1.3	Latino Influence and the 1992 Elections	32
1.4	Turnout and Victor's Margin in Congressional Races with Latino Candidates, 1992	36
2.1	Reported Voting and Registration in New Mexico Presidential Elections, 1980-1992, by Race and Hispanic Origin	54
3.1	The Distribution of Latinos in Colorado, Most Heavily Hispanic Counties	76
3.2	Latino Voting Patterns in Denver County, 1992	79
3.3	Latino Voting Patterns in Adams County, 1992	80
3.4	Latino Voting Patterns in Pueblo County, 1992	81
3.5	Latino Voting Patterns in Conejos County, 1992	82
3.6	Latino Voting Patterns in Costilla County, 1992	83
3.7	Latinos and the 1992 Colorado Presidential Vote	92
4.1	Mean Household Income, by Race and Ethnicity, for Arizona and Major Counties, 1979, 1989	97
4.2	Voter Turnout for Presidential Election in Maricopa County Precincts with High Latino Population	107
5.1	Distribution of Latinos in Texas, by County	115
5.2	Voter Distribution and Turnout for 1992 Presidential and Vice-Presidential Candidates, by County	120
5.3	Voter Distribution and Turnout for Judge, Court of Criminal Appeals, Place 3, by County	122
6.1	Support for Major Party Candidates, by Race and Ethnicity, 1988 and 1992	138
6.2	Characteristics of Congressional Districts Won by Latinos, 1992, Los Angeles County	140

6.3	Characteristics of Vacant Assembly Districts Won by Latinos, 1992, Los Angeles County	142
7.1	Selected Socioeconomic Indicators for Latinos, Whites, and African Americans in Cook, Du Page, Kane, Lake, McHenry, and Will Counties	151
7.2	Illinois Cities with Greatest Latino Population	152
7.3	Population of the City of Chicago, by Race and Hispanic Origin	152
7.4	Vote Totals, by Region, Illinois 1992 Presidential Primary	157
7.5	1992 Chicago Presidential Primary Election, Vote by Ward Composition	158
7.6	Latino Vote in the Presidential Primary, by Ancestry	159
7.7	Illinois 1992 Presidential General Election, by Region	159
7.8	Chicago 1992 Presidential General Election, Vote by Ward Composition	161
8.1	Dade County's Changing Hispanic Population	172
8.2	Voting in Dade County, by Race and Ethnicity, 1992 Presidential Election	173
8.3	Hispanic Support for Democratic Presidential Candidates, Dade County Precincts	173
8.4	Hispanic Support for Democratic Candidates in Statewide Races, Dade County Precincts	179

Foreword

Bruce E. Cain

At the start of each new presidential election cycle, political reporters engage in the ritual of writing background stories about the American electorate. In recent years, these include articles about the potential political influence of the Latino community. Will Latinos finally wield the kind of influence in the upcoming election that their population numbers suggest they should have, they ask, or is this the year that the Republican party will make significant inroads into the Latino vote? Often, the press looks to party operatives and political consultants for answers to these questions, and the professionals, ever mindful that expectations matter greatly in politics, "spin" their responses with careless disregard for the evidence of recent history.

In fact, the best answers to these questions lie in the results of the last couple of elections. While normal electoral patterns occasionally undergo sweeping and dramatic political shifts due to extraordinary events, major crises, or charismatic individuals, change tends more typically to be evolutionary and incremental. Fortunately for political scientists, groups and interests show remarkable continuity in their behavior over time even when individuals act less predictably. Recent history, it turns out, does contain lessons for those who are willing to learn.

The value of this volume and its predecessors is that they establish a historical record about Latinos and national elections that enables us to distinguish between constant and variable behavior from one election to the next. Also, instead of the projective spin that political operatives offer, the scholars in this volume have tried very carefully and dispassionately to determine precisely how influential Latinos were in the 1992 election.

There is much useful descriptive detail in the pages that follow, but at the same time, all of the authors have tried to do more than simply detail what happened in each state. They have also attempted to come to grips with the questions of what it means to have influence over an election, and whether Latinos met those conditions in 1992. Several themes emerge from the experiences of the states discussed in this volume.

The first is that the federalist structure of U.S. elections mediates the influence of Latinos in various ways, some positive and some negative. The presidential election itself has two components: the popular vote and the electoral college. In theory, a group of any size could potentially decide an election, but the odds of being "decisive" (i.e., having a change in a group's vote would result in a change in electoral outcome) vary positively with size. Consequently, year in and year out, larger groups will have a greater chance of being decisive in the popular vote outcome. For this reason, Latinos, constituting only 9 percent of the national population and less than 5 percent of the actual presidential electorate, cannot count on being decisive in the popular vote except in very close elections.

The situation, however, is somewhat different in the electoral college, and it is in this sense that the federalist structure of U.S. elections helps all geographically concentrated minorities, such as Latinos. If a minority group is concentrated in large enough numbers in a state where the competitive balance is even, that group can be electorally decisive at the state level. Given the winner-take-all allocation of electoral college votes to the winning candidate in a state, a group can therefore be decisive in the electoral college even when it is not decisive in the popular vote. In this sense, the electoral college structure gives minorities multiple political leveraging opportunities.

This is important to bear in mind as one reads the accounts of what happened in each of the states. As de la Garza and DeSipio point out in Chapter 1, the curious feature of the 1992 election was that the swing states in which Latinos were decisive to the outcome were not the "large states with significant Latino populations" but, rather, the smaller states and the states with smaller Latino populations. In Colorado, for instance, Rodney Hero concludes that Latino support was essential to Clinton's narrow 4 percent margin of victory over Bush in 1992. On the other side, Moreno and Warren find that the heavy support of Cuban Americans for Bush was essential to Bush's narrow eighty-six-thousand-vote victory in Florida. Latinos were not decisive in the popular vote or in the states with the largest concentrations of Latinos like California and Texas, but they were decisive in a couple of states in an election where electoral votes mattered. In other words, the system gives minority groups like Latinos a number of opportunities to be decisive, and the mere fact that *ex ante* their vote could make the difference in any of a number of state outcomes guarantees that the candidates, being risk averse, will have to pay attention to them.

The prospect of being decisive in state elections brought some measure of responsiveness from the candidates (although not as much as some of the authors would have preferred). For instance, the Cubans were able to secure the endorsements of both Bush and Clinton for the Torricelli bill. By contrast, most of the authors believe that Mexican Americans got far less in the way of specific, targeted promises because promises ran against the grain of Clinton's strategy of trying to win back middle-class voters for the Democratic party. Thus, he carefully avoided making specific commitments to the Mexican American community.

Even so, we learn that the National Hispanic Leadership Agenda was permitted to testify before the Democratic party platform committee and was "pleased with the degree to which Latino community needs were included in the final platform" (de la Garza and DeSipio). In addition, several authors point out that the Republicans based their messages to Latinos on the weakness of Clinton's record in Arkansas with respect to English only and minority business preferences. It cannot be said that the candidates totally ignored issues of interest to Mexican Americans.

A second federalist element that works to the advantage of minority groups like Latinos is the importance of Congress and state legislatures. The American system provides many points of entry for those who would influence public policy. As the authors of this book document, Latinos were able to make gains in a number of states following the 1990 round of redistrictings. In Congress, the number of Latino-held districts increased from 11 to 17, and in the state legislatures, they increased from 131 to 157. Among the more significant gains, Cuban Americans picked up several state legislative seats in Florida, and Mexican Americans picked up one congressional and three assembly seats in California. Many of these gains could be attributed to the enforcement of the 1982 amendments to the Voting Rights Act of 1965. Recent decisions such as *Shaw v. Reno* raise the prospect of smaller gains in the next round of redistricting.

Another major theme in this volume is that the conditions for being maximally influential are very strict and hard to meet. Several of the articles develop or elaborate on existing lists of conditions for political influence. For the purposes of making a simple, but important, point, I would organize these conditions into three categories. The first is luck or circumstance. Latinos, we are told, will be maximally influential when elections are competitive in a state or nationally. The closer the margin between the two candidates, the more likely that a minority can be the swing group. But what determines whether the election is competitive? For the most part, a number of things that Latinos cannot control by themselves, such as whether both parties field strong candidates, what others in the majority groups think of those candidates, and how effectively those candidates and their consultants use their resources in the campaign. By themselves, Latinos cannot make a presidential race competitive, and thus the condition of competitiveness is a matter of exogenous circumstance, or, to put it another way, a matter of luck.

Other conditions fall into the category of skill. The ability of elites to stay unified is one example, and except for the case of Puerto Ricans in New York, the Latino leadership has been relatively successful in that regard in recent years. Substantive advocacy on behalf of the Latino community is another example, and here we can point to the efforts of the NHLA (the National Hispanic Leadership Agenda) and Hispanic PAC-USA. Whether either demonstrated great skill is apparently a debatable question. De la Garza and DeSipio maintain that while the NHLA carefully and thoughtfully identified an agenda of issues important to the Latino community (including civil rights, education, health, housing, and economic opportunity), officials in both the Clinton and the Bush campaigns accused them of not being well organized and not getting proposals to them in a timely fashion. With respect to Hispanic PAC-USA, it is simply too early to say whether pooling money in this way will substantially increase Latino political power.

The last set of factors can be categorized as effort. How much effort is put into making the Latino community a political force in a given election? Did Latino organizations and incumbents make major attempts to register Latinos? Was there any get-out-the-vote? A number of authors allude to the fact that the motivation to provide effort is influenced by various factors, such as whether Latinos think that they might be decisive, whether there are issues of importance to Latinos on the ballot, and whether any of the lower-level races are going to be competitive. Unfortunately, since many of the majority Latino seats are competitive only in the primary (if at all), the safety of these districts undercuts the incentive to turn out in November.

Ironically, turnout can rise even though luck or circumstance inhibits real effort. This seems to have been the case in 1992. The national Democratic party put little sustained effort into Latino registration or mobilization yet turnout among Latinos was up. Even more remarkably, Clinton wrote off Texas, yet turnout among Latinos in that state rose 6 percent. In other words, the forces driving up participation in the electorate as a whole were also driving it up among Latinos.

This brings up an important point, namely, that, *ceteris paribus*, luck is more important in determining Latino political influence than is skill or effort. If the circumstances are right, Latinos can be maximally influential with little effort or skill. However, if conditions are not right, no amount of effort or skill will overcome that advantage. What saves the situation for Latinos is that the fractured, federalist American electoral system provides enough opportunities so that circumstances can be right in at least a few places. On the margin, effort and skill can leverage those opportunities into well-defined policy gains.

A question that is not posed in this volume, but one that surely deserves an answer, is whether promises extracted during an election mean anything in the long run anyway. They certainly are problematic if those promises run against the current of majority opinion. As the 1994 election demonstrated, the anti-immigrant themes of the Buchanan campaign foreshadowed the Proposition 187 campaign in California. The importance of the Latino vote to the Democratic coalition helps keep the Democratic party on the more moderate side of these issues, but the electoral logic of heeding the salient, strongly felt positions of the majority is compelling. Interest groups in the United States generally are most effective in securing promises in areas that are not salient and important to the electoral majority. The median voter's power in U.S. elections is such that targeted promises that are opposed by a caring majority are probably not worth the effort or skill it takes to secure them.

The large role that luck plays in these matters helps to explain a curious third theme of this volume, namely, that, even though many of the formal conditions for maximal political influence were missing in 1992, Latinos managed to make some gains in that election. On the face of it, the conditions in 1988 were better suited for Latinos. Dukakis owed his victory in Texas to the Latino voters in that state. Dukakis had a better record on minority rights than Clinton and was not running a campaign deliberately targeted to the white middle class. But in the end, luck is the key. Perot siphoned off disaffected Bush voters, and Clinton had just enough of the rest to win. Latinos could not be decisive in the big states like California or Texas, but they did swing a couple of small states and could claim to be an important part of Clinton's election constituency. Clinton proved to be fairly responsive to women and minorities in his appointments and has stood with the Latino community on NAFTA, immigration, and affirmative action.

The problem turned out not to be the promises made by the incoming Democratic administration, but, rather, the shifting sands of public opinion among the majority white population. De la Garza and DeSipio and Guerra and Fraga mention that one of the critical factors in Latino influence is the ability to minimize white backlash. In a sense, this is critically true, but at the same time, it is also an almost impossible demand to make of the Latino leadership. At one level, this view asks Latinos to try to control something they cannot control—the positions that white voters will take. But even if they could, there is a curious dilemma implicit in this strategic question. Not to push specific, targeted demands is to pass up the opportunity to use the system to advantage, but to be too successful risks incurring the backlash of the majority. The optimal electoral strategy has to take into account not only the short-term consequence of securing a given promise, but also the long-term consequences of winning those promises—and all of this in an environment where chance is a major factor. Winning political influence is not an easy matter, as this volume amply demonstrates. Latino leaders should not be too hard on themselves if what they achieve is not all that they hoped for.

Bruce E. Cain
Berkeley, CA

PART ONE

National Overview

	United States 1992
Population	251,447,000
Latino population	22,096,000
% Latino of total population	8.8
% Mexican American of Latino population	63.6
% Puerto Rican of Latino population	10.6
% Cuban American of Latino population	4.7
% Other Hispanic of Latino population	21.1
Voting population	113,866,000
Latino voters	4,238,000
% Latino of voting population	3.7
Latino adult noncitizens	5,910,000
Electoral votes	538

1

Latinos and the 1992 Elections: A National Perspective

Rodolfo O. de la Garza and Louis DeSipio

For Latino politics, 1992 was an unusual year.[1] Throughout the presidential campaign, Latino organizations and leaders played a diminished formal role compared with their involvement in the 1988 presidential election. None of the presidential candidates staked their candidacy on expectations of Latino support. In the primaries, Latino voters played no particular role in conferring either party's nomination. While both parties offered symbolic and substantive roles to Latinos in crafting the party platforms and in the convention, neither presidential candidate used the period between the primaries and the general elections to reach out to Latinos specifically or to raise the salience of Latino issues within the national debate. The general election campaign moved away from the large states with significant Latino populations, such as California, Illinois, New York, and Texas, and toward states with few Latino voters, such as in the industrial Midwest, or to small states with significant proportions of Latino voters, such as New Mexico, Colorado, and New Jersey. All of the indicators thus suggest that Latinos had less impact on the 1992 election than on the 1988 election.

Ironically, however, Latino voters had a greater effect on the results of the 1992 election than they have had on any election since 1960. Thus, Latino communities may well have emerged from this election in a good position to influence policy outcomes during President Clinton's first term.[2] In this chapter, we compare these results to the expectations created by the role Latinos played in the 1988 campaign. We then seek to explain how all this came about. We will also analyze the Latino role in major 1992 state-level elections as well as the communities' own efforts to shape the national policy agenda.

The Role of Latinos in National Elections

In a series of studies, we have joined others in exploring Latino political participation as well as candidate and party outreach to Latinos. In a parallel study to this volume, we examined the interaction between Latino electorates and national-level candidates in the 1988 campaign nationally and in eight states (de la Garza and DeSipio 1992). We also studied the 1990 elections through a narrower focus on Latino community-level politics in five core Latino barrios (de la Garza, Menchaca, and DeSipio 1994). In a separate volume offering descriptive results from the Latino National Political Survey (LNPS), we reported on the partisan leanings, political values, and policy preferences of Mexican American, Puerto Rican, and Cuban citizens and noncitizens (de la Garza et al. 1992). The LNPS has also spawned a series of academic papers that analyze various aspects of Latino electoral participation (Falcón et al. 1991; DeSipio and de la Garza 1992; García et al. 1992) and electoral nonparticipation (de la Garza and DeSipio 1993; DeSipio 1993).

Other recent studies have also grappled with Latino political participation. Hero (1992) has offered a structural explanation for how Latino electoral success has been limited. Pachon (1991) has identified high rates of noncitizenship as the single most important factor that has limited Latino electoral participation (also see Pachon and DeSipio 1994). Shorris (1992) questions the idea of a common Latino political identity in a manner that nicely complements the findings of the Latino National Political Survey. Chávez (1991) argues that the only limitation on Latino political empowerment is a self-serving and out-of-touch Latino leadership that serves its own ends, not those of a Latino community in need only of assimilation. The work of the National Association of Latino Elected Officials (NALEO) has documented the rapid gain in Hispanic elected officials at the local level (NALEO 1992a; Pachon and DeSipio 1992). Several studies of ethnic relations at the state and local levels complement these national, theoretical examinations of Latino politics (Arian et al. 1991; Jackson and Preston 1991; Grenier and Stepik 1992).

While it is not possible to do justice here to the findings of this diverse range of literature, those results helped us frame this analysis and influenced our expectations regarding the role Latinos would have in the 1992 presidential race.

A recurring theme of these studies is that rarely do Latinos significantly influence state or national electoral outcomes. This belief flies in the face of many unsubstantiated claims that the Latino vote is important because of the rapid growth of this population over the past two decades. Why is this the case and why did we anticipate that Latinos would again play a relatively minor formal role in the 1992 elections? There are two reasons. The first relates to Latinos' demographic characteristics. The second looks to how political institutions have failed to mobilize Latinos into the electoral process.

Four demographic characteristics of the Latino communities need to be understood before discussing Latino political participation. Mexicans and Puerto Ricans, who together constitute three-fourths of the Latino population, are younger, poorer, less educated and have a much higher rate of noncitizenship than Anglos (DeSipio and Rocha 1992; Pachon et al. 1992). Consequently, they are much less electorally active than Anglos. When income, education, and youth are controlled for statistically, however, Mexican American voting rates are slightly higher than those of Anglos (Wolfinger and Rosenstone 1980). A study of Latinos in California also found that "once one compares [U.S. citizens] of similar socioeconomic position, differences in participation evaporate" (Uhlaner, Cain, and Kiewiet 1989: 210).[3]

The effects of noncitizenship are particularly significant. In 1988, for example, among all U.S. citizens, 70.4 percent of adults were registered and 60.7 percent of all adults voted. Among Latino U.S. citizens, 56.6 percent were registered and 45.9 percent voted (U.S. Bureau of the Census [hereafter Census] 1989). When noncitizens and citizens are combined, Latino rates drop even further. In 1984, while 48.0 percent of Latino citizens voted, only 32.6 percent of all adult Latinos voted (Pachon and DeSipio 1988: 4). It should also be noted that noncitizenship rates among Latino adults vary considerably from a few percent in New Mexico to as many as 50 percent in California.

Candidates, campaigns, and political professionals are knowledgeable about Latino turnout rates. While they may not understand or care about the reasons, they understand the bottom line: investment in traditional voter mobilization in Latino neighborhoods generates relatively few votes because it will reach large numbers of noncitizens and equally large numbers of citizens who are less likely to vote. This does not mean that all statewide campaigns ignore the Latino vote. It does mean that such campaigns look to Latino electorates to influence electoral outcomes much less frequently than one might think, given the population's swelling numbers.

Another demographic trait, however, serves both to increase the importance of Latinos and to make them more likely to play a role in close state and national elections, such as the 1992 presidential campaign. Latinos are geographically concentrated in nine states, including five of the six most populous. These states contain 75 percent of the electoral votes needed to win the presidency. As a result, any close race will have to target some or all of these states.

Yet demographics alone do not explain Latino voting patterns. Voter mobilization, or its absence, is also an important factor in explaining low rates of Latino voting. Until the mid-1970s, discrimination and voter intimidation prevented many Mexican Americans and other Latinos from participating in American politics with the same freedoms and protections as other Americans. Although the extension of the Voting Rights Act virtually eliminated the institutionalized discrimination and intimidation, it did nothing to mobilize newly enfranchised electorates (de la Garza and DeSipio 1993). Parties, candidates, and campaigns also did not reach out to these newly enfranchised voters. Instead, they have increasingly targeted those who are already electorally active (Pachon and Argüelles 1993). Consequently, electoral institutions have virtually no presence in high-density, low-income Latino neighborhoods.

Immigration influences and helps reproduce the justification for the electoral marginalization of these barrios. Immigrants, who tend to reside in low-income neighborhoods, are introduced to American elections by this political vacuum. Most U.S.-born children of immigrants—U.S. citizens by birth—are reared in households where U.S. electoral participation is not an option because their parents tend not to naturalize and they live in neighborhoods bereft of electoral institutions. As a result, immigrants and their children are socialized into nonparticipation. Thus, the failure of electoral institutions to penetrate barrios and to mobilize Latino voters helps explain Latino nonvoting, not simply among older Latinos, who faced electoral discrimination prior to 1975, but also among new citizens and immigrants' children who are U.S. citizens. How these demographic and institutional factors interact to dampen Latino voting is more fully developed in de la Garza and DeSipio (1993) and in de la Garza, Menchaca, and DeSipio (1994: chap. 1).

Given Latinos' very limited influence in 1988, what, then, did we expect from Latino electorates in the 1992 presidential elections? The answer emerges from our analysis of both 1988 and 1990 elections. We began with Guerra's (1992) conclusions that Latinos in any given state could play a key role in presidential contests if

1. they united behind one candidate;
2. the contest was very close and the respective states were important to national victory;
3. long-term strategies for voter registration and mobilization were in place;
4. they were visible in the nominating convention and subsequent campaign;
5. the general election included state- and local-level Latino candidates and addressed issues of importance to Latino communities; and
6. either the party or the campaign had a strategy for mobilizing Latino voters without alienating the general electorate.

Although these conditions narrow the occasions when Latinos can influence national electoral outcomes, they establish a more realistic picture for Latino influence than do predictions based solely on the size of the Latino population.

Our 1988 study also documented that Latinos were more influential in the primaries and in the period around the party conventions than in the general election. Further, it indicated the importance of Latino elites, who acted as intermediaries between campaigns and potential Latino voters. Finally, it documented what had previously been anecdotal evidence of a slow migration by some Mexican American Democrats to the Republican party and the Republican party's concomitant efforts to attract the Mexican American electorate.

The study of Latinos in the 1990 elections reinforces and supplements the factors Guerra identified. First, local issues play a fundamental role in mobilizing Latino voters. In what was admittedly an off-year election in each of the five study sites, potential voters were primarily concerned with local problems and issues. Neighborhood residents repeatedly complained that candidates and campaigns failed to discuss such concerns. Further, the research on the 1990 elections demonstrated that candidate- or party-driven voter outreach or mobilization in most high-density Latino areas was virtually absent. Thus, our concern was that if Latinos were to play a significant role in the 1992 elections (or any role greater than their role in 1988), there would have to be extensive voter mobilization and direct candidate and campaign outreach in addition to there being close statewide races. Our research, however, has shown that outreach of this nature is increasingly rare.

Going into the 1992 presidential race, then, it appeared to us that Latinos could again have an important role in the primaries. Although candidates did not explicitly stake their candidacy on Latino votes, as was the case in 1988, the wide-open Democratic field raised the possibility that a cohesive electorate in a large state with an early primary could be influential. Mexican Americans in Texas, Latinos in Illinois, and Puerto Ricans in New York were well-placed to fill this role. Further, because the presidential race seemed to be close, we anticipated that the period around the party conventions would again see outreach to the Latino electorates. This targeted outreach is a safety device that candidates use to assure that they can turn to Latinos if needed later in the election. Finally, because the election remained close, we anticipated that both candidates would compete for Latino votes in large states such as Texas, Illinois, California, and New York.

We expected, in sum, that the 1992 election met most or all of the conditions necessary for Latinos to play a major role. For Latinos and other electorates, however, the election defied expectations.

Throughout this chapter and this volume, we will return to the questions of when Latinos can and do influence candidate selection and electoral outcomes. Following the model established in our study of the 1988 elections (de la Garza and DeSipio 1992), we examine the primaries, the period around the party conventions, and the general elections as discrete phenomena.

The Primaries

The 1992 presidential campaign differed from many of its predecessors. The campaign season began quite late and many of the major potential Democratic candidates decided not to compete. While their reasons were never made public, party luminaries such as Jesse Jackson, Mario Cuomo, Jay Rockefeller, Al Gore, and Lloyd Bentsen opted out of the race. The media characterized the eventual field—Bill Clinton, Paul Tsongas, Jerry Brown, Tom Harkin, Bob Kerrey, Douglas Wilder, and Larry Agran—as second-string if not second-rate.

The decisions by the first tier of Democrats to avoid the race reinforced an image of George Bush as largely invincible. In addition to the benefits of incumbency, he enjoyed high popular support due to the Gulf War. Yet, despite this perception of invincibility, Bush faced two Republican opponents—Pat Buchanan and David Duke. While neither of these candidates lasted beyond the early primaries, they deflated the incumbent president's aura of invulnerability.

The Democratic Primaries

Latino voters did not play a decisive role in the Democratic party primaries in 1992. The promise of Latino primary votes did not entice candidates into the field, as it had in 1988. Further, the candidates who did run did not create a specific message targeted to Latino voters in any of the primary states. While Latinos did play a role in several primaries, the nature of their support followed the tendencies of other Democratic voters in these states, so they could not claim responsibility for a candidate's victory. This is in sharp contrast to 1988, when Texas's Mexican American Democrats could point to their votes as the difference between victory and defeat for Michael Dukakis (de la Garza 1992a).

Nonetheless, several of the Democratic candidates made efforts to reach out to Latinos. Bill Clinton and Tom Harkin appointed Latino constituency directors (María Echaveste and Alberto José Cardelle, respectively). Clinton also had Latino staff in Little Rock and in the primary states. At the campaign's peak, five of Clinton's thirty-two field staff and one member of the senior staff were Latino. It is also important to note that, for the most part, these staff members were not placed in Latino constituency positions, but were instead spread throughout the campaign organization. Furthermore, most of these appointees were neither tied to nor deeply involved with traditional Latino organizations. María Echaveste, for example, was appointed because of a long-standing association with Hillary Clinton that developed when they served on the board of the New World Foundation. Marcella Sandoval, who by the campaign's end was Clinton's field director for the western states, became involved in the campaign as a result of organizing a "Young Washingtonians for Clinton" initiative. Jerry Brown's much more informal campaign always mentioned Latinos as part of his core constituency of the politically excluded.

Clinton's campaign actively sought Mexican American votes, particularly in Texas. During one of his first campaign trips, Clinton visited South Texas and earned endorsements from prominent local elected officials (Hight 1991). Commentator Jesse Treviño (1991) noted that "many of the same Hispanic politicians who got behind Dukakis early have materialized in Clinton's corner." Clinton also attended the annual conference of the (Texas) Mexican American Democrats (MAD). His strategy of actively seeking these votes early in the race paid off. In January, he received MAD's endorsement with an overwhelming 97 percent of the vote (Hight 1992a). This endorsement came the same weekend that the state Democratic Executive Committee endorsed him, making Clinton the odds-on favorite in the Texas primary.

Clinton received these endorsements despite what would come to be described as his history of insensitivity to Latino issues. For example, as governor, Clinton had signed legislation making English the official language of Arkansas and defining "minority businesses" as only African American enterprises. Although some MAD leaders were informed about this record, it was not brought to the attention of the Mexican American electorate before the Texas primary.

Although not as strongly as the MAD delegates, Latino voters supported Clinton on primary election day. Super Tuesday saw the first competition for Democratic Latino votes in Texas and Florida. In Texas, Clinton beat his two remaining opponents by a large margin—64 percent for Clinton to 19 percent for Paul Tsongas and 9 percent for Jerry Brown (Southwest Voter Research Institute [SVRI] 1992).[4] Clinton received majority support among all gender, age, education, income, and ideological categories of Texas Latinos, except for those with college degrees (49 percent) or with annual incomes of sixty thousand dollars or more (42 percent). Exit polls in Florida did not capture a sufficient number of Latinos to report on their preferences (*New York Times* [March 11, 1992]).

In the Illinois primary the following week, Clinton captured 60 percent of the Latino vote. Tsongas received 23 percent of the Latino votes and Brown garnered 9 percent (Midwest-Northeast Voter Registration and Education Project 1992).

In the next major primary state with significant numbers of Latino voters, New York, Clinton again bested his opponents. Earning 63 percent of the Latino votes, Clinton beat Brown's 26 percent and Tsongas's 10 percent (*Los Angeles Times* [April 9, 1992]). Even before the final round of primaries, which included California and New Mexico, Clinton had already assured his nomination.

The *New York Times* (July 12, 1992) aggregated the results of its primary election exit polls from the twenty-nine states with primaries. It found that 51 percent of Latinos supported Clinton, 30 percent supported Brown, and 15 percent supported Tsongas. While Clinton's support is somewhat lower and the rate for Brown somewhat higher than in the other exit polls reported here, the *Times* recap indicates an important point about Clinton's Latino support. Across all electorates, Clinton received 50 percent of the vote. Support among whites was 47 percent, and among blacks, 70 percent. Thus, Latinos gave Clinton slightly more support than did the population as a whole, but not too much more. This pattern holds in each of the states with large numbers of Democratic Latino voters.

In the Texas Democratic primary, for example, 64 percent of Latinos voted for Clinton. Although this number is substantial, 66 percent of Texas Democrats voted the same way. As a result, it is hard to argue that Latinos were integral to the Clinton victory in Texas. In Illinois, Clinton received 51 percent of the primary vote and 60 percent of the Latino vote. Without Latino support, Clinton's margin of victory would have been smaller. Thanks to Latino voters, he fashioned a majority victory in a multicandidate election. The Latino impact was more marked but less decisive in New York. Latino New York Democrats gave Clinton 63 percent of their votes. Statewide, he carried 41 percent of the vote to Tsongas's 29 percent and Brown's 26 percent. Although the gap between Latino and statewide voters was greater in New York than in the other states, New York Latinos do not make up a sufficient percentage of the statewide Democratic electorate to account for his 12 percent margin of victory. Thus, while we do not wish to diminish the importance of Latino Democratic voters, it is important to recognize that their votes were not decisive in any of the primary races.

The Republican Primaries

Latino voters were also marginal to the outcome of the Republican primaries. George Bush relied on their support, but did not actively campaign for the votes of Republican Latinos. Instead, the Republican party machinery used the primary period to prepare a Latino campaign for the general election. Latinos did, however, play contrasting symbolic roles in the competition to unseat George Bush as the Republican standard-bearer. Republican challengers both courted Latino votes and attacked Latino immigrants in their efforts to galvanize Republicans against George Bush. There are neither polling data nor anecdotal evidence to gauge the effectiveness of these efforts.

George Bush did not need Republican Latino voters to win his party's nomination. Although his campaign was shocked by Pat Buchanan's showing in New Hampshire, it had controlled the damage by the time Latino votes became important in the Super Tuesday primaries. According to a poll conducted the week before the primary, Bush was handily beating Buchanan in Florida by a margin of 68 to 19 percent (Sharp and Keen 1992). If this poll measured the true rates of Latino voting on election day, Bush's showing was to be several points short of his victory margin in 1988, which hinted, perhaps, that his base in the Cuban community might be weaker in the general election. Bush's margin in Texas was much stronger. According to *New York Times* exit polls, he beat Buchanan 83 percent to 17 percent (March 11, 1992). Indicative, perhaps, of animosity toward Buchanan's anti-immigrant message, Bush's victory margin among Texas Hispanics exceeded his margin among white voters by 13 percent.[5] President Bush did not face serious opposition in the primaries in other states with large Latino Republican constituencies.

While Bush faced some opposition early in the primary season, his campaign's efforts to reach Latino voters always focused on the general election. A *USA Today* poll early in the election year suggests the reasons for this strategy. In January respondents were asked whether they had voted for George Bush in 1988 and whether they anticipated that they would in November. Among all respondents, support for Bush declined from 53 percent to 47 percent. Among Hispanics, on the other hand, support increased from 30 percent to 46 percent (January 13, 1992). Only one other group—black women—saw a large increase (an increase of 50 percent over 1988). Bush's support among black women remained weak, however, increasing to only 15 percent.

Bush and his supporters within the Republican party used the period before the general election to strengthen traditionally weak ties to non-Cuban Latinos. For example, he spoke to the National Association of Hispanic Journalists by satellite. Unlike in 1988, however, he did not attend the annual conference of the League of United Latin American Citizens (LULAC). To counter Democratic party criticisms of its Hispanic record, the Republican party prepared an eighteen-page document describing Bush administration policies that benefited the Hispanic community ("The Hispanic Community and the Republican Party: The *Real* Record" 1992). The report lists Hispanic appointments to federal posts and names policy initiatives concerning education reform, economic growth, housing, crime, drugs, health care, civil rights and quotas, and the North American Free Trade Agreement (NAFTA). The document, essentially a series of negative sound bites, also describes Democratic flip-flops on key policy issues. Although it does not identify its audience, it seems to be a kit for local party leaders on how to conduct a reelection campaign for President Bush and how to sell the Republican party to traditionally Democratic Latinos.

Despite President Bush's seemingly wide support from Republican Latinos, both of his opponents in the primary campaign attempted to use the Latino communities, though in very different ways. David Duke brought his presidential campaign to the Miami Cuban community early in the campaign. In December 1991, he visited the city and found the nexus of Cuban political discussion—the radio call-in show (Kenen 1991). By this point in the campaign, Duke's strategy had narrowed to a focus on the Super Tuesday primaries, and Florida was integral. Seeking to distinguish Miami's Cubans (who are largely immigrant in origin) from his otherwise anti-immigrant position, Duke noted that Cubans have been a "tremendous asset" to the United States and that "they're Christian people, they're anti-communist" ("Inside Politics" 1991).

Duke's message was muted by the uproar over his presence in Miami at the invitation of controversial talk-show host Felipe Rivero (Stencel 1991). The Cuban leadership in Miami followed the lead of establishment Republicans nationwide and repudiated Duke. Jorge Más Canosa, president of the Cuban American National Foundation (CANF), said that "it is a disgrace that a Cuban invited him to Miami" (*Times of the Americas* [January 8, 1992]). Their fears proved groundless. At the time of his visit, Duke was supported by just 6 percent of Florida's Republicans. By the time of the Florida primary, Duke had largely dropped from the race and received few Cuban votes in Miami.

Pat Buchanan took a different tack. Instead of courting Cuban voters, he seemed to lump all Latinos into an undifferentiated negative category and used them to rally Republicans disaffected with President Bush and more broadly with changes in the composition of American society and American values. To protect national purity, he called for the "Buchanan Fence," a fenced-in trench along the U.S.-Mexico border that he promised would halt 90 percent of undocumented migration. The promise of the fence was just part of a broader, more cynical strategy to articulate the fears of a loss of American culture. Buchanan noted that "we're getting record amounts of immigration at the same time these institutions are breaking down—the family, the church, the schools.... All these things if you will are an assault on American culture at the same time you have masses of immigration coming in and you are deciding the character of your nation in [the] year 2025" (*Chicago Tribune* [December 24, 1991]). He added an economic threat to the cultural threat and attributed it to "many, or some Hispanics." He charged that these Hispanics wanted to "retain Spanish as a separate language and to require it in various places... People used to come here to be Americans... but a lot of folks are coming now, in the Southwest, coming to get the benefits of the welfare state" (Decker 1992).

More so than David Duke, Pat Buchanan was able to introduce his themes into the national debate. Although his electoral success steadily declined after a surprisingly strong showing in the New Hampshire primary, Buchanan continued to use immigration policy as a rallying cry. After the Los Angeles riots, for example, he charged that "foreigners are coming into this country illegally and burn[ing] down one of the greatest cities in America" (Brownstein 1992). Despite Buchanan's assurances that his comments were not anti-Latino, community leaders felt otherwise. Raúl Yzaguirre of the National Council of La Raza (NCLR) called his approach "racist, mean-spirited, and xenophobic" (*Los Angeles Times* [March 17, 1992]). In response to Buchanan's comments about the immigrant roots of the Los Angeles riots, Richard Martínez of the Southwest Voter Registration and Education Project (SVREP) accused Buchanan of "scaring people" and "appealing to literally the dark side of the soul, a fear of the other" (Brownstein 1992).

While there is no measure of the mobilizing effect of this rhetoric on the white vote, Buchanan's success among Latinos was limited. Despite opening a campaign office on Miami's Calle Ocho, he received the support of just 19 percent of the Republican Hispanics polled one week before the Florida primary (Sharp and Keen 1992). He did not seek Mexican American Republican votes in Texas, the other Super Tuesday state with Latino voters. By the time of the primaries in other states with large Latino Republican populations, Buchanan was in effect out of the race.

Between the Primaries and the General Elections: Establishing the Styles of the Presidential Race

George Bush was assured of winning his party's nomination by mid-April. Bill Clinton had to wait until late May, though he was relatively assured of the nomination by mid-April. This early conclusion to the primary season offered each campaign a long period to prepare for the fall. The entrance of Ross Perot into the race, however, confused both candidates' plans and continually created new imperatives that could not be anticipated in April.

The Democrats and Governor Clinton

With the end of the primary campaign season, Bill Clinton began to reach out to specific Democratic party constituency groups in preparation for the general elections. While he performed many of the traditional tasks to court blocs of voters, Clinton also used this period to distinguish his effort from those of recent Democratic nominees, particularly Walter Mondale and Michael Dukakis. Clinton spoke of inclusion for all Americans and was less likely to appear to pander to "special interest" groups within the society (Márquez 1992a; Szulc 1992). This difference was particularly marked in his dealings with the black community in general and with Jesse Jackson in particular, but was also felt by Latino leaders.

Clinton's new approach did not preclude some specific outreach to Latinos. As we have mentioned, Clinton sought MAD's endorsement and appointed a Latino constituency director during the primaries. Like Bush, he spoke to the annual meeting of the National Association of Hispanic Journalists in April (*Houston Chronicle* [April 25, 1992]). After the primary season ended, he attended the national LULAC convention (Ratcliffe 1992; Shannon 1992) and spoke to the annual meeting of NALEO by satellite. He also promoted José Villareal, a San Antonio attorney, from assistant general counsel to the campaign to deputy campaign manager.

Despite these activities, Clinton's campaign sought to speak to the needs of *all* Americans, not just Latinos or any other component of the Democratic coalition. This inclusiveness appeared in both the campaign's rhetoric and its actions. In a press release announcing that the candidate would attend the LULAC convention, Clinton is quoted as saying, "I come here to pledge to you an administration that looks like America, that feels like America, that understands the pain and promise of this country and will involve you and all Americans in the struggle to make it better ("Clinton Meets with Latino Leaders," July 2, 1992). In another visit, the campaign took its announcement of a national education plan to East Los Angeles College. Yet, it framed the proposed policy of federal college tuition assistance, job training for high school dropouts, and school choice in terms of the needs of all Americans (Boyarsky 1992; Ifill 1992a). Clinton's choice of Senator Al Gore as his running mate also reflected, to many, a betrayal of traditional Democratic efforts to balance the ticket among party constituencies. As a harbinger of how Latino leaders would respond to Clinton's strategy, Los Angeles County Supervisor Gloria Molina showed surprise and disappointment with Clinton's choice by describing the candidates as "two white men from the South" (Benanti 1992).

The Democratic party convention demonstrated the dualism as well. On the one hand, the convention and platform did not specifically reach out to Latinos or address Latino issues. On the other, Latinos had a more significant role in the convention than at any previous party convention. Hispanic delegates and alternates numbered approximately 373 out of the 4,928 delegates and alternates (*National Hispanic Reporter* [July 1992]).[6] According to the Midwest-Northeast Voter Registration Project, approximately 71 percent supported Clinton (Márquez 1992a).[7] The 373 Latino delegates in 1992 exceeded the 358 in 1988 and the 340 in 1984.

Latino leaders also played major formal party and convention roles. Gloria Molina cochaired the Rules Committee. Congressman Edward Roybal served as cochair of the convention and emceed the nomination of Al Gore. Congressman Bill Richardson chaired the platform's drafting committee. Congressman Esteban Torres and Speaker of the New Mexico House of Representatives Ray Sánchez served on the Rules Committee. Texas Attorney General Dan Morales, Texas Railroad Commissioner Lena Guerrero, and U.S. Representatives Kika de la Garza and José Serrano addressed the convention, though many of these speeches came during the ill-attended and poorly watched afternoon sessions (Szulc 1992). The party had two Latino vice-chairs, Carmen Pérez and Jack Otero. Thus, the convention and the Democratic party demonstrated that Latinos had senior roles.

The Democrats reported that this would be the first Spanish broadcast of a party convention available nationally (Payne 1992). The Democratic party made arrangements to broadcast podium activity in Spanish on C-SPAN. In addition, Univisión interviewed Clinton during convention week.

The Republicans and President Bush

For two reasons, the Bush campaign did not use the period between the end of the primaries and the general election as well as it did in 1988 to reach out to constituencies that were not traditionally Republican, such as Latinos. First, Ross Perot entered the debate, if not the race. Second, the extreme tone of the Republican convention alienated many who had voted Republican in 1988, including moderate Republicans and "Reagan Democrats." Following the convention, therefore, the Bush campaign was distracted by Perot and concentrated on regaining its 1988 constituencies, which left little time for courting Hispanics.

The impact on the Bush campaign of Ross Perot's consideration of a race for the presidency has been (and will be) extensively analyzed and need not be discussed at length here (Ceaser and Busch 1993: chap. 4; Pomper et al. 1993). Instead, it is important to note that the Bush campaign was in disarray almost from the beginning. The Perot challenge exacerbated these problems, and, beginning in April,[8] the Republican effort focused more on Perot and on preserving core Republican constituencies than on reaching out to potential new Republican voters.

Despite this confusion within the campaign, the Republican National Committee and its Hispanic staff continued their well-established Latino outreach initiatives. While counting on high levels of support from Cuban Americans, the party also sought to increase Republican support among Mexican Americans and Puerto Ricans. The Republican National Committee conducted "surrogate training sessions" for local Hispanic Republican leaders. These sessions, conducted by senior-level campaign professionals, were designed to provide individual Republican activists with the skills to spread the party message. Once trained, Hispanic staff kept these activists informed with frequent fax messages discussing the daily message of the Bush campaign and providing them with talking points for the local press.

The party's Latino outreach strategy included attacking Clinton's record as governor vis-à-vis Latinos so as to distance Hispanic voters from Bill Clinton. It focused on five issues: (1) Clinton signed a bill making English the official language of Arkansas; (2) during Clinton's tenure as governor, Arkansas failed to pass a civil rights law, one of just two states without such a law; (3) Clinton failed to appoint Latinos to positions in Arkansas government; (4) Clinton signed into law a bill that defined minority businesses as those owned only by African Americans; and (5) the Arkansas state police implemented a policy during the Clinton administration that allowed them to stop cars with drivers meeting a profile that included "looking Hispanic" and having Texas license plates. By the end of the campaign, the Bush campaign and the Republican party had distributed over one hundred thousand bilingual fliers emphasizing these criticisms. Some or all of these points appear in almost all interviews with Republicans talking about the Latino vote, and they were the topics of speeches at Viva Bush! rallies.

The nurturing of a new generation of Latino Republicans, which had been under way for over a decade, continued at the Republican convention. According to the party, 238 of the 4,414 delegates and alternates were Latino. Six Latinos served on the Republican platform committee and 13 spoke before the convention. Among these, Orange County Supervisor Gaddi Vásquez directed the platform debate on economic policy and addressed the convention in Spanish and English. Colorado delegate Gloria Gonzales-Roemer seconded the nomination of President Bush. Other prominent Republican convention speakers included Florida U.S. Representative Ileana Ros-Lehtinen, Hispanic Chamber of Commerce President José Niño, Treasurer of the United States Catalina Villalpando, and New Jersey Assemblyman José Sosa. Houston restaurateur Ninfa Laurenzo served as convention cochair and opened the convention with the Pledge of Allegiance. These Hispanic Republican speakers were from each of the major Latino national-origin groups (seven Mexican Americans, four Cuban Americans, and two Puerto Ricans). Further, relative to the total number of Hispanics in the Republican and Democratic parties, Hispanic Republicans were better represented at their party's convention than were Hispanic Democrats at theirs. Responding to the Democrats' broadcast of their convention in Spanish, the Republicans also made arrangements with C-SPAN to carry a broadcast in Spanish of party activities (Payne 1992).

Perhaps the strongest advocate of Hispanics for Bush was the most unexpected—George P. Bush, the president's grandson and the son of Jeb and Columba Bush. Speaking on family night, George P. presented a polished and loving defense of his grandfather's devotion to family. "Family," he said, "is what makes my grandfather tick." He finished his statement, some said as an afterthought, with a shout of "Viva Bush." After an evening of negative and narrow messages about family, George P. electrified the convention (de la Isla 1992).

Despite these record high levels of Latino participation in the Republican convention, the stridency of the party's extremists turned off the Hispanic delegates. The party platform called for the use of the "tools, technologies, and structures necessary to secure the border," which angered and offended some Latino Republican delegates.[9] At their insistence, the party passed a resolution stating explicitly that the language of the platform did not mean a wall. While advocating ethnic diversity, the platform also warned that illegal immigration "threatens the social compact on which immigration is based" (Raasch 1992).

The party's turmoil also affected Republican Latinos when a rumor spread through the convention that Secretary of Interior Manuel Luján would be asked to step down in President Bush's second term. Although he was not mentioned by name, many interpreted the president's promise of new faces in the second term to signify Luján's departure (Eldridge 1992). Finally, one Latino added to the negative and moralistic messages of some convention speakers, which alienated many non-Republicans. U.S. Treasurer Villalpando dismissed Henry Cisneros's support for Bill Clinton because both he and Clinton were "skirt-chasers." This comment caused the president of LULAC, a Republican, to condemn Villalpando. "She has chosen to wage a personal assault on an individual [Cisneros] considered to be one of the most highly respected and talented public figures in the country," he noted (Franks 1992). Cisneros was more philosophical. "Desperate people," he said, "do desperate things" (Contreras 1992).

Few outside observers noticed the prominent positions of Latinos at the convention. The strident tone and intolerant message of many of the convention's leading speakers obscured the gains that Latinos had made within the party and the success of the party's efforts to include Latinos and other nontraditional Republicans in newly prominent roles (Contreras 1992; "The Politics of Exclusion" 1992).

Ross Perot

As Ross Perot began to consider running for the presidency, the only sure thing was that his campaign would be different. In terms of outreach to Latinos, he was either different or retrograde, depending on one's reading of American history. Prior to withdrawing from the race during the Democratic convention in July, he made no effort to reach out to Latinos as individuals or as a constituency. He spoke to no Latino groups, and there is no record that he named any Latinos to his National Advisory Panel of one hundred (the group was not fully formed at the time of his withdrawal) (De Witt 1992). Although he did make more of an effort to reach out to African Americans, the enduring legacy of this attempt was his controversial "you people" comment in a speech before the National Association for the Advancement of Colored People. He also visited Los Angeles after the riots. His focus, however, was the African American community and not Latinos (Stall 1992). This lack of outreach caused resentment among some Latinos and African Americans (Nagourney and Pesce 1992).

Curiously, despite the distance Perot maintained from Latinos in his early consideration of a campaign for the presidency, he appealed to many Hispanics. Exit polls taken during the California primary indicated that 34 percent of California Latinos favored Perot. While this was less than the 44 percent of whites supporting him, it exceeded the 24 percent support from the African American community (Page 1992). These numbers say little about the eventual support Perot would have received had he stayed in the race. Instead, they suggest an openness to Perot among some blacks and Latinos, despite a lack of active outreach to these groups or their leaders. Perot's message to the country as a whole rather than to groups was a model that Clinton had articulated but strayed from in the primaries, and that he would follow in the general election.

The General Election

Between January and Labor Day, the presidential election campaign experienced three distinct shifts. As we have indicated, President Bush was perceived as largely invincible by all but the Republican Right early in the race. Beginning in April, Ross Perot had come to lead in some polls, despite not yet being a candidate. Beginning with the Democratic convention (and Perot's withdrawal), Clinton led. This lead, though weak nationally, was particularly strong in several of the larger states with large numbers of electoral votes such as California, Illinois, and New York. Thus, the context of the discussion of the final stage of the 1992 campaign is Clinton leading Bush, at times by large margins in the electoral college, with Perot nearby on the sidelines.

The "Dukakis–Not" Democratic Campaign

As soon as the Democratic convention ended, Bill Clinton and Al Gore sought to distinguish themselves from the party's 1988 nominee. Where Dukakis had returned to Massachusetts to attend to state business and to take a vacation after the convention, Clinton and Gore immediately took the first of their highly successful bus tours. Throughout the fall, Clinton did things differently from Dukakis and other Democrats before him. This difference extended to many aspects of the style of the Clinton Latino campaign. Specifically, the campaign included Latinos and relied on Latino campaign staffers throughout the campaign. Yet, it did have a separate, or autonomous, strategy to win Latino votes. Clinton's personal efforts to reach out to Latinos appeared only at the end of the campaign, when the focus shifted to get-out-the-vote activities.

At a formal level, the most important aspect of the Clinton Latino campaign was "Adelante con Clinton!" This strategy was in the tradition of previous attempts by the Democrats to target constituency groups. María Echaveste, the campaign's Latino coordinator, directed the effort. The model for Adelante con Clinton! was the Viva Kennedy! clubs of the 1960 election. These clubs had galvanized and mobilized Mexican Americans for John Kennedy and may well have assured his victory in Texas and New Mexico, which in turn assured his victory in the electoral college (García and de la Garza 1977).

Clinton's Latino staff, led by José Villareal and María Echaveste, was initially opposed to developing a specific Latino component to the campaign. They preferred having Latinos integrated into the regular campaign structure, and their view temporarily prevailed. The established Latino leadership—including organizational leaders, union representatives, and elected officials—insisted on a traditional, targeted approach, however, and ultimately carried the day. Following a late August meeting in Little Rock with between sixty and one hundred traditional Latino Democratic leaders, the campaign acceded to their demands. Nonetheless, to emphasize that this was a new era, Villareal and Echaveste insisted on discarding the Viva nomenclature in favor of a fresh image; Adelante con Clinton! was launched.

Participants in the August meeting also helped design the tactics of Adelante con Clinton! They noted that Governor Dukakis did not meet with Latino leaders until two weeks before the election. Clinton's organization would work with each state's coordinated campaign to assure that these campaigns included a Latino outreach component. The coordinated campaigns were state- and congressional-district level voter outreach efforts designed by party chair Ron Brown to assure that state and local parties included traditional Democratic constituencies. Once established, Adelante con Clinton! distributed printed materials, reviewed (but did not create) English- and Spanish-language media directed to Latinos, assured that Latinos were appointed to senior positions within the coordinated campaigns in key states, responded to the concerns of Latino leaders and elected officials, and, generally, troubleshot.

Adelante con Clinton! also acted as an umbrella for state organizations. These efforts coordinated voter registration and get-out-the-vote drives. The most active of these was in Texas. Polls showed the presidential race in a virtual dead heat in early September. As a result, the Texas Adelante con

Clinton! effort launched a voter registration drive targeting thirty-three counties with high concentrations of Hispanics. The Texas effort also promised to undertake a get-out-the-vote campaign during Texas's early-voting period.[10] This undertaking, however, never developed because the Clinton campaign began in the early fall to move resources out of Texas to place them in states where it believed it had a better chance of victory.

The Latino initiative was dissonant with the tone of the Clinton campaign. As we have indicated, Clinton sought to unify, as opposed to creating distinct interest groups. For the most part, the campaign stuck to its philosophy; Adelante con Clinton! was the only visible race- or ethnic-based support group that received campaign funds. African American leaders complained that Clinton did not undertake targeted black outreach (Ifill 1992b).

The campaign's ambivalence about the Adelante con Clinton! initiative is reflected in its day-to-day activities. Field staff perceived Adelante as a parallel campaign that did not do field-work and merely produced some materials that they themselves did not necessarily even use. Moreover, it was viewed primarily as a political necessity rather than as a mobilizing tool.

The ambivalence may also be reflected in some of the products of the campaign. Traditional Latino Democratic activists complained that some of the campaign's Spanish-language materials were poorly translated and that it was unclear who in the campaign was responsible for such materials. They complained that many key Latino campaign operatives were novices regarding Latino issues. Evidence of this inexperience is the initial Adelante con Clinton! poster, which featured the candidate with his left hand raised in a fist. This pose alienated the Cuban community, which associated the symbolism with Castro and communism. The poster had to be reprinted in reverse so that Clinton's right hand was raised in the air.

Thus, Adelante con Clinton! should be seen as the campaign's attempt to respond to demands from Latinos, yet not to change the campaign's basic opposition to constituency-based campaigning. While the general campaign staff seems not to have resented it, they may not have understood the necessity of this exception to the overall strategy of the campaign. Further, as the focus of the campaign shifted away from states with large Latino populations, the relative importance of Adelante con Clinton! within the campaign declined.

The fall campaign saw only one other targeted outreach to Latinos. Unexpectedly, perhaps, considering their high levels of support for Republican presidential candidates, Cuban Americans were the target of this effort. In April, Clinton endorsed the Cuban Democracy Act (also known as the Torricelli bill) at a fund-raising event in Miami's Little Havana (Rother 1992). The legislation was designed to further tighten the economic embargo on Cuba.

Clinton's early endorsement put President Bush in a difficult position. Traditionally, Bush had been very supportive of Cuban community interests (Moreno and Warren 1992), but he did not endorse this legislation because many U.S. allies opposed it on the grounds that it limited the ability of international subsidiaries of U.S.-owned companies to trade with Cuba. These allies contended that this violated international law. The Republicans feared that Jorge Más Canosa, the head of the CANF, had used the promise of Cuban votes to win Clinton's support for the legislation, knowing that this would also force President Bush to support the Torricelli bill. Recognizing Clinton's political calculus and the need to carry Florida in the fall elections, Bush soon followed Clinton in endorsing the bill and signed it into law in October.

By the fall, Clinton's early support of the bill and his lead in the polls offered him an entree into the Florida Cuban community (Evans and Novak 1992a). He and his campaign capitalized on this. In addition to endorsing the Torricelli bill, Clinton spoke out against Castro in ways that distinguished him from many previous Democratic presidential nominees:

> For over 30 years, the people of Cuba have been subjected to repression and deprivation. Under Fidel Castro, the Cuban people are denied their most basic human rights. At a time when most of Latin America has joined the community of democratic nations, his regime stands firmly against the tide of history.
>
> The dissolution of the Soviet Union offers the United States an important opportunity to increase the pressure for democracy in Cuba. The Cuban Democracy Act addresses this important issue by tightening the economic embargo against Fidel Castro. ("Statement by Governor Bill Clinton on the Signing of the Cuban Democracy Act" 1992)

Clinton offered more than token backing. Senior Clinton aides reported that he genuinely supported the goals of the Cuban Democracy Act. Also, soon after Bush signed the bill, Clinton met with Jorge Más Canosa. After the meeting, Más Canosa and three other CANF directors issued a statement saying, "Any fears that the Cuban American community may have had about a Clinton administration with regard to Castro's Cuba have dissipated today" (Clary 1992).

Despite Más Canosa's previous endorsement of Bush, many saw this statement as a blessing to Cubans who wanted to support Clinton. Even Más Canosa could not so easily get away with this level of political opportunism (or treason, as some in the Miami Cuban community called it). Two days after releasing the statement on Clinton, Más Canosa released another statement: "My affiliation is Republican, my vote is for President Bush, but my work for Cuba is much more important than my partisan preferences" (Clary 1992).

Despite the Adelante con Clinton! campaign and its flirtation with the

Miami Cuban community, the Clinton campaign was true to its strategy of not conducting ethnic campaigns. Nonetheless, the campaign continuously emphasized diversity. Indeed, the image of campaign institutions reflecting America echoes through many Clinton campaign speeches. As we have indicated, the campaign staff represented this commitment by having Latinos active in all aspects of the campaign. With the exception of Adelante con Clinton! coordinator Echaveste, Latino staff did not have positions tied to researching, polling, mobilizing, or otherwise interacting with Latino communities. Echaveste herself had many responsibilities beyond Latino outreach. There is some indication that, toward the end of the campaign, ethnic considerations influenced field staff assignments. For example, Marcella Sandoval, a bilingual senior field organizer who had worked in Illinois, Wisconsin, and New Jersey earlier in the campaign, was assigned to coordinate activities in New Mexico as election day drew near. Her ethnicity was, in her judgment, irrelevant to this assignment, and the effort she directed targeted Democrats, not Latinos. Thus, the Clinton campaign largely succeeded at broadly involving Latinos while not stigmatizing them as capable of doing only Latino outreach.

The campaign also incorporated Latinos at state and local levels. Unlike the Dukakis strategy of bringing in outsiders and controlling state and local efforts from the campaign headquarters in Boston, Clinton relied extensively on local residents. When field staff (outsiders) opened local offices or coordinated local efforts, they staffed the operations with local volunteers. The grass-roots aversion to "white boys from Boston" assured that interested Latinos and non-Latinos alike could play an active role in the campaign, especially in those states that remained important to the Clinton campaign.

The campaign also included senior Latino elected officials in advisory roles. Soon after the Democratic National Convention, Clinton named Los Angeles County Supervisor Gloria Molina as the campaign's national cochair (Tobar 1992). Interestingly, in announcing her appointment, the campaign emphasized her experience in grass-roots politics and the likelihood that she would help the Democrats win California; it did not stress her ethnicity or her role in Latino outreach. In August, former San Antonio Mayor Henry Cisneros resigned from the board of the Federal Reserve Board of Dallas to campaign for Clinton. "My greatest usefulness to him," Cisneros reported, "is working the concentrations of Hispanics in states that can be won, but a large turnout will be necessary" (Eskenazi 1992). He also served on Clinton's Strategic Planning Group. As we have mentioned, José Villareal served as one of Clinton's deputy campaign managers. Reports from both within and outside the campaign suggest that his role was substantive and not symbolic.

The direction that the competition took in October and early November facilitated the campaign's ability to avoid ethnic campaigning. By mid-October, the election was effectively over in the four states with the largest number of Latinos, with the Republicans conceding California, Illinois, and New York to Clinton, and the Democrats conceding Texas to Bush. The one exception among the states with large numbers of Latino votes was Florida, where, as we have indicated, Clinton ran a more ethnically focused campaign.

This unexpected turn of events reduced the need for Clinton to campaign in or commit resources to these big states. So, the states with Latino votes sought after by the Democrats were not those rich in electoral votes, as many analysts had predicted (including us), but, instead, three states with few electoral votes—New Jersey, New Mexico, and Colorado. In these, Clinton addressed his message to all voters, without singling out any one group. In the final few weeks of the campaign, Clinton made repeated visits to these states to spur turnout. Campaign field-workers and Adelante con Clinton! efforts tried to mobilize Latino voters along with non-Latino voters. They continued to reject ethnic appeals in favor of targeting all voters likely to vote Democratic.

The decision not to invest organizational or media resources in Texas confused many and caused resentment among many leading Texas Democrats (Burka 1992). Throughout the general election season, Clinton led or was a close second in state opinion polls. State Democratic party leaders insisted that with an investment of resources the campaign could win the home state of both of his opponents. Yet, Little Rock, and campaign manager James Carville in particular, never believed that Texas was winnable and withdrew resources by mid-October. They did continue a low-budget organizational campaign supplemented by Clinton visits during the campaign's final weeks to keep the race close enough that Bush had to spend limited campaign resources (some say as much as $2.5 million) to assure victory. Arizona Democrats also believed the party could carry their state. They, too, reacted angrily to Carville's decision to concede the state to Bush.

The campaign used Spanish-language media extensively in only one state, and there only reluctantly. In New Mexico, the Clinton campaign ran Spanish-language radio advertisements in response to negative Spanish-language ads run by the Bush campaign. In Texas, the campaign did not use Spanish-language media, despite the Republicans' use of Spanish-language radio.

In the final week of the campaign, the focus shifted to get-out-the-vote. Though largely confident of victory in the electoral college, the Clinton strategists realized they had to make sure that the voters did not become overconfident. The focus on turnout shifted the campaign schedule to include visits to states (and, more precisely, media markets) where a large number of voters could see Clinton, even if the states had not been targeted in the months leading up to the election. Among these was Texas, particularly urban and South Texas, where Clinton visited several times in the campaign's last few days. New Mexico, New Jersey, and Colorado, which had been the focus of campaign organization efforts, also received last-minute visits. In fact, the campaign's last visits included the Rio Grande Valley at about midnight on election eve and Denver on the morning of election day. Despite the overwhelmingly Mexican American audience in McAllen, Clinton held firm to his commitment not to speak to just Mexican Americans. "This is a big election about big issues," he noted. "My opponents have spent too much time in this election attacking me. If he had spent so much time attacking your problems, we'd be in a lot better shape today and so would he. Let's go after our problems and face them" (National Public Radio [November 3, 1992]).

The Democratic party made efforts to prevent Latinos and Asians from facing harassment at the polls ("Democrats Trying to Prevent Voter Intimidation" 1992). In previous presidential elections, state and local Republican parties had operated "ballot security" efforts.[11] The stated objective of these Republican efforts was to guarantee that only registered voters voted. They resulted, however, in intimidation and reminded many older Mexican Americans of the manipulation of the Latino vote prior to the extension of the Voting Rights Act in 1975 (de la Garza and DeSipio 1993). In order to guarantee as high a voter turnout as possible among Mexican Americans, the Democrats coordinated efforts to monitor polling places and litigate where necessary to assure that voters were not intimidated. Party efforts were supplemented by two voter rights hotlines operated on election day. The first was an 800 number available in Texas and answered by staff members of Texas Attorney General Dan Morales. The second was a national Hispanic voting rights hotline (also an 800 number) operated by the Mexican American Legal Defense and Education Fund (MALDEF), NALEO, and the Puerto Rican Legal Defense and Education Fund.

The combination of long-term Clinton campaign organization in key states and last-minute get-out-the-vote campaigns in other states proved successful on election day. Clinton carried all but one of the states that he had targeted early in the campaign, including California, New York, New Jersey, Illinois, New Mexico, and Colorado. The campaign was driven by a series of overlapping imperatives. Most important, of course, was victory. This dictated that resources be dedicated to states where Clinton could win, but where he was not assured of victory. Within these competitive states, Clinton concentrated on groups likely to produce high numbers of Clinton voters. As a result, there was no unique Hispanic outreach effort, yet Latinos were among those constituencies who were recognized as being able to offer large blocs of votes on election day.

The Republican Campaign: Confusion, Homilies, and Attack Ads

The Bush campaign was ill-prepared for the contest it was to face in 1992. The early challenge from Duke and Buchanan, the entrance of Perot into the race, the misunderstanding of the popular perception of the economy, and, ultimately, the lack of vision united to create a confused campaign uncharacteristic of the Republicans. Yet, behind this confusion was the well-oiled and well-financed Republican machine, which had been organizing for years to bring some traditionally Democratic Mexican Americans and Puerto Ricans into the Republican fold. Interestingly, both the confusion of the Bush campaign and the long-term strategy of the Republicans to convert Democratic Latinos worked to guarantee outreach to some Latinos. Bush's loss of support from middle-class Anglos increased the importance of traditionally more marginal electorates. Thus, the long-term Republican strategy of outreach to Latinos continued amidst the confusion in the president's campaign and offered the potential to offset some of the core Republican votes that would be lost to Clinton and Perot.

The Bush campaign had polling data comparable to that held by Democrats. Early in the general election race, Republicans saw that they could not win several states with Latino electorates. Among the big states the Republicans usually win, California was the first to be acknowledged as lost (Reinhold 1992). By mid-October, Republican strategists also acknowledged Illinois as lost and withdrew staff (Cobb 1992). New York, often a Democratic state even in Republican landslides, also was recognized as an unlikely Republican victory early in the race. The Bush strategists viewed the remaining states with large Latino populations—Texas, Florida, New Mexico, New Jersey, Colorado, and Arizona—as competitive (Evans and Novak 1992b). For a Bush victory, however, these states had to be more than just competitive. Because of the electoral college, the campaign's acknowledgment that they would probably lose in several of the largest states (as well as in several others in the Northeast, the South, and the West) required that Bush win virtually all of these remaining states. As the Perot campaign leached some traditional Republican support, the importance of Latino electorates to the Bush campaign increased.

The Bush campaign followed a more traditional pattern in Latino outreach than did Clinton. Its efforts involved both ongoing party efforts to move Latinos away from the Democratic party and local Viva Bush! campaigns.[12] As we have indicated, the national party's effort began with the training of local Latino activists. During the general election campaign, these trained local activists received daily faxed media messages from Washington. Their efforts were coordinated by the party's national director of Hispanic affairs, Roberto de Posada. The national coordination efforts included preparing materials (fliers, posters, etc.), designing the media campaign, assisting Viva Bush! campaigns, and developing a media strategy.

The Bush Latino strategy was defined early: it was not to win the entire Latino vote, or even a majority; instead, the party and the campaign hoped to enlist the support of components or coalitions within the electorate, for example, businesspeople or the religiously motivated. The strategy was to develop any combination of Latino support that resulted in more than 30 percent of the statewide Latino vote in any state (except Florida). Republican strategists perceived this goal as reasonable if the local parties cooperated with the Hispanic outreach efforts.

Like Clinton, Bush relied on surrogates to carry his message to Latinos. Reflecting the relative weakness of Republicans among Latinos, these Bush Latino surrogates were less well known than their Democratic equivalents. They included the president's grandson George P. Bush and the president's daughter-in-law Columba. The Latino campaigners also included Treasurer Villalpando, Secretary of Interior Luján, Surgeon General Antonia Novello, drug czar Bob Martínez, Representative Ileana Ros-Lehtinen, Orange County Supervisor Gaddi Vásquez, New Jersey Assemblyman José Sosa, and former Texas attorney general candidate Roy Barrera (Moreno 1992).

These surrogates carried two messages. First, they emphasized the accomplishments (particularly economic) of the Reagan and Bush years as documented in "The Hispanic Community and the Republican Party: The *Real* Record." Second, they highlighted the five Clinton negatives. Notably, this balance did not offer a vision for the future or a sense of what four more years of Bush and Republican rule would offer Latino communities.

One of these surrogates, Villalpando, proved an embarrassment to the campaign. At the opening rally of the Texas Viva Bush! bus tour in Austin, she charged that Clinton had burned the American flag while abroad.[13] The Bush campaign retracted this statement even before the Clinton campaign had time to object (Hight 1992*b*). In late October, Villalpando was indicted for taking payoffs from her former employer and had to take a leave of absence from her office and her role in the campaign. Involved in the same scandal was Ernest Olivas, Jr., director of the Bush/Quayle Hispanic campaign. He had worked for the same firm and had his home raided by the F.B.I. at the same time that Villalpando's was raided. He resigned from the campaign a week before the election ("Treasurer Probe Grows" 1992).

The Bush campaign also placed Latinos in prominent roles in the campaign. There were, however, fewer Latinos than there were in the Clinton campaign and for the most part they were more narrowly focused on Latino issues. Lionel Sosa, a leading Latino media consultant, joined the Bush campaign in a formal role to oversee advertising, media relations, and communications strategy. His responsibilities included both Latino and non-Latino media issues. Olivas directed the Bush Hispanic campaign. Shiree Sánchez, White House director of public liaison to the Hispanic community, also served in an unofficial role.

These surrogate efforts supplemented a party-driven effort to bring attention to the five Clinton weaknesses. The party and Bush/Quayle Hispanic coordinators traveled to the competitive states with Latino populations to seek local press coverage for their anti-Clinton message. As in 1988, these Republican operatives were able to have small-town newspapers and Spanish-language publications carry campaign propaganda under the guise of news stories or unsigned editorials. Again, this negative campaign did not speak to the future of a second Bush term (Paulson 1992; Scott 1992). In Colorado and New Mexico, the Democrats organized a response to these anti-Clinton attacks.

Late in the campaign, the president supplemented his surrogates with campaign trips to Texas, New Jersey, Florida, New Mexico, and Colorado. His daughter and son also visited New Jersey and Florida. These efforts reached Latinos, though they did not appear to be the sole targets in any state except Florida. As we have indicated, Clinton's overture to the Miami Cubans caught the Bush campaign by surprise. Bush responded strongly and personally. He went to Miami to sign the Cuban Democracy Act into law and made several other visits to South Florida late in the campaign.

The Bush campaign relied on a Hispanic media strategy to a greater degree than did Clinton. While the Clinton campaign largely used the same message for everybody, Bush's strategists designed a specific message for Latinos. They also seemed more sensitive to language issues. Clinton relied almost exclusively on English media to reach Latinos. The Bush strategists reported that the majority of their media was in English, yet Spanish constituted a significant minority.[14] The ads targeting Latinos were attack ads emphasizing the five Clinton negatives that drove the Bush Hispanic campaign. The goal, according to one campaign staffer, was to "prove to Hispanics that . . . they weren't comfortable with Clinton." The states receiving the most Latino media money were Illinois, Texas, New Mexico, and Colorado. Neither California nor New York received significant media money. As was true with other aspects of the campaign, Florida Latino (Cuban) Republicans directed their own media undertaking.

Like Adelante con Clinton!, Viva Bush! was the grass-roots voter mobilization strategy. Washington staff coordinated local activities, supplied local campaigns with materials, and encouraged local parties and Bush/Quayle campaigns to develop Viva Bush! campaigns. Among the most successful of these was the Texas campaign. In late October, it coordinated a fifteen-hundred-mile bus trip starting in Austin and moving through San Antonio to South Texas. At different points, the tour included First Lady Barbara Bush, George P. Bush and his mother, Columba, Catalina Villalpando, and Roy Barrera.

The rallies drew Latinos and non-Latinos alike. The contradiction that had been evident at the convention between the anti-Latino rhetoric of key speakers and the party's efforts to bring Latinos into the party surfaced again during the Viva Bush! campaign. The initial rally in Austin drew more non-Latinos than Latinos. The message, however, was clearly aimed at Latinos—the speakers trumpeted that a Mexican American, George P. Bush, was a member of the first family. More significantly, the speakers contrasted Governor Clinton's support for legislation making English the official language of Arkansas with the president's support for bilingual education and opposition to official English. Many Anglo Texas Republicans, however, have supported the Official English movement and opposed bilingual education. Thus, while the Latinos in the crowd cheered these declarations, many Anglos reacted with quiet puzzlement.

When asked, the Republican National Committee staffer responsible for Viva Bush! indicated that the campaign did not concern itself with providing conflicting messages to Anglos and Latinos. Instead, the mainstream campaign and the Latino campaign operated semiautonomously, linked by the desire to re-elect George Bush. This contrasts with the careful effort of the Clinton campaign to speak to common American themes to the greatest degree possible.

As should be indicated by this discussion of different aspects of the Bush campaign, the Latino message was essentially negative. It was delivered by surrogates, campaign staffers, and the Viva Bush! campaign. In the end, the strategy may have been effective. Clinton's support among Latinos reached a historical low for a Democrat. Given that Bush's total Latino vote was also down relative to Republican totals from 1980–1988, however, this probably reflects support for Ross Perot among traditional Latino Democrats rather than defection to the Republican party.

Perot: The Quintessential Nonethnic Campaign

Little can be reported of the Perot Hispanic strategy as there does not seem to have been one. From his reentry into the race on October 1 through election day, he made little effort to reach out to any specific electorate. He made only a few campaign appearances and focused his attention on the three presidential debates, talk show appearances, and infomercials. His campaign organization was loosely organized and decentralized. His communications director reported that they did not make special appeals to any group. "The Perot message is for all Americans," he said. Thus, the National Hispanic Leadership Agenda's attempts to open a dialogue with Perot were ignored. Perot did, however, try to get his message to Latino voters. National Public Radio reported that Perot ran advertisements in Spanish, and the campaign tried "to make use of Spanish-speaking volunteers" (Gamerman 1992).

Despite this lack of outreach or strategy, Perot received support from Hispanics. One poll of Hispanics in five states in early October (just after

Perot had reentered the race) gave him between 4 and 9 percent of the Latino vote (Hispanic Business and Telemundo Group 1992).

The Results

The results of the 1992 elections offer both positive and negative indicators for the potential role of Latino electorates. On the one hand, the race was sufficiently close that Latino votes influenced electoral outcomes in as many as six of the nine states where Hispanic populations are concentrated. On the other hand, the rapid increases in Latino turnout and Latino share of the national vote that had occurred in national elections between 1980 and 1988 slowed such that the increase in the number of Latino votes barely exceeded the increase in the number of adult Latinos who did not go to the polls.

Slowed Increase in Latino Turnout Relative to the 1980s

In the 1992 election, the turnout percentage among *all* voters increased over the 1988 elections. The 63.0 percent voter turnout rate was the highest since the 1972 elections,[15] reversing, at least temporarily, the steady decline in voter turnout (Census 1993). The spurt in voter turnout, combined with the slow increase in the national adult population, resulted in an 11 percent increase in the number of voters between 1988 and 1992.

Latino turnout also increased over 1988, with 48.3 percent of Latino U.S. citizens going to the polls compared with 45.9 percent in 1988. The 1992 Latino turnout rate exceeded the previous community high of 48.0 percent, set in 1984. The number of Latino voters increased by 14.2 percent, from 3.710 million in 1988 to 4.238 million in 1992.

While this record turnout and significant increase in the number of Latino voters appear to bode well for Latino electoral impact, it must be noted that the increase in voters did not match the growth rates achieved between 1980 and 1988 and barely kept pace with the growth in the Latino adult population. Between 1980 and 1984, the number of Latino voters increased by 26.0 percent. Between 1984 and 1988, the increase measured 20.0 percent. Had the number of people voting increased between 1988 and 1992 by the average of these two levels of increase (23.0 percent) instead of the actual increase of 14.2 percent, slightly more than 4.5 million Latinos would have gone to the polls (Pachon et al. 1992: fig. 4). Further, while the number of Latino voters increased by 14.2 percent, the number of Latino nonvoters increased by almost as much, 13.8 percent. Thus, the rapid increase in voters barely outpaced the increase in adults not eligible or unable to participate.

Finally, Latinos had been able to steadily increase their share of the national vote during the 1980s because Latino turnout was increasing rapidly during a period of very slow growth in overall turnout. That flip-flopped in 1992. The increase in Latino turnout slowed while the overall turnout increased rapidly. Thus, the Latino share of the national vote increased only marginally, from 3.6 percent in 1988 to 3.7 in 1992; this is a small increase relative to the growth between 1980 and 1988, from 2.6 to 3.6 percent.

The share of Latino vote varied in the nine states with significant Latino populations (see Table 1.1). Ranging from 3.0 percent in Illinois to 25.5 percent in New Mexico, these Latino turnouts offered varying opportunities for influence. As we will indicate, share of the total vote is just one of several factors that influence Latino impact, and not necessarily the most important.

The change in the number of Latinos turning out varied considerably by state (see Table 1.2). Arizona and California saw increases in Latino turnout exceeding 30 percent.[16] At the other extreme, Colorado and New York saw declines in the actual number of Latinos voting. As we have indicated, New York was largely uncompetitive at the presidential level. While this noncompetitiveness might partly explain the decline in turnout among New York's Latinos, other states with no national campaign, such as California and Illinois, saw increases in Latino turnout.

National Influence in Close State Races

Despite the relatively slow growth in overall Latino turnout and actual decline in two states, the overall closeness of the race assured that Latino votes had the potential to influence state-level outcomes in as many as six of the nine states with Latino population concentrations (see Table 1.3). In the remaining three states (California, Illinois, and New York), the victor's overall margin was greater than the total number of Latino votes. Hence, Latinos, no matter how unified, could have little influence in these states.

TABLE 1.1 Latino Share of the 1992 Statewide Vote, Selected States

State	Total Vote	Latino Vote	% Latino of Statewide Vote
Arizona	1,728,000	156,000	9.0
California	11,789,000	1,135,000	9.6
Colorado	1,688,000	136,000	8.1
Florida	5,772,000	411,000	7.1
Illinois	5,650,000	171,000	3.0
New Jersey	3,572,000	173,000	4.8
New Mexico	675,000	172,000	25.5
New York	7,613,000	382,000	5.0
Texas	6,817,000	927,000	13.6

Source: Authors' compilations based on U.S. Bureau of the Census 1993: Table 4.

TABLE 1.2   Latino Voter Turnout, by State, 1988 and 1992

State	1988 Vote	1992 Vote	% Change
Arizona	119,000	156,000	31.1
California	827,000	1,135,000	37.2
Colorado	137,000	136,000	-0.7
Florida	361,000	411,000	13.9
Illinois	154,000	171,000	11.0
New Jersey	141,000	173,000	22.7
New Mexico	161,000	172,000	6.8
New York	411,000	382,000	-7.1
Texas	854,000	927,000	8.5
National	3,710,000	4,238,000	14.2

Note: Current Population Survey (CPS) data rely on self-reporting of race and ethnicity. For Hispanics, this is determined by ancestry in Latin America. Many New Mexico and some Colorado Latinos trace their ancestry to migrants from Spain prior to Mexico's independence. As a result, CPS data on New Mexico and Colorado underestimate the influence of Latino voters.
Source: Authors' compilations based on U.S. Bureau of the Census 1989: Table 4; 1993: Table 4.

The influence in the six states with a possible Latino impact varied. In four states with narrow margins between Bush and Clinton (Colorado, Florida, New Jersey, and New Mexico), the majority of Latinos voted with the majority of the state's voters. Thus, holding other factors constant, their impact was direct: the majority of Latino votes contributed to the victor's victory margin.

The probability that the Latino votes could realistically have led to an alternative outcome is low. Latinos in each state have regular patterns of support for each party and regular turnouts. The exact level of this "core" support varies by state (DeSipio and de la Garza 1992). In two-person races, 60 to 70 percent of Latinos generally support the Democrats in each of the nine states with large Latino populations, with the exception of Florida. In Florida, Republicans can usually count on approximately 70 percent of the Latino vote. The customary degree of core support, however, did not hold in 1992. The presence of Ross Perot in the race reduced the levels to which the Democrats and the Republicans could count on their traditional core electorates.

In the three states in which Latino votes were integral to narrow Democratic victories, Clinton needed at least 49.1 percent of Colorado's Latino votes, 45.9 percent of New Jersey's Latino votes, and 28.4 percent of New Mexico's Latino votes. Indeed, Latino Democratic votes at these levels are well within the traditional patterns of their core adherence, even accounting

TABLE 1.3 Latino Influence and the 1992 Elections

Margin Between Bush and Clinton, Selected States

State	Clinton Vote	Bush Vote	Clinton Victory Margin[a]	Absolute Difference As % of State Vote
Arizona	543,050	572,086	−29,006	2.0[b]
California	5,121,325	3,630,575	+1,490,750	13.5
Colorado	629,681	562,850	+66,831	4.3
Florida	2,071,651	2,171,781	−100,130	1.9
Illinois	2,453,350	734,096	+719,354	14.3
New Jersey	1,436,206	1,356,865	+79,371	2.4
New Mexico	261,617	212,824	+48,793	8.6
New York	3,444,450	2,346,649	+1,097,801	16.0
Texas	2,281,815	2,496,071	−214,256	3.5

Latino Votes As a Share of the Winning Margin, Selected States

State	Winning Candidate	Latino Vote for Winning Candidate	Winner's Margin Had No Latino Voted for Winner	Impact
Arizona	Bush	40,560[c]	−11,474	Clinton victory
California	Clinton	737,750	+753,000	No change
Colorado	Clinton	106,080	−39,249	Bush victory
Florida	Bush	304,140	−204,010	Clinton victory
Illinois	Clinton	104,310	+615,044	No change
New Jersey	Clinton	86,500	−7,129	Bush victory
New Mexico	Clinton	110,080	−61,287	Bush victory
New York	Clinton	240,660	+857,141	No change
Texas	Bush	222,480	−8,224	Clinton victory

Notes:

[a] For ease of presentation, we represent the margin as the Clinton vote minus the Bush vote. Thus, a plus represents a Clinton victory and a minus a Bush victory.

[b] State vote includes Perot totals. Because electoral college delegates are awarded based on winning a plurality of votes, however, the margin between the first- and second-place candidates is the significant margin.

[c] These Latino vote totals for the winning candidates are derived from U.S. Bureau of the Census Current Population Survey Data, which overestimate turnout and from Voter Research and Surveys exit polls.

Sources: DeSipio (1993: 136), based on Voter Research and Surveys exit polls; Pomper et al. (1993: 136–137), based on *Congressional Quarterly Weekly Report* 51 (January 23, 1993); U.S. Bureau of the Census (1993: Table 4).

for the impact of the Perot candidacy. Further, 1992 exit polls indicate that the Democratic ticket did receive at least these levels of support. Thus, it would have taken gross neglect of the Latino electorate or its alienation to have driven Democratic support below these levels in New Jersey, New Mexico, and Colorado.

In Florida, the core Republican vote proved integral to a Republican victory. The narrow Republican victory required at least 24.4 percent of the Republican Latino votes. Again, 1992 exit polling and traditional core levels of Florida Republican Latino partisanship assured that the Republicans would receive at least this much support. Realistically, it would have been hard for a Republican ticket to drive away Latinos to get a lower share of the vote than this necessary level. Thus, in these four states, the cohesiveness of the Latino vote proved an important component of the victor's margin in a series of close races.

Latino minorities also may have had an influence in two states. To assure Republican victories in Arizona and Texas, the Republicans had to garner at least 18.6 percent and 23.1 percent, respectively, of Latino votes. In two-person races, the Republicans could be largely assured of Latino support at these levels. In 1992's three-person race, these necessary levels of Latino support are on the high-but-still-possible end of Latino support that the Republicans could reasonably expect. In both cases, the exit poll results are sufficiently close to these levels to be within the poll's sampling error for their small Latino voter samples.

Had the Republicans been able to carry the three states—Colorado, New Mexico, and New Jersey—in which core Latino Democratic votes assured victory, Clinton would still have carried the electoral college with a sizable 342 to 196 margin. Had the Democrats been able to carry the three states—Florida, Texas, and Arizona—in which Latino votes contributed to the Republican majority, Bush would have lost 65 of his 168 electoral votes, making the magnitude of his defeat comparable to Michael Dukakis's in 1988.

In as many as six states, then, Latino votes contributed to the margin of victory in close elections. For campaign strategists, these results offer important lessons. In several states, Latinos deliver a cohesive bloc of votes that can be tapped by either party in close elections. Their numbers offer resources for both Democrats and Republicans. The 1992 experiences of Republicans in Texas and Arizona, however, demonstrate that the race must be very close for Republicans to benefit more than the Democrats (in all states but Florida).

Strategists should also note that the ability of Latino voters to contribute to state-level outcomes was achieved in 1992 with unexceptional increases in most states' Latino voter turnouts and an outright decline in two states, including Colorado (see Table 1.2). The 1992 voters, then, were the core

Latino voters. Thus, a candidate seeking more Latino votes, even if it meant a reduced overall share of the Latino vote, could undertake a strategy based on mobilization of previously nonvoting Latinos.

Latino Candidates and Campaigns at Other Levels

The 1992 elections were the first after the redistrictings and reapportionment that followed the 1990 census. Redistricting assured that Latinos would increase their hold on elective office from Congress through local offices. The 1992 elections followed the expected patterns, with Latinos being elected to a host of new offices. These results continue a trend that seems likely to continue over the next several years. Yet, Latinos failed to gain some of the more important seats that were created with the very intent of electing Latinos and further failed to hold onto gains made through appointment to elective offices. Moreover, most of the newly elected Latinos occupied seats in which a majority of the constituency was Latino. Thus, the 1992 gains did not come from non-Latino constituencies.

As in 1982, there were exaggerated expectations regarding the increase in Latino members of Congress that would follow reapportionment. In what may have been efforts to mobilize voters, as the presidential campaign got under way, many Latino leaders cited continued population growth as evidence that Southern California would be home to three additional Latino members of Congress and Texas would deliver at least two more. Others, taking political factors as well as population growth into account, accurately predicted a maximum increase of six (de la Garza and DeSipio 1989).

Election day did see the largest one-year gain in the number of Latino members of Congress. Prior to the election, there were eleven Latinos in the House; afterwards, they numbered seventeen. Their diversity also increased. Prior to the election, the Latino members represented six states, afterward, eight. The number of Republicans increased from one to three. The number of Cubans increased from one to three, and Puerto Ricans, from one to three. In a departure from the past, voters elected a Democratic Cuban (from New Jersey) and a Republican Mexican American (from Texas). This Texas election set two precedents. The victor, Henry Bonilla, beat an incumbent, Albert Bustamante (who faced a criminal investigation). In addition, Bonilla was the first Republican Mexican American elected to national office from a southwestern state other than New Mexico.

Despite this significant increase in Hispanic members and their growing diversity, 1992 again was witness to how political factors may be more important than population when designing Latino congressional districts (de la Garza and DeSipio 1989). The redistricting processes in Florida and New York could have added two Latino majority seats, but did not. Perhaps more important, the Texas legislature created a Latino majority seat with the assumption that a Mexican American would win election. In a bitterly fought primary and two runoffs (the courts dismissed the results of the first runoff), Gene Green bested Ben Reyes for the Democratic nomination; Green went on to win the general election.[17]

Four Latino majority seats did not see serious competition from Latinos. Although these districts can be viewed as likely sites for increasing Latino representation prior to the post-2000 census redistricting, each has high rates of non-U.S. citizenship. Only two minority Latino districts elected Latinos to Congress—incumbent Bill Richardson from New Mexico and newcomer Robert Menéndez of New Jersey.

This pattern of not generating as many seats as expected, losing some seats designed to elect Latinos, and failing to win non-Latino majority seats was repeated in state capitals across the country. The number of Latino state legislators increased from 131 to 157. The number of Latino elected officials at all levels also increased considerably, from 4,202 to 4,994 (NALEO 1992*b*). While this number represents a 20 percent increase over the previous year, it includes approximately 650 local school board members in Chicago who had not previously been counted as *elected* officials. If these newly enumerated elected officials are excluded from the count, the one-year increase is a more reasonable 3.5 percent. Latinas have steadily increased their share of elective offices, increasing to 30 percent of Hispanic officeholders.

In Texas, Latino candidates lost two races for statewide office—Lena Guerrero for Railroad Commission and Pete Benavides for Circuit Court of Appeals. Both were unelected incumbents, having been appointed by Governor Ann Richards. Guerrero faced a scandal after having inflated her academic credentials. Although she resigned her office, many did not feel she was appropriately contrite. According to an SVRI exit poll, both Guerrero and Benavides carried 80 percent or more of the Latino vote, but lost the statewide vote.

Thus, the 1992 elections saw a continuation of the steady pattern of increasing numbers of Latinos in elective office. The pattern at the congressional level of not quite reaching expected levels should not diminish these accomplishments. Further, while discussions such as this often emphasize the election of new Latinos to office, many who have been elected over the past two decades are achieving seniority. At the congressional level, Latinos lost Edward Roybal to retirement. Two senior Latino members of Congress continue to serve as committee chairs (Kika de la Garza and Henry B. González) and others are being groomed for leadership (particularly New Mexico's Bill Richardson) (Hickox 1992). In 1992, Congressman Roybal was the only Latino on the House's powerful Appropriations Committee; in 1993, Latino representation on Appropriations increased to four. The delegation of seventeen assures that Latinos serve on most House committees.

No Latinos ran for the U.S. Senate or for governor in 1992.

Noncompetitive Congressional Races

The November elections in even-numbered years fill national offices. In most jurisdictions, races for local offices are held at a different time, often in the spring. Despite their national importance, the congressional, senatorial, gubernatorial, and presidential races may not be the most important ones for mobilizing Latino voters. Recent research indicates that local races and local issues are more likely to incorporate previous nonvoters (de la Garza, Menchaca, and DeSipio 1994). Of these races decided in November elections, the congressional is the one closest to many communities. As a result, congressional campaigns serve a potentially important role in mobilizing new voters.

Few 1992 congressional races with Latino candidates, however, were competitive (see Table 1.4). Three Latino candidates, including two first-time members of Congress—Lincoln Díaz-Balart (R-FL) and Frank Tejeda (D-TX)—faced no opposition in the general election (Tejeda faced no primary opposition, either). By comparison, among all the nation's congressional seats, only eleven candidates faced no major-party opposition in the general election. Further, only one Latino victor had a margin of less than 60 percent to 40 percent (Solomon Ortiz [D-TX]).

TABLE 1.4 Turnout and Victor's Margin in Congressional Races with Latino Candidates, 1992 (Major Party Candidates)

State/District	Vote	%	Candidate
Arizona 2	83,873	70.4	Ed Pastor (D)
	35,253	29.6	Don Shooter (R)
California 23	108,152	56.4	Elton Gallegly (R)
	83,543	43.6	Anita Pérez Ferguson (D)
California 30	45,502	71.5	Xavier Becerra (D)
	18,150	28.5	Morry Waksberg (R)
California 31	64,430	63.1	Matthew Martínez (D)
	37,729	36.6	Rubén Franco (R)
California 33	30,235	67.8	Lucille Roybal-Allard (D)
	14,383	32.2	Robert Guzmán (R)
California 34	86,721	64.7	Esteban E. Torres (D)
	47,357	35.3	J. "Jay" Hernández (R)
California 46	49,633	55.0	Robert Dornan (R)
	40,587	45.0	Robert John Bañuelos (D)

(continues)

TABLE 1.4 (continued)

State/District	Vote	%	Candidate
California 50	71,251	66.4	Bob Filner (D)
	35,942	33.5	Tony Valencia (R)
Colorado 1	155,037	68.8	Patricia Schroeder (D)
	70,407	31.2	Raymond Díaz Aragón (R)
Florida 18	104,715	66.8	Ileana Ros-Lehtinen (R)
	52,095	33.2	Magda Montiel-Davis (D)
Florida 21	Unopposed		Lincoln Díaz-Balart (R)
Illinois 4	83,340	77.5	Luis V. Gutiérrez (D)
	24,246	22.5	Hildegarde Rodríguez-Schieman (R)
New Jersey 13	87,034	67.5	Robert Menéndez (D)
	41,869	32.5	Fred J. Theemling, Jr. (R)
New Mexico 1	125,056	62.5	Steven Schiff (R)
	75,114	37.5	Robert Aragón (D)
New Mexico 2	94,826	56.5	Joe Skeen (R)
	73,118	43.5	Dan Sosa, Jr. (D)
New Mexico 3	118,257	69.2	Bill Richardson (D)
	52,755	30.8	F. Gregg Bemis, Jr. (R)
New York 12	51,608	78.7	Nydia Velásquez (D)
	13,945	21.3	Angel Díaz (R)
New York 16	81,632	91.2	José Serrano (D)
	7,868	8.8	Michael Walters (R)
Texas 14	137,184	71.5	Greg Laughlin (D)
	54,567	28.5	Humberto Garza (R)
Texas 20	Unopposed		Henry B. González (D)
Texas 23	97,888	60.7	Henry Bonilla (R)
	63,423	39.3	Albert G. Bustamante (D)
Texas 27	87,517	56.8	Solomon P. Ortiz (D)
	66,485	43.2	Jay Kimbrough (R)
Texas 28	Unopposed		Frank Tejeda (D)

Source: Authors' compilation.

Not only were many of these races noncompetitive, they shared a second characteristic: they had low turnouts, particularly in California. The three California races with the lowest number of votes had Latino candidates (Lucille Roybal-Allard in California's 33rd District, Xavier Becerra in California's 30th District, and Robert John Bañuelos, the loser in California's 46th District). The three races were the only ones nationally in which the winner won the election with fewer than fifty thousand votes. In the Roybal-Allard victory, the two major-party candidates received fewer than fifty thousand votes between them. These low vote totals reflect high concentrations of non-U.S. citizens in each of these districts *and* low voter mobilization. This pattern of highly noncompetitive congressional races and low turnout reduces the incentive for candidates to mobilize new voters that would be present in more competitive electoral environments (de la Garza and DeSipio 1993).

Latino Efforts to Influence National Political and Policy Outcomes

The Latino communities organized in new and effective ways to influence political and policy outcomes around the 1992 election cycle. Among these efforts was a newly unified and diverse approach to agenda development and new drives at demand making for Latino campaigns and candidates.

Agenda Setting

While the presidential candidates paid less attention to Latinos than in previous elections, Latino undertakings to develop a united voice to make themselves heard reached new levels of success. In 1988, several organizations prepared national policy agendas for the candidates. The confusion created by this duplicative effort limited their impact (Roybal 1988). In anticipation of the 1992 elections, the leaders of the two most significant Latino agendas, the National Hispanic Leadership Conference and the National Hispanic Agenda, merged to form the National Hispanic Leadership Agenda (the NHLA).[18] This organization produced a forty-five-page policy summary and distributed it to the parties and the presidential candidates in the summer of 1992 (National Hispanic Leadership Agenda 1992). The production of the document was not to be the end of the project. Instead, the NHLA hoped to follow the agenda's issues through the entire administration and to monitor the administration's compliance with the reported needs of the Latino communities. While this had been a goal of agendas from the 1976, 1980, 1984, and 1988 elections, the directors of the NHLA hoped that the independence of this organization and funding separate from its member organizations would assure that this goal would be reached.

The NHLA sought to emphasize a few core issues that united all of the

Latino communities. These issues—empowerment and civil rights, education, health, housing, and economic opportunity—were identified by a diverse fifty-member board of directors. The bipartisan board included the chief officers of twenty-five national Latino organizations plus twenty-five individuals from government, academia, corporate America, and other fields. The cochairs for 1992 were Representative Ileana Ros-Lehtinen, Bronx Borough President Fernando Ferrer, Henry Cisneros, MALDEF's Antonia Hernández, and NCLR's Raúl Yzaguirre. The chair of the Congressional Hispanic Caucus, Solomon Ortiz, was an honorary cochair.

To explore each of the five core issues, between September 1991 and March 1992 the NHLA held fourteen daylong hearings throughout the country to assess local Hispanic leaders' perceptions of the communities' needs. Based on its findings, the NHLA prepared a policy summary that was then presented to the presidential candidates and the party platform committees. These local meetings not only assured that local views and needs would shape the Agenda, but also guaranteed extensive local media attention to Hispanic issues in the months leading up to the 1992 campaign (Broom 1991; "Comeback Trail" 1991; Garza 1991, as examples).

It should be noted that the selection of these five core issues reduced any potential controversy among different Latino national-origin groups. According to NHLA Executive Director Frank Newton, this narrower focus was deliberately undertaken to emphasize commonalties among the groups and to form a basis for a future expansion of the consensus.

The NHLA's accomplishments were diminished in part by two of the three major candidates' lack of interest in the Agenda. Only the Democrats and Bill Clinton responded to NHLA's request that the Agenda be included in the party platform and for a meeting between the organization and the candidate. Drafters of the Agenda presented testimony before the Democratic platform committee and were pleased with the degree to which Latino community needs were included in the final platform (Márquez 1992b). The NHLA also made a presentation before Hispanic delegates to the Democratic National Convention. This caucus adopted the NHLA Agenda as its own. Finally, the NHLA met with Clinton in September.

The Bush and Perot campaigns did not pursue contacts with the NHLA. The Bush campaign liaison with Hispanic groups found the NHLA to be disorganized. In his judgment, NHLA came along too late to influence the Republican platform (it asked to make a presentation just three days before the deadline) and made its request to meet with the president too late. The Republicans also reported that Clinton had received very little media coverage for meeting with the Agenda and embarrassed both himself and the Agenda by not demonstrating an understanding of the issues at a postmeeting press conference. According to Newton, despite repeated contacts, the Perot campaign expressed no interest in NHLA.

Despite its accomplishments, Latinos were somewhat critical of the NHLA. These criticisms ranged from claims of disorganization relative to 1988 and a perception that its major purpose was not to create community unity, but was instead to serve as a vehicle for Henry Cisneros's political ambitions. Perhaps the most damning criticism came from the NHLA liaison in the Clinton campaign. She reported that the Agenda was ill-timed. While the campaign was organizing to get a candidate elected, the NHLA was discussing policy. She argues that the Agenda would have been more important during the transition period, when its organizers were largely silent.

Hispanic Political Demand Making

As their numbers have grown, the Latino communities have become increasingly sophisticated practitioners of American politics. While most political activity has been regional or local in emphasis, 1992 saw strategies to supplement the presidential campaigns that made for a truly Latino politics. Although nascent, several examples from the 1992 election exhibit this growing sophistication. The first consists of new forms of national Latino political endeavors. The second type is Hispanic political activity in unexpected places.

Hispanic PAC USA was formed and held its first major fund-raiser during the Democratic National Convention. Although it had no discernible impact on the 1992 campaign, this organization holds the potential to fund national Hispanic candidates. Following the lead of the presidential campaigns, Hispanic elected officials journeyed outside their traditional bases of support to campaign for the Democratic ticket. Illinois congressional candidate Luis Gutiérrez joined New Jersey candidate Robert Menéndez on a bus tour through northern New Jersey in support of the Clinton/Gore ticket. Hispanic leaders from the Northeast met for the first time to discuss ways of pushing their agenda at the national level (Arce 1992).

In the waning weeks of the campaign, the NCLR raised the issue of the role of Latinos in the campaigns. In a study entitled "Not Invited to the Party: Hispanics and the 1992 Presidential Campaign," NCLR (1992) charged that Hispanics were underrepresented on the campaign staffs of both Bush and Clinton. According to the report, just 1 percent of Bush's staff and 5 percent of Clinton's staff were Latino. Both campaigns reacted angrily to these allegations and indirectly defended each other by suggesting that the report had overlooked Latinos who were not involved in Latino-specific initiatives. As one senior member of Clinton's staff said, "What's sad is people like me never got mentioned. We weren't part of the Hispanic outreach." The report also charged that the party platforms neglected Hispanic issues and that the Clinton campaign had failed to develop campaign materials addressing Hispanic issues (although it had such materials for women, the elderly, the disabled, and gays and lesbians). Both candidates were charged with failing to speak before Hispanic organizations. The timing of the report's release and the allegation that it was wrong in its major charge limited its impact.

Latino political organization also appeared in unexpected places and from atypical groups. Hispanics in both Connecticut and Massachusetts organized to support the Clinton/Gore ticket ("Hispanics Rally for Clinton" 1992; Seline 1992). These efforts included targeted information dissemination and get-out-the-vote drives. Support for Clinton also came from unexpected places. Cuban women in Florida formed Cuban Women for Clinton because, they said, four more years of Bush would be "intolerable." These Cuban women also looked on Clinton with slightly less concern because of a family member—Hillary Rodham Clinton's brother is married to a member of Miami's Cuban exile community.

Although these undertakings pale in comparison with the endeavors of the presidential campaigns to mobilize Latino support, they bear monitoring. The success of the National Hispanic Leadership Agenda indicates that a narrow focus can create a common Latino political agenda. These other ventures, though individually unimportant, could capitalize on the same type of success as the elite-driven Agenda and develop other linkages among the Latino communities.

Conclusion

The experiences of the 1992 presidential race further refined our understanding of the role that Latinos can play in state and national elections. As demonstrated in the 1988 presidential race, the occasions when Latinos can significantly influence electoral outcomes are rare. The 1992 campaign demonstrates, however, that the conditions that create such occasions are somewhat more varied than we had originally calculated.

The Clinton campaign showed that, contrary to our expectation, explicit outreach to Latinos may not be an absolute requirement for Latinos to play an important role. This is the ultimate irony of the 1992 presidential race. In Colorado, New Mexico, and New Jersey, the Democrats needed their core supporters, including Latinos, to turn out in high numbers. Furthermore, in New Mexico and Colorado, the Latino vote was the crucial margin in Clinton's victories. Yet the campaign, despite its Latino component, maintained its strategy of running a campaign for all Americans and did not target its message to the audience.

Thus, campaigning on issues of concern to Latinos such as educational reform and job training, but describing those issues in terms that appealed to all Americans, proved to be a win-win strategy. It prevented Anglo backlash while generating Latino votes. Moreover, from the Latino perspective, this approach in no way diminished the ability of Hispanics to make demands regarding issues that most concerned them, since these were at the core of Clinton's agenda (de la Garza 1992b).

Clinton's victory also countered our expectations regarding the states in which Latinos would make a difference. We expected that Latinos in states rich in electoral college votes would have a major role in a competitive election. Instead, 1992 saw the relatively small Latino populations of smaller states become significant while Latinos in California, Illinois, New York, and Texas were essentially irrelevant to the election's outcome.

The Bush campaign also demonstrated the complexity of developing rules for Latino political significance. Its strategy did not require majorities of the Latino vote or wholesale shifts of Latinos from Democrat to Republican. Instead, it sought incremental shifts of blocs of Latino voters to the Republican fold. The Bush campaign and Viva Bush! are part of a much longer term Republican strategy to assure steadily increasing Latino support. Though Latinos did not move in great numbers to the Republicans in 1992, party strategists can be pleased that the combined effect of the Bush and Perot campaigns gave the Democrats their lowest share of the Latino vote in history.

Underlying these partisan victories and defeats, however, is the continuing dilemma of low levels of Latino electoral participation. Yet, ironically, those Latinos who voted in November 1992 had much more of an impact than those who voted in 1988. Mexican Americans in the Southwest, Puerto Ricans in New York, and Cubans in New Jersey were essential either to victories in key states or to the overall vote total that created President Clinton's tenuous mandate. Nonetheless, demographics and the dearth of voter mobilization in high-density barrios tell us that many more Latino adult citizens did not participate in 1992 than in 1988. The 1980s offered a period of rapid increases in the Latino share of the national vote. Had the pattern for the 1980s continued, Latinos would have come to vote at roughly the Latino adults' share of the U.S. citizen population by the year 2020. If, on the other hand, the pattern of the rate of change of the Latino share of the national vote between 1988 and 1992 continues, this parity in voter turnout will never be reached, and Latinos will never match their electoral potential. Latino leaders, then, must focus their attention on citizenship and voter mobilization with vigor equal to candidate support and agenda building.

Notes

1. Throughout this volume, we use the terms "Latino" and "Hispanic" interchangeably to refer to people who can trace their ancestry to the Spanish-speaking regions of Latin America and the Caribbean. When data are available, we discuss specific national-origin groups.

2. We use the term "Latino communities" to recognize the perceived heterogeneity among the major Latino national-origin populations in the United States. See de la Garza et al. 1992.

3. There is no comparable study of Cubans or other Latinos. Several recent Florida elections indicate that Miami Cubans who are U.S. citizens participate at *higher* rates than do Anglos.

4. The SVRI exit poll had the largest sample of Texas Latino voters. Two other exit polls with sufficient Latino samples found comparable rates of Texas Latino support for Clinton. The *Los Angeles Times* reported 68 percent for Clinton, 19 percent for Tsongas, and 10 percent for Brown. Voter Research and Surveys reported 64 percent for Clinton, 19 percent for Tsongas, and 10 percent for Brown.

5. The *Times* exit poll does not distinguish between Hispanic whites and non-Hispanic whites. As a result, this underestimates the true gap between non-Hispanic white Republicans and Hispanic Republicans. Hispanics constitute 10 percent of the Republican electorate in Texas.

6. The number of Latino delegates and alternates to the Democratic convention is disputed. Another source reports just 330 (Roth 1992).

7. This delegate poll indicated that the delegates identified a policy agenda similar to that discussed by Latino leaders. The delegates' top three domestic issues were education, employment, and discrimination. The named foreign policy issues were immigration policy, NAFTA, and relations with Latin America. Among those delegates stating an opinion, statehood was perceived as the best option for Puerto Rico's future. Just two-thirds as many delegates preferred an enhanced commonwealth status for the island.

8. April was when Perot's campaign took off. A poll early in the month gave him 16 percent of the presidential vote. By the end of the month, 30 percent supported his candidacy.

9. Some of the Latino delegates dismissed the platform language as mere hyperbole. "Just because it's in the platform doesn't mean it's the law," said an Abilene, Texas, delegate (Franks 1992).

10. Texas allows and encourages in-person voting before the election. The "no excuses" voting caught on in 1992 and as many as one-third of those registered had voted in advance of election day.

11. In response to the efforts of the Orange County Republican party to place guards at select minority polling places in 1988, the California legislature passed a law forbidding uniformed guards at polling places.

12. These efforts sometimes came together. Bush's efforts to reach the Cuban vote in Florida were entrusted to local Cuban party officials. Although they were reportedly taken by surprise by Clinton's outreach to Cubans, they recovered with a surrogate and talk radio-driven word-of-mouth campaign about Clinton's visit to Russia. In the end, the Bush campaign "scared" the Cuban support away from Clinton.

13. Villalpando said: "Is it a slap in the face when you have a person that wants to be in the White House as our leader when he doesn't even honor those of our community that have shed blood and have gone when their country demanded it, instead of dodging the draft, and instead of going to another country to burn our flag. . . . Is that the kind of person you want in the White House? I don't want that kind of person" (Ramsey 1992).

14. The reliance on English media is a departure for the Republicans since 1988 (Subervi 1992), resulting from several realizations. First, the Bush strategists noted that Latinos received most of their news in English. Second, Spanish media are perceived as more difficult to use relative to payoff. Finally, there was some concern that local Spanish-language media, particularly newspapers, see advertising as a quid pro quo for coverage in the news sections.

15. We derive these data from Current Population Survey (CPS) estimates of voter registration and turnout (Census 1993). Although the data overestimate registration and voting, there is no other source of national- and state-level data with a sufficient sample size to analyze the registration and voting patterns of race and national-origin groups. There is no evidence that the levels of overestimation vary by race or ethnicity (Census 1990).

16. CPS state-level estimates, particularly for a specific racial or national-origin group, are subject to high sampling error. We are suspicious of the reported level of turnout among California Latinos. A more realistic level based on 1980, 1984, and 1988 turnouts would be slightly more than one million.

17. In what could have been a similar outcome, incumbent Stephen Solarz, who lost most of his existing district to redistricting, ran in a nearby Latino majority district. Differences between New York and Texas electoral law impeded Solarz's victory. New York gives victory to the recipient of the most votes in party primaries. Texas, on the other hand, requires the winner to receive 50 percent of the vote. By requiring a runoff, the Texas law encourages the top Latino vote getter to compete with the top non-Latino vote getter in what is likely to become an ethnic battle.

18. The NHLA distinguished itself from previous efforts in six ways. It would (1) have full-time staff; (2) carry on beyond the election; (3) have nationwide grass-roots input; (4) bring the Agenda to the attention of people in the new administration and the new Congress; (5) assure visibility in the general public and the media; and (6) take the Agenda back to the grass roots.

References

Arce, Rose Marie. 1992. "Party Leaders Pricing Votes among Latinos." *Newsday* (February 23).

Arian, Asher; Arthur S. Goldberg; John H. Mollenkopf; and Edward T. Rogowsky, eds. 1991. *Changing New York Politics.* New York: Routledge.

Benanti, Mary. 1992. "Democrats Face Challenge of Attracting Hispanics." Gannett News Service (July 19).

Boyarsky, Bill. 1992. "The Presidential Race Turns Serious." *Los Angeles Times* (May 15).

Broom, Jack. 1991. "Hispanics Meet to Form Agenda for '90s." *Seattle Times* (November 20).

Brownstein, Ronald. 1992. "Buchanan Links Riot to Border Problem; GOP: He Says a Strong Primary Tally for Him in California Would Force His Immigration Proposals onto Bush's Agenda." *Los Angeles Times* (May 14).

Burka, Paul. 1992. "Bill's Bungle: Why Clinton Lost Texas—and What It Means." *Texas Monthly* (December).

Ceaser, James, and Andrew Busch. 1993. *Upside Down and Inside Out: The 1992*

Elections and American Politics. Lanham, Md.: Littlefield Adams Quality Paperbacks.

Chávez, Linda. 1991. *Out of the Barrio: Toward a New Politics of Hispanic Assimilation*. New York: Basic Books.

Clary, Mike. 1992. "Cuban American Bloc May be Splitting; Politics: Powerbroker's Kind Words for Clinton Have Caused an Uproar. Some Say Shift Away from GOP Has Been Underway for Some Time." *Los Angeles Times* (October 31).

"Clinton Meets with Latino Leaders." 1992. Clinton for President Press Release (July 2).

Cobb, Kim. 1992. "Defying Recent History, Clinton Making Big Inroads in Illinois." *Houston Chronicle* (October 25).

"Comeback Trail." 1991. *National Journal* (May 4).

Contreras, Maggie. 1992. "Politically Invisible." *Hispanic* (October).

Decker, Cathleen. 1992. "Buchanan Uses Whatever It Takes in Long-Shot Bid." *Los Angeles Times* (January 14).

de la Garza, Rodolfo O. 1992a. "From Rhetoric to Reality: Latinos and the 1988 Election in Review." In Rodolfo O. de la Garza and Louis DeSipio, eds., *From Rhetoric to Reality: Latino Politics in the 1988 Elections*, pp. 171-180. Boulder, Colo.: Westview Press.

———. 1992b. "Ignoring Latino Voter Proves to be a Blessing." Pacific News Service (November 7).

de la Garza, Rodolfo O., and Louis DeSipio. 1993. "Save the Baby, Change the Bathwater, and Get a New Tub: Latino Electoral Participation after Seventeen Years of Voting Rights Act Coverage." *University of Texas Law Review* 71 (7) (June): 1479-1539.

———, eds. 1992. *From Rhetoric to Reality: Latino Politics in the 1988 Elections*. Boulder, Colo.: Westview Press.

———. 1989. "The Changing Hispanic Political Landscape." In William P. O'Hare, ed., *Redistricting in the 1990s: A Guide for Minority Groups*, pp. 43-54. Washington, D.C.: Population Reference Bureau.

de la Garza, Rodolfo O.; Louis DeSipio; F. Chris García; John García; and Angelo Falcón. 1992. *Latino Voices: Mexican, Puerto Rican, and Cuban Perspectives on American Politics*. Boulder, Colo.: Westview Press.

de la Garza, Rodolfo O.; Martha Menchaca; and Louis DeSipio, eds. 1994. *Barrio Ballots: Latino Politics in the 1990 Elections*. Boulder, Colo.: Westview Press.

de la Isla, José. 1992. "In Houston, a Defining Moment for Hispanics." *Houston Chronicle* (August 23).

"Democrats Trying to Prevent Voter Intimidation." 1992. United Press International (October 29).

DeSipio, Louis. 1993. "Counting on the Latino Vote: Latinos as a New Electorate." Ph.D. dissertation, The University of Texas at Austin (forthcoming from the University Press of Virginia).

DeSipio, Louis, and Gregory Rocha. 1992. "Latino Influence on National Elections: The Case of 1988." In Rodolfo O. de la Garza and Louis DeSipio, eds., *From Rhetoric to Reality: Latino Politics in the 1988 Elections*, pp. 3-22. Boulder, Colo.: Westview Press.

DeSipio, Louis, and Rodolfo O. de la Garza. 1992. "Will Latino Votes Equal Political

Clout? Core Voters, Swing Voters, and the Potential Vote." Paper prepared for presentation at the Annual Meetings of the American Political Science Association, Chicago. September.

De Witt, Karen. 1992. "The 1992 Campaign: Undeclared Candidate Perot to Begin Forming a National Advisory Panel." *New York Times* (July 7).

Eldridge, Earle. 1992. "Hispanics Say Dumping Luján Isn't Good Politics." Gannett News Service (August 19).

Eskenazi, Stuart. 1992. "Leaders Use Different Campaign Approaches." *Austin American-Statesman* (August 23).

Evans, Rowland, and Robert Novak. 1992a. "Bush's Collapsing Cubans." *Washington Post* (October 18).

———. 1992b. "Bush's Texas Shuffle." *Washington Post* (September 18).

Falcón, Angelo; Rodolfo O. de la Garza; F. Chris García; and John García. 1991. "Modes of Political Participation of Mexican Americans, Puerto Ricans, and Cubans: Preliminary Data from the Latino National Political Survey." Paper prepared for presentation at the Annual Meetings of the American Political Science Association, Washington, D.C., September.

Franks, Jeff. 1992. "Republican Party May Be Fencing Out Hispanics." *Reuter Library Report* (August 19).

Gamerman, Ellen. 1992. "Who's Wooing the Hispanic Vote? Bush, Clinton Camps Keep Tailor-Made Appeals in Check." States News Service (October 23).

García, F. Chris, and Rodolfo O. de la Garza. 1977. *The Chicano Political Experience: Three Perspectives*. North Scituate, Mass.: Duxbury Press.

García, F. Chris; Rodolfo O. de la Garza; John García; and Angelo Falcón. 1992. "The Effects of Ethnicity on Partisanship and Partisanship's Impact on Ethnicity: The Case of Mexicans, Puerto Ricans, Cubans, Anglos in the United States." Paper prepared for presentation at the Annual Meetings of the Western Political Science Association, San Francisco. March.

Garza, Melita Marie. 1991. "Hispanics Seek Voice in Politics." *Chicago Tribune* (October 14).

Grenier, Guillermo, and Alex Stepik III. 1992. *Miami Now! Immigration, Ethnicity and Social Change*. Gainesville: University of Florida Press.

Guerra, Fernando. 1992. "Conditions Not Met: California Elections and the Latino Community." In Rodolfo O. de la Garza and Louis DeSipio, eds. *From Rhetoric to Reality: Latino Politics in the 1988 Elections*, pp. 99-110. Boulder, Colo.: Westview Press.

Hero, Rodney. 1992. *Latinos and the U.S. Political System: Two-tiered Pluralism*. Philadelphia: Temple University Press.

Hickox, Katie. 1992. "First Hispanic Wins Congressional Leadership Post." States News Service (December 7).

Hight, Bruce. 1991. "Democrat Clinton Starts Presidential Parade in Valley." *Austin American-Statesman* (December 1).

———. 1992a. "Candidate Clinton Sweeps Support of Mexican-American Democrats Group." *Austin American-Statesman* (January 12).

———. 1992b. "Flag-burning Claim Fans Fire at Bush Rally." *Austin American-Statesman* (October 17).

Hispanic Business and Telemundo Group. 1992. *Hispanic Voters in the United States, October 3-6, 1992.*

"The Hispanic Community and the Republican Party: The *Real* Record." 1992. Unpublished mimeo.

"Hispanics Rally for Clinton." 1992. *Boston Globe* (October 18).

Ifill, Gwen. 1992a. "Clinton Offers National Education Plan." *New York Times* (May 15).

———. 1992b. "Some Leaders Feel Ignored: Clinton Waves at Blacks As He Rushes By." *New York Times* (September 20).

"Inside Politics." 1991. *Washington Times* (December 29).

Jackson, Bryan O., and Michael B. Preston, eds. 1991. *Racial and Ethnic Politics in California.* Berkeley: University of California Institute for Governmental Studies Press.

Kenen, Joanne. 1991. "Duke Brings Presidential Campaign to Cuban Exile Community." Reuters (December 26).

Márquez, Sandra. 1992a. "Latinos at Democratic Convention Focus on Unity." *Hispanic Link Weekly Report* (July 20).

———. 1992b. "Party Platforms Have Strengths, Faults, Say Analysts." *Hispanic Link Weekly Report* (August 31).

Midwest-Northeast Voter Registration and Education Project. 1992. "The Hispanic Vote in the Illinois Primary Election." (March 17).

Moreno, Roberto. 1992. "On the Road to Washington: Will Hispanic Campaign Staffers Hitch a Ride to the White House?" *Hispanic Business*. October.

Moreno, Dario, and Christopher L. Warren. 1992. "The Conservative Enclave: Cubans in Florida." In Rodolfo O. de la Garza and Louis DeSipio, eds. *From Rhetoric to Reality: Latino Politics in the 1988 Elections*, pp. 127-146. Boulder, Colo.: Westview Press.

Nagourney, Adam, and Carolyn Pesce. 1992. "Perot's Minority Gap: 'Big Daddy' Image, Wealth Are Concerns." *USA Today* (June 8).

NALEO. 1992a. *National Roster of Hispanic Elected Officials.* Washington: NALEO Educational Fund.

———. 1992b. "Number of Hispanic Elected Officials Grows by 800 in 1992: 4,994 Hispanic Elected Officials Set a New Record at State, Federal, and Local Level." Press Release (December 17).

National Council of La Raza (NCLR). 1992. *Not Invited to the Party: Hispanics and the 1992 Presidential Campaign.* Washington, D.C.: National Council of La Raza.

National Hispanic Leadership Agenda. 1992. *1992 Policy Summary.* Washington, D.C.

Pachon, Harry. 1991. "U.S. Citizenship and Latino Political Participation in California." In Bryan O. Jackson and Michael B. Preston, eds., *Racial and Ethnic Politics in California*, pp. 71-88. Berkeley: University of California Institute for Governmental Studies Press.

Pachon, Harry, and Louis DeSipio. 1994. *New Americans by Choice: Political Perspectives of Latino Immigrants.* Boulder, Colo.: Westview Press.

———. 1992. "Latino Elected Officials in the 1990s." *PS: Political Science and Politics.* 25(2): 212-217.

———. 1988. "The Latino Vote in 1988." NALEO Background Paper #7. Washington, D.C.: NALEO Educational Fund.

Pachon, Harry, and Lourdes Argüelles. 1993. "Grassroots Politics in an East Los Angeles Barrio: A Political Ethnography of the 1990 General Election." In Rodolfo O. de la Garza; Martha Menchaca; and Louis DeSipio, eds., *Barrio Ballots: Latino Politics in the 1990 Elections*, pp. 137–160. Boulder, Colo.: Westview Press.

Pachon, Harry; Louis DeSipio; Juan-Carlos Alegre; and Mark Magaña. 1992. *The Latino Vote in 1992*. Washington, D.C.: The NALEO Educational Fund.

Page, Clarence. 1992. "Three Way Race Gives New Clout to Black Voters." *Chicago Tribune* (June 10).

Paulson, Michael. 1992. "GOP Hispanics Claim Clinton Discriminated." *San Antonio Light* (October).

Payne, Chris. 1992. "GOP to Broadcast Convention in Spanish." *Houston Chronicle* (July 10).

"The Politics of Exclusion." 1992. *New York Times*. Editorial (August 19).

Pomper, Gerald M.; F. Christopher Atherton; Ross K. Baker; Walter Dean Burnham; Kathleen A. Frankovic; Marjorie Randon Hershey; and Wilson Carey McWilliams, eds. 1993. *The Election of 1992: Reports and Interpretation*. Chatham, N.J.: Chatham House Publishers.

Raasch, Chuck. 1992. "GOP Platform Calls for 'Structures' on the Border." Gannett News Service (August 17).

Ramsey, Ross. 1992. "GOP Apologizes for Treasurer's Remark." *Houston Chronicle* (October 17).

Ratcliffe, R. G. 1992. "Clinton Vows to Promote Ethnic Diversity." *Houston Chronicle* (July 2).

Reinhold, Robert. 1992. "Poll Ratings Low and Anger High, Bush Seems to Concede California." *New York Times* (September 24).

Roth, Bennett. 1992. "Convention 92: Hispanics Are Urged to Boost Activism in Local Political Arena." *Houston Chronicle* (July 15).

Rother, Larry. 1992. "Clinton Sees Opportunity to Break G.O.P. Grip on Cuban Americans." *New York Times* (October 31).

Roybal, Edward. 1988. "Hispanic Agendas in a Presidential Election Year." *NALEO National Report* (Spring).

Scott, S. 1992. "GOP Hispanics Attack Clinton Record." *San Antonio Express News* (October 29).

Seline, Anita. 1992. "Hispanic Activists Seek Leverage at Polls: Hispanics Seek to Influence Policy through Electoral Process." *Hartford Courant* (October 31).

Shannon, Kelly. 1992. "'Mi Casa, Su Casa,' Clinton Tells Group." *Austin American-Statesman* (July 2).

Sharp, Deborah, and Judy Keen. 1992. "Cuban Vote Not Sure Bet for President." *USA Today* (March 5).

Shorris, Earl. 1992. *Latinos: A Bibliography of the People*. New York: W. W. Norton.

Southwest Voter Research Institute. 1992. *Southwest Voter Research Notes* (March).

Stall, Bill. 1992. "Perot Slips into L.A., Focuses on Minority Issues." *Los Angeles Times* (June 18).

"Statement by Governor Bill Clinton on the Signing of the Cuban Democracy Act." 1992. Clinton/Gore Campaign Press Release (October 23).

Stencel, Mark. 1991. "Duke Tries to Woo Conservative Cuban Exiles in Florida." *Washington Post* (December 28)
Subervi, Federico. 1992. "Republican and Democratic Mass Communication Strategies: Targeting the Latino Vote." In Rodolfo O. de la Garza and Louis DeSipio, eds., *From Rhetoric to Reality: Latino Politics in the 1988 Elections*, pp. 23-42. Boulder, Colo.: Westview Press.
Szulc, Tad. 1992. "How Can 29 Million People Be Politically Invisible to Democrats?" *Los Angeles Times* (July 26).
Tobar, Héctor. 1992. "Clinton Gives Molina Role in the Campaign." *Los Angeles Times* (July 29).
"Treasurer Probe Grows; Republican Official Quits" 1992. *Houston Chronicle* (October 31).
Treviño, Jesse. 1991. "Candidate Needs Latino Vote to Capture State Democratic Primary." *Austin American-Statesman* (December 16).
U.S. Bureau of the Census. 1993. *Voting and Registration in the Election of November 1992*. Current Population Reports, Series P-20 #466. Washington, D.C.: U.S. Government Printing Office.
―――. 1990. *Studies in the Measurement of Voter Turnout*. Current Population Reports. Special Studies, Series P-23 No. 168. Washington, D.C.: U.S. Government Printing Office.
―――. 1989. *Voting and Registration in the Election of November 1988*. Current Population Reports, Series P-20 #440. Washington, D.C.: U.S. Government Printing Office.
Uhlaner, Carole; Bruce Cain; and D. Roderick Kiewiet. 1989. "Political Participation of Ethnic Minorities in the 1980s." *Political Behavior* 11 (3): 195-232.
Wolfinger, Raymond, and Steven Rosenstone. 1980. *Who Votes?* New Haven, Conn.: Yale University Press.

PART TWO

The Old Reliables: Mexican Americans in Small Western States

	New Mexico 1992	Colorado 1992	Arizona 1992
Population	1,581,000	3,470,000	3,832,000
Latino population	623,000	459,000	755,000
% Latino of total population	39.4	13.2	19.7
Voting population	675,000	1,688,000	1,728,000
Latino voters	172,000	136,000	156,000
% Latino of voting population	25.5	8.1	9.0
Latino adult noncitizens	45,000	11,000	116,000
Electoral votes	5	8	8

2

Conventional Politics Under Unusual Circumstances: Latinos and the 1992 Election in New Mexico

F. Chris García

It is widely recognized that the situation of Hispanics in New Mexico is considerably different from that of Latinos in most other places in the United States.[1] New Mexican Hispanics generally are much more incorporated into the social, economic, and political systems of the state than is commonly the case elsewhere in this country (García and Wrinkle 1971; García 1974; Vigil 1978, 1979; Sierra 1992). This high level of incorporation reflects the history of the Hispanic people in New Mexico. The Hispanos of New Mexico have a long history of residence in the area, antedating the period when the region became part of the United States following the war between Mexico and the United States in 1848. Prior to the conquest, there was a relatively large population of Hispanics in the area, numbering about sixty thousand. They lived in vital communities with thriving religious, economic, and political institutions. Many of these settlements predated the establishment of the nation of Mexico following its successful War of Independence against Spain in the early nineteenth century. Thus, unlike their experience in much of the United States, Hispanics in New Mexico had a long-established, vital society for more than two centuries prior to the imposition of U.S. institutions pursuant to the Treaty of Guadalupe Hidalgo in 1848.

Because of this sequence of events, Hispanics and Anglo Americans in New Mexico have been much more accommodating in their relationships than has been the case in most other areas. This is not to say that there has not been any ethnic conflict or a sometimes painful adjustment process. However, especially when compared with other parts of the United States, in New Mexico there is considerably less separation and considerably more integration of Hispanic and Anglo American people and institutions. This is perhaps more true of the political process than of economic relationships (García 1974; Sierra 1992).

Hispanics in New Mexico have been significant political players throughout their history as U.S. citizens. While some political distinctiveness drives an ethnic dimension in New Mexico's politics, Hispanics are much more mainstream and less distinctive than in other states. This point is salient to an understanding of the politics of Hispanics in New Mexico.

The level of political participation of New Mexican Hispanics is, in some elections, comparable to that of non-Hispanics. For example, in 1980, 56.3 percent of New Mexico's Hispanics voted, compared with 60.4 percent of New Mexico's whites. While this gap widened in the 1980s and in 1992, it is narrower than in other states with large Latino populations. In 1992, Hispanic voter registration and participation was only 11 to 12 percent lower than for Anglos, rather than the more typical 20 to 30 percent lower found in other states (see Table 2.1).

There are much greater percentages of Hispanics in political organizations and in public office in New Mexico than are found elsewhere (Sierra 1992). In 1993, six of the ten statewide elected executives were Hispanic. The speaker of the house of representatives and the senate majority leader were Hispanic. Hispanics are major "grass-roots" components in both major parties, composing about 25 to 30 percent of the Republican party identifiers and 40 to 60 percent of the Democrats. In fact, Hispanics have been such a

TABLE 2.1 Reported Voting and Registration in New Mexico Presidential Elections, 1980-1992, by Race and Hispanic Origin

	% Reported Registered		
Election	White %	Hispanic %	Difference %
1980	68.3	65.1	3.2
1984	70.7	62.1	8.6
1988	66.6	57.9	8.7
1992	68.0	56.8	11.2
	% Reported Voted		
Election	White %	Hispanic %	Difference %
1980	60.4	56.3	4.1
1984	62.9	51.1	11.8
1988	57.1	47.4	9.7
1992	63.8	51.3	12.5

Sources: Adapted from Sierra (1992); U.S. Bureau of the Census (1993).

major part of the state's Democratic party for so long that the state party chair feels that the "Hispanic group is really the backbone of the Democratic party" (Powell 1993).

So while Hispanics are still distinctive enough to warrant attention and analysis in New Mexico politics, they are less distinctive than in other regions. In some ways, this makes analysis more difficult, since the group is closely intermingled with the "mainstream." In fact, outright denial of any ethnic factor in New Mexico politics is a social norm. Since the predominant thinking in the state is that "Hispanics are just like everyone else," election data broken out by ethnicity are rare.

In other ways, however, the blurring of ethnic distinctions makes the phenomenon analytically more interesting. New Mexican Hispanic involvement in politics may be of particular interest because it could very well be a harbinger of Hispanic American politics elsewhere, in a future in which Hispanics increasingly are being incorporated into all facets of American life.

The role of New Mexico Hispanics in the 1992 election was typical. Even though the national parties and campaign organizations felt that they were making special efforts to target Hispanics in New Mexico, very little targeting was actually observed in the state. With the exception of a newsworthy incident or two occasioned by visits by dignitaries and candidates, every observer of the local political scene agreed that no extraordinary targeting of Hispanics was visible. The campaign strategies and tactics were the usual ones, and the results of the elections, both in turnout and direction, also did not indicate anything but typical New Mexico politics. Voter turnout was average, or slightly below average; the top-of-the-ticket Democrats won with the typical level of support from the Hispanic voters; and New Mexico continued to be the single state most reflective of the national presidential vote since 1912.

The 1992 Primary in New Mexico

New Mexico has always had a problematic history with regard to its political nominating procedures (Hain and García 1981). The state has vacillated between conventions and primaries. It even attempted to incorporate both into a "preprimary nominating convention" system. For the last few elections, both parties have held direct primary elections followed by state conventions that ratify the vote of the rank and file and that also decide who those particular individuals will be who will carry the primary election results to the national convention.

Another major obstacle to generating voter interest has been New Mexico's typically late primary, usually in early June. The major national party nominees are already known by the time the presidential primary is held in this state. Further, New Mexico's primary is often held on the same day as that of other more electorally significant states such as California and New Jersey. Compared with these states, New Mexico has relatively few delegates—thirty-four to the Democratic National Convention and twenty-five to the Republican in 1992.

Republicans face an additional barrier to mobilizing voters in presidential primaries. The Republicans in New Mexico are definitely a minority party, disadvantaged by a 1.7 to 1 negative registration ratio to the Democrats. Most of the meaningful primary action is almost always in the majority party, the Democratic party. New Mexican Hispanics are predominantly Democratic in registration—70 to 75 percent in recent years—but also are quite important, if less so, in the state's Republican party (Sierra 1992: 49-50; Zia Research Associates 1992*b*).

To a large extent, this typical situation existed in 1992. The New Mexico primary was held in June. By this time, the Republican primary competition was over. Although the nomination was not formally guaranteed for the Democratic nominee, Bill Clinton, he was recognized as the party's probable nominee.

Despite the formal irrelevance of the primaries, important officials in both of the major parties had decided that the general election was likely to be close and, consequently, paid a great deal of attention to the state of New Mexico as early as May. As New Mexico has only five electoral votes, this attention was unprecedented in the modern era. Seldom in recent history had presidential candidates visited New Mexico personally, at either the primary or the general election stage. The last visit of a serious presidential contender had been in 1968, when Bobby Kennedy was one of the front-runners for the Democratic presidential nomination. The election of 1992 proved to be very different, and New Mexican voters were surprised and flattered by the many visits that began during the primary season.

The formal campaign began on a controversial note. The Bernalillo County (Albuquerque) Democratic party held a preprimary caucus for Democratic candidates in late March. Bernalillo County is by far the most populous county in the state. Democrats in Bernalillo County compose 28 percent of statewide Democratic registration and Republicans make up 42 percent of Republicans statewide. Holding a caucus of Central Committee members was criticized by some Democrats, who saw it as giving an unfair advantage to the person whom the county Democratic chair, Art Trujillo, Governor Bruce King, and state party chair Ray Powell wanted at the top of the ticket in the fall, namely, Bill Clinton. In fact, one of the dissenters—contending that the caucus was de facto an illegal preprimary nominating convention—sought a legal opinion from the state's attorney general. The attorney general rejected the contention. The complainant conceded that the meeting would be fine, but "there is no need to take a vote. Sure, have a mariachi band come by, hold a raffle. What's the purpose of a poll if it's not to stack the cards in favor of some candidates?" (Nelson 1992a). In spite of complaints, the preprimary caucus was held among approximately eight hundred Bernalillo County Democratic party regulars on March 20 and 21, and a straw poll was conducted. Arkansas governor Bill Clinton received 509 of the Central Committee votes and former California governor Jerry Brown garnered 185 (Robertson 1992a). Former Massachusetts senator Paul Tsongas won 13 votes, even though he had withdrawn from the contest the previous week.

The caucus was seen as a kickoff for a tentatively scheduled campaign stop in Albuquerque by Bill Clinton on April 13. Supporters of Jerry Brown were seemingly unperturbed by Clinton's show of force at the caucus and proudly stated that they would be bringing their candidate into the state in May. Several candidates for state and local office, as well as ward leaders, were interviewed at this caucus (Robertson 1992a). Many of these were Hispanics. For example, State Senator Martín Chávez reported that he had been campaigning door-to-door and that he had been finding very strong anti-incumbent sentiment. Longtime Albuquerque Democratic leader Manuel Sánchez, in his sixtieth year as a ward chair, predicted that President Bush would be ousted in November because of voter backlash. The ninety-year-old ward chair said that he thought it was a Democratic year because of the lack of jobs and generally poor shape of the economy.

Other straw votes brought Hispanic candidates to the fore. For example, for the 1st Congressional District, whose constituents almost entirely comprise Bernalillo County residents, the number-one straw vote gatherer was Robert Aragón. In the race for state corporation commissioner, incumbent Jerome Block, who is Hispanic, was the leader in the straw vote. Supreme Court candidate Francesca Lobato finished second to Stanley Frost, but she still received a significant number of votes.

The first major candidate actually to visit the state was Vice-President Dan Quayle, who visited Albuquerque on May 4. Since Quayle's visit followed on the heels of a visit to the recently devastated areas of South-Central Los Angeles, his itinerary included attending a meeting with Youth Development, Inc., a not-for-profit organization that works largely with barrio and gang youth. He also attended a political fund-raiser held by private residents (Linthicum 1992). Some of the media reported that Hispanics in the area seemed unimpressed with Quayle's visit (Asher 1992). The major complaint was that he appeared more interested in media coverage than in the concerns of the community. Of Quayle's visit to the South Valley, an area that is heavily Hispanic, one local Hispanic resident joked that Valley residents had received no hot dogs and free Cokes, which Muhammad Ali had supplied on his visit to the area. Other South Valley residents were more concerned about Quayle's motives. A Hispanic city hall employee reasoned that, because people like Quayle are not in touch with Hispanic communities, she could not believe that he even appeared there. A Hispanic landscaper was quoted as stating that Quayle believed he was impressing the community when he really was not. There was a widespread feeling that Quayle's visit was really an insult to the intelligence of the Valley's Hispanic residents (Asher 1992).

On May 19, it was announced that there would be visits from Democratic presidential candidates Bill Clinton and Jerry Brown, and that the Democratic party had high hopes for these visits (Robertson 1992b). The central role played by Hispanics in the Democratic party is illustrated in how these visits were managed. Lieutenant Governor Casey Luna, a Hispanic and a Clinton supporter, reported that, even though there had not been a "whole lot of hoopla" about the visits, they knew that the visits would be very productive for the Clinton campaign. It was announced that several Hispanic notables, including longtime Rio Arriba County Party Chair Emilio Naranjo and former District Judge Patricia Madrid, would appear on a stage full of New Mexico Democrats supporting Clinton. Clinton had been endorsed by many of the state's top elected Democrats as well as by the New Mexico AFL-CIO, which has a large Hispanic membership. Endorsements came from the state's only Hispanic member of Congress, Bill Richardson, who announced in a prepared statement that he believed Clinton had "innovative proposals to stimulate the economy, improve education, enact a national health care plan, and enhance America's competitiveness overseas." He also said that he had no doubt that "Clinton would make a great president."

The *Albuquerque Journal* reported that Clinton's visit would be followed by an appearance by his wife, Hillary Rodham Clinton. She was tentatively scheduled to be in Santa Fe a few days later to meet with First Lady Alice King on family and youth issues.

On the day before Clinton's visit, a Hispanic homemaker stated in the *Albuquerque Tribune* that she believed Clinton was "going to be another John Kennedy" (Nelson 1992b). The *Tribune* also mentioned Clinton's longheld backing by New Mexico's Democratic power brokers, including Governor Bruce King, House Speaker Raymond Sánchez, Corporation Commissioner Eric Serna, and Land Commissioner Jim Baca. Their support was fortified by a 150-person steering committee and hundreds of other volunteers for Clinton.

The *Tribune* headlines on Wednesday, May 20, reporting the visit of Bill Clinton, read "Time-Squeezed Clinton Scatters Promises to Crowd." His visit turned out to be a mixed blessing; it certainly was not an optimal start toward winning the support of Hispanics. Despite the numerous promises offered to a number of New Mexicans, the constraints of a tight schedule meant that Clinton would disappoint many, particularly Hispanic leaders.

The cause of the dissatisfaction was a decision by the Clinton campaign not to have Clinton attend the national IMAGE, Inc., conference, after a tentative agreement to attend. IMAGE's membership comprises primarily Mexican American government employees; it advocates employment, education, and other civil rights issues. IMAGE leaders had believed that sixty Latino representatives attending the conference would meet with Clinton.

Clinton's New Mexico director, Ray Martínez, took the blame for the confusion. He stated that the meeting with the Hispanic IMAGE conferees had not been cleared with the campaign staff. He reported that the staff had gone "out of the way to accommodate IMAGE [leaders]" and assured everyone that this would not happen again. However, Frank Trujillo, Taos Democratic party chair and head of a group of northern New Mexico Hispanic political leaders, said it was he who had arranged the IMAGE meeting with Clinton through Governor King and Lieutenant Governor Luna; he blamed Clinton's security force for denying the IMAGE group a meeting with Clinton. The *Albuquerque Tribune* reported that, probably in part as an apology, several of IMAGE's leaders had been able to meet briefly with Clinton in a closed-door photo-taking session that had originally been designed only for large donors (Nelson 1992c).

Tomás Gómez, IMAGE president, said that he told the Arkansas governor that Hispanics were not going to be "used" by the Democratic candidates. Gómez further stated that, "if Clinton expected to have the support of Hispanic people, he was going to have to listen to them." He complained that the cancellation served as one more instance in which the Hispanic community had been taken for granted. He vowed to make the national Hispanic leadership aware of the disrespect with which Hispanics had been treated in Albuquerque and went on to argue that Clinton's cancellation exemplified yet another instance of "political deafness to Hispanic voters." He stated that Hispanics had been attempting to get candidates to listen to their issues, as opposed to simply having photo opportunity sessions with Hispanics (Moreno 1992).

Another incident illustrating the less-than-auspicious first visit of Clinton to the state, at least with regard to courting Hispanic votes, involved the local press and one of its Hispanic female reporters (Robertson 1992c). Clinton's aides had told local news organizations that a $125-a-plate fundraising lunch would be closed to reporters. Local reporters, however, showed up anyway, and several were admitted to the Albuquerque Convention Center ballroom before being asked to leave. Emile Gonzales, a reporter for KOB-TV, claimed that she was punched in the kidney by a security guard after she questioned the eviction of the press.

Disappointment with Clinton was not universal among New Mexico's Hispanic leaders. Santa Fe District Judge Steve Herrera, for example, welcomed Clinton's message of "cooperation and values." Herrera said that he thought that Hispanics were going to be very attracted to Clinton's message (Moreno 1992).

In contrast to the highly publicized, if ill-fated, visit of the Democratic front-runner, the next day's visit by candidate Jerry Brown went very smoothly, was low key, and explicitly courted the ethnic vote. On Wednesday, May 20, the former California governor arrived in Albuquerque. He spoke at the Indian Pueblo Cultural Center on a six-hour swing through the city. Reporting on his visit, the May 21 *Tribune* (Nelson 1992d) described Brown as a candidate who maintained a number of "handy themes," for example, creating ethnic and gender balance in his cabinet. Brown apparently conducted a number of give-and-take sessions, allowing groups to define their own agendas.

While Clinton had arrived surrounded by Secret Service guards and a number of aides, Brown was viewed as more accessible to the people. His arrival, however, had been met by no New Mexico Democratic party officials. He held a meeting with Hispanic leaders similar to the one he held with the Indian Pueblo Council. Brown's visit to the IMAGE convention won him admiration as he "touted his record of appointing Hispanics while he was Governor of California" (Rodríguez 1992). At the meeting, he discussed the Hispanics he had named to high-level positions, including Mario Obledo, who had headed California's Health and Welfare Department, and Cruz Reynoso, who had served as State Supreme Court justice, the first Hispanic ever appointed to that position. Brown also remained firm in his opposition to the free trade agreement between the United States and Mexico, for he believed that U.S. companies would simply flee to Mexico "to exploit a cheaper labor force and relaxed environmental standards." He claimed the agreement would be disastrous and pointed out how living conditions in Tijuana and Juárez were already substandard (Powell 1992d). IMAGE president Gómez hugged Brown and thanked him for appearing and for caring about Hispanic needs. "We finally have somebody who understands Hispanic issues and someone who is willing to take charge," waxed Gómez ("Brown Wins Praise of Hispanic Group Ignored by Clinton" 1992). Herb Sanabria, national IMAGE's chief of staff, stated, "He took time to be here, no structure, no body guards" (Nelson 1992d). Sanabria believed the meeting gave Brown some extra Hispanic votes. An IMAGE member compared the two candidates: "Clinton was rude. Brown is intrinsically sincere when he talks about Hispanic issues." The love fest, however, was less than unanimous; a member of IMAGE formerly from California explained that she could no longer listen to Brown, as she remembered him as governor. She stated that she did not trust him and issued a gloomy verdict for his campaign among Hispanics.

At his speech at Los Amigos Stables in Albuquerque's North Valley, Brown explained that no one else running for president, senator, or governor could say that he or she had pushed through, along with César Chávez, the "most far-reaching farm labor law" in the history of the country (Rodríguez 1992). He also said that, unlike his opponent Bill Clinton, he had pushed through bilingual and bicultural education and "none of these English-only laws." Further criticizing Clinton's last-minute cancellation, one of Brown's supporters from IMAGE stated that, by not giving the organization the time of day, Clinton was exemplifying how he took the Hispanic community and the Southwest for granted.

For the next couple of weeks, Bill Clinton's spin doctors worked at controlling the damage caused by their candidate's visit (Nelson 1992e). Concerns over perceived snubs of Hispanics in Albuquerque on May 20 had already included a series of spins, including calls to reporters and a quiet meeting with Hispanics in Santa Fe. On Tuesday, June 2, the campaign named Albuquerque businessperson Ed Romero state cochair. Late the previous week, the campaign had released a list of New Mexican Hispanics backing Clinton. At least one of them, State Senator Martín Chávez, was somewhat surprised by his inclusion. Chávez stated, "I told them they could use my name but not to play ethnic politics." A *Tribune* reporter opined that, "with the expected general election entrance of Ross Perot, minority votes will play an even more critical role for Clinton" (Nelson 1992e). Rumors now abounded that Clinton would speak to a June convention of Hispanic elected officials in Santa Fe, but Little Rock had not yet promised anything definite.

As primary day approached, questions abounded as to how much effect, if any, the visits of these candidates had. Would there be any backlash against the candidate favored by the Democratic party hierarchy, including most of the state's Hispanic political leaders? Two influential Hispanic political leaders favored yet other candidates. Former governor Jerry Apodaca was among many well-known Democrats supporting Paul Tsongas. Tom Harkin had the support of Mary Sue Gutiérrez, former director of the state's AFL-CIO committee on political education. Would IMAGE national leaders' condemnation of Clinton have any noticeable effect on the usual centrist-moderate position of Hispanic Democratic voters in New Mexico? Would Jerry Brown's "radical" position, a posture typically rejected by New Mexican Hispanics, be overlooked because of his overt appeals to the ethnic vote?

A statewide preelection poll by Zia Research Associates (1992a) cast some light on these unknowns. The statewide survey of registered voters revealed some interesting, although not large, ethnic differences in patterns of support between Anglos and Hispanics. The poll showed that Clinton had the support of 44 percent of the Anglos and 38 percent of the Hispanics. The "uncommitted delegate" voters included 13 percent of the Anglos and 5 percent of the Hispanics. A small but similar number of Anglos and

Hispanics (8 percent) supported Jerry Brown. Tsongas received 6 percent of the Anglos' support and 3 percent of the Hispanic support. Perot had 6 percent Anglo support and 4 percent Hispanic support. The largest difference between Anglo and Hispanic preferences was among the undecided Democratic voters; twice as many Hispanics as Anglos were undecided a few days prior to the primary election. Fully 41 percent, the largest plurality of Hispanic voters, were not sure whom they were going to vote for as their party's nominee, compared with just 20 percent of Anglos. Perhaps Clinton's less than fully successful visit, criticized by IMAGE leaders, the alleged treatment of the female Hispanic reporter, and the doubts cast by Jerry Brown and others about southerner Clinton's record on Hispanic appointments and issues did weaken the enthusiasm of rank-and-file Hispanic Democrats, in spite of the endorsements by most of the state's Hispanic party elites.

Among Republicans, Bush had the support of 59 percent of the Anglo Republicans and 63 percent of the Hispanic Republicans. The Republicans for uncommitted delegates were slightly more Hispanic than Anglo, 15 to 13 percent. Votes for Buchanan were minimal, although Hispanics favored him relatively more than did Anglo Republicans, 15 to 10 percent, respectively. Anglo Republicans were slightly more supportive of Perot than were Hispanic Republicans, 7 to 3 percent, respectively, while 17 percent of Anglos and 10 percent of Hispanics were undecided.

State and Local Races

In addition to the presidential contests, there were a few other races involving Hispanics that conceivably could have increased Hispanic turnout. However, most pundits perceived a relatively low level of interest in this primary, featuring as it did the cross-pressures described above, no gubernatorial or senatorial contests, and a generally high level of negativism or cynicism among the public across the state and the nation. Even though redistricting of the congressional and state legislative districts had occurred, there were few changes expected; virtually all incumbents (and most state legislative candidates in both parties) ran without serious challenges.

In New Mexico's 1st Congressional District (Bernalillo County), four Democrats competed for the right to challenge one-term incumbent Republican Steve Schiff. A former state legislator, Robert Aragón, was the only Hispanic candidate among the four contenders.

In New Mexico's 2nd Congressional District, three Democrats ran in the primary for the right to oppose another long-term incumbent Republican, Joe Skeen. The only Hispanic challenger was Dan Sosa, Jr., former state supreme court justice, from Las Cruces. Sosa contended that incumbent

Skeen had not done a good job serving anyone in the district, especially Hispanics and those with lower incomes.

In the third of New Mexico's congressional districts, another long-term incumbent, Democrat Bill Richardson, faced no primary challengers (Richardson's mother was Mexican and he is a member of the Hispanic Congressional Caucus).

The New Mexico primary elections were held on June 2. Turnout was slightly below average for recent presidential primaries—47.1 percent, with 51 percent of registered Democrats and 41 percent of registered Republicans voting in their respective primaries.

The results were pretty much as expected, with Bush winning a large majority of the Republican voters and Clinton taking a bare majority of Democratic primary voters. In the GOP primary, George Bush received 64 percent of the 86,078 votes cast. The next highest proportion (27 percent) went for "uncommitted" delegates. Patrick Buchanan garnered only 9 percent of the total. Most of the other races on the Republican ballot were uncontested. Democrats cast a majority (53 percent) of their ballots (179,649) for Bill Clinton. He was followed by "uncommitted" (19 percent), Jerry Brown (17 percent), Paul Tsongas (6 percent), Tom Harkin (2 percent), Larry Agran (1 percent), and Lyndon LaRouche (1 percent).

In the 1st Congressional District, the only Hispanic candidate, Robert Aragón, received the party's nomination with 45 percent of the 49,862 votes cast. The majority of votes were cast for his four Anglo opponents, but split four ways; Aragón's closest contender was James Nance, with 30 percent (14,860 votes). Judging from preprimary polls, ethnicity was a major consideration, as Hispanics overwhelmingly supported Aragón while the Anglo vote was divided among Aragón and the four Anglo candidates. A similar situation emerged in the 2nd Congressional District. The one Hispanic among the three candidates, Dan Sosa, Jr., won with a plurality of 47 percent.

The same ethnic bloc voting pattern emerged in the statewide Corporation Commission contest. Hispanic Jerome Block won a plurality (74,395) of the votes cast, with a majority of the votes (90,073) split between his two Anglo female opponents.

Between the Primaries and the General Election

After the June 2 primary, the state's Democratic party met on Saturday, June 13, to elect twenty-six national delegates, who would join the eight super delegates at the national presidential convention (Yeager 1992). Two dozen of the thirty-four-member delegation supported Bill Clinton, but supporters of Governor Jerry Brown and Ross Perot were also included. Although it did not make many of the party regulars happy, one of the convention delegates was qualified under party rules to run as an uncommitted delegate because someone had to be selected to reflect the 19 percent uncommitted vote in the primary, which largely was a vote for Ross Perot. Jerry Brown supporters sent three committed delegates to the convention.

The platform passed at the Democratic state convention included opposition to tax increases, unless they were necessary; support for governmental appointments based more on merit than on partisan loyalty; support of stronger ethics, financial disclosure, and conflict-of-interest laws; a call for government partnership and labor to foster economic development; a call for full employment; and conditional approval for opening the Waste Isolation Pilot Plant. The platform also called for a return to preprimary nominating conventions, which had given party regulars greater say about candidates in primary elections. Later, the state Democratic chair would characterize the issues as being important to Hispanics as well as Anglos, but he could not recall any issues as being intended as strictly Hispanic issues.

The platform committee chair, Patrick Apodaca of Albuquerque, commented on the diversity of the state in observing that "there are a lot of Democrats, fortunately, but Democrats have different views." The list of convention delegates revealed six Hispanics among the eighteen supporting Bill Clinton; none of the five pledged to Jerry Brown; no Hispanics among the uncommitted delegates; and three of the eight super delegates, U.S. Representative Bill Richardson, Bernalillo County Democratic Chair Art Trujillo, and former governor Toney Anaya (Yeager 1992). Overall, the proportion of Hispanic delegates reflected roughly their proportions among both Democratic party ranks and supporters of Clinton. Nine of the thirty-four (26 percent) delegates to the Democratic National Convention were Hispanic.

One of New Mexico's super delegates was heard from during the Democratic party's national convention. Toney Anaya, former governor of New Mexico, received publicity for his comments on national television regarding what he saw as the Clinton organization's neglect of its traditional ethnic minority base, particularly Hispanics.

The GOP state convention also took place on Saturday, June 13. Only Bush backers were among the twenty-five delegates selected to the national convention in Houston in August. Since there was a substantial proportion of Republican primary voters not voting for Bush in the GOP primary, only seventeen were official Bush delegates; the others were officially uncommitted, although supporters of President Bush in practice. The vote for Ross Perot was discounted by former state GOP chair Edward Luján, who stated that "Perot is not a Republican, this is not his convention." Thus, the sixty "uncommitted" state convention delegates were upset because they could not seek election to the national convention. At the state GOP convention, a Hispanic woman, Laree Pérez of Albuquerque, was elected the state's national committeeperson. The Republican delegates to the national convention included eight Hispanics among the twenty-seven delegates (30 percent), including U.S. Interior Secretary Manuel Luján, Jr.

The General Election

In the general election campaign, New Mexico Hispanics continued to play a substantial role in electoral activities, but were not a particularly distinctive segment. Only minimal efforts specifically targeted the Hispanic vote. These efforts mainly consisted of having luminaries from each party visit areas of substantial Hispanic population and give some speeches on behalf of their candidates.

I contacted party officials in New Mexico who headed or were heavily involved in the campaigns of the presidential candidates. All felt that their respective national parties had at least hoped or intended to make special efforts to win Hispanic support. The GOP coordinator for Hispanic affairs in the state, David Archuleta, said he and other New Mexican Republican leaders had been trained by the national party to speak out on issues on behalf of President Bush—mainly on the economy and a criticism of the Clinton record. National GOP committeeperson Laree Pérez stated that the Republicans cared about and had made an effort to reach Hispanics, citing as one example a whole week of "caravan tours to every little community in northern New Mexico" by state party Chair John Lattuzio, senior U.S. Senator Pete Domenici, and several in-state Hispanic activists and leaders. Democratic party officials, including several Hispanic party officials and leaders, had also gone to sessions outside the state to be "trained" for a special effort to win the support of Hispanic voters, largely through public speeches in heavily Hispanic areas and publicity through the media. These speaking tours are very traditional and typical of campaigning in New Mexico. Given the fact that Hispanics in New Mexico historically have fairly stable partisan voting patterns favoring the Democratic presidential candidates—usually from 60 to 70 percent—it seemed that in the state neither party seemed willing or able to break out of the traditional patterns.

Ray Martínez, the Clinton state director, was a Texas Hispanic who had previously served on the staff of the Texas attorney general, Dan Morales. In an interview with me, Martínez asserted that the Democratic party was making some effort to tie the state campaign to the national Adelante con Clinton! campaign or, at least, to use the slogan, which was being put forth nationally. He wanted to emphasize that the Democratic party was not taking the state's Hispanics for granted and that the organization was using a "community oriented, bottom-up, inclusive approach" to the Hispanic community. For example, Martínez mentioned that they were bringing in

Hispanic celebrities, such as Henry Cisneros, to speak for Clinton. In keeping with the agenda set by Governor Clinton, however, the emphasis from this Hispanic coordinator in a 40 percent Hispanic state was on an "all-inclusive agenda." In fact, Martínez felt that Hispanics in New Mexico and elsewhere would have the same agenda as mainstream America, if not entirely so in 1992, certainly in the near future. Nonetheless, Martínez stressed that they were paying special attention to Hispanics and were working, for example, with organizations such as LULAC to distribute bilingual campaign materials and to bring in well-known Hispanic political figures to address the Hispanic communities in New Mexico.

An example of the latter occurred on October 18, when Henry Cisneros, described by the press as "a Bill Clinton advisor and former mayor of San Antonio," talked to residents of the predominantly Hispanic South Valley area of Albuquerque (*Albuquerque Journal* [October 19, 1992]). Addressing a crowd of about five hundred at the Third Annual Festival de Otoño, Cisneros stressed the importance of change through the vote and particularly through the Hispanic vote. In fact, Cisneros stressed the theme of "su voto es su voz" (your vote is your voice). While emphasizing the importance of voting for the future of America, he deemphasized any partisan themes or candidates. This approach was echoed by a former and soon-to-be-re-elected state legislator, Delano García, who stated that Cisneros's message was exactly what was needed and that "we should not be complacent." Cisneros had spent the day speaking in three other much smaller, but largely Hispanic, cities: Las Vegas, Española, and Taos. In these northern New Mexico towns, Cisneros spoke in Spanish at old-fashioned political rallies on the plazas.

Joining him was U.S. Representative Bill Richardson. Richardson was much more partisan than Cisneros. Also speaking in Spanish, he told people not to forget that the Democratic party was the party of Franklin Roosevelt, John F. Kennedy, Jimmy Carter, and now Bill Clinton. Richardson continued, "If you want a government in Washington that represents the old people, the children, and the veterans, all of the interests of the Hispanic people, vote for Bill Clinton." Cisneros, continuing in Spanish, mentioned the importance of a Clinton administration in bringing about health care and addressing the problem of unemployment.

The Democratic state chair felt that, while there was some intent to pay special attention to Hispanics, for example, the speaker training sessions and the appointment of an Adelante con Clinton! coordinator in the state, the actual result was more of an "overlay" of this on the typical campaign rather than a distinctive "targeting" effort. He epitomized the prevailing view of Hispanics in New Mexico politics when he reiterated that any and every Democratic campaign in New Mexico was going to "*automatically* be directed at Hispanics since they are such an integral part of the party" (Powell 1993).

It is interesting that, while the Democratic candidates were addressing primarily Hispanic audiences in their campaign speeches, New Mexico's senior senator, Republican Pete Domenici, was talking to a group of Asian Americans and advocating less regulation, fewer taxes, more free enterprise, and support of small businesses. The event was sponsored by the Chinese for Bush Coalition. Some of the Chinese Americans in attendance supported Bush for his position on family and stated that the Chinese had had the same family values for thousands of years, which President Bush shared. Senator Domenici added that Clinton's home state of Arkansas was one of only two states in the Union without a civil rights law.

When the issue of Arkansas's failure to pass a civil rights law was raised to Clinton state coordinator Martínez, he explained that it was the result of political necessity. Clinton supported such legislation, but he was opposed by a nearly unanimous legislature. Further, he reminded his interviewer that less than 1 percent of Arkansas' population is Hispanic.

The verbal rhetoric of celebrities continued a few days later when Marilyn Quayle visited Albuquerque on October 21 (*Albuquerque Journal* [October 23, 1992]). Flanked by Albuquerque Republican Hispanic leaders, she accused Clinton of being anti-Hispanic. The wife of the vice-president also said that the Republican party stand on abortion would not hurt their re-election effort, but in fact would be well received by the Hispanic community. Mrs. Quayle spoke to over one hundred persons at a closed-door breakfast sponsored by the Albuquerque Chapter of the Republican National Hispanic Assembly. In a brief news conference afterward, she related that President George Bush had a special feeling for the Hispanic community. "The strides that have been made in the United States for people of Hispanic origin are tremendous, and we cannot break that stride," Mrs. Quayle said. "With President Bush you know that you would be moving forward; Bill Clinton . . . would set Hispanics back in the United States."

Excerpts of statements from San Antonio pollster, Lionel Sosa, a senior adviser to the Bush campaign, were read by former State Republican party chair Ed Luján and by David Archuleta, chair of the Bush/Quayle campaign in New Mexico. Archuleta reminded the crowd that Clinton had not included any Hispanics in policymaking positions within his state administration and also brought up again that Clinton had signed a law in Arkansas establishing English as the official language. This drew a rebuttal from the Clinton campaign's Martínez, who said that Archuleta's statement was "a false charge." "The fact of the matter is Governor Clinton has an excellent record on giving ethnic minorities as well as women opportunities to serve," Martinez retorted. Archuleta continued, however, "I would like to challenge those Hispanic leaders who are supporting Clinton, those same leaders who fought hard against discrimination, against English-only, for civil rights, for inclusion, and for business opportunities to explain to the

Hispanic voters how they can in good conscience support a man who stands for everything that they are against." Martínez explained that Clinton had signed the official English-only law because it had already been passed by veto-proof majorities in the Arkansas legislature. He added that the governor inserted language ensuring that public schools would continue to provide equal educational opportunities to all.

Aside from these brief verbal jousts occasioned by the visits of partisan celebrities, there was very little focus on Hispanics in the media. Only a few spot announcements were heard on Spanish-language radio. The issues that were brought up by the campaign leaders and spokespersons never ignited a general debate or even sustained interest as Hispanic issues. If the media did not overtly downplay these personal appearances, they either downplayed or deemphasized the issues as well as the ethnic aspects of them. GOP leader Archuleta expressed frustration with the state's media and felt they thwarted much of his party's attempts to get out the message, especially those designed to appeal to Hispanics. (Archuleta 1993).

In short, there was little or no evidence at the grass-roots level of any extraordinary effort at targeting or mobilizing the Hispanic vote as a distinctive ethnic voting bloc involving unusual organizational activity, new leadership, or a focus on primarily Hispanic issues.

Campaign Results

A preelection statewide opinion survey conducted by Zia Research Associates broadcast on KOAT-TV on November 2 revealed quite traditional patterns of preferences that seemed little affected by any specifics this particular campaign had generated (Zia Research Associates 1992b). The election, according to the survey results, seemed to be, as it was on a national scale, primarily a referendum on the economic performance of the Bush administration. Hispanics (19.7 percent) reported they were less likely to feel that they were better off than four years previously (30 percent of Anglos felt that way). Hispanic registered voters were also much more likely than Anglos to be critical of the performance of George Bush as president. A few days before the election, 57 percent of Hispanic registered voters favored Bill Clinton and Al Gore, compared with one-third of Anglo voters. Only 22 percent of Hispanics favored the Republican ticket of George Bush and Dan Quayle, compared with 42 percent of Anglo registered voters. Ross Perot and James Stockdale had twice as much Anglo as Hispanic support, 15 percent to 7 percent, respectively. Hispanics were slightly more undecided (14 percent) than were Anglos (10 percent) in their preference for a presidential candidate.

Ethnic presidential preferences were less important than were partisan differences, as 64 percent of the Democrats favored Clinton and Gore and

63 percent of the Republicans favored Bush and Quayle. Still, ethnicity was a significant factor even among Clinton's partisan supporters. Among the 64 percent of the Democrats who supported Clinton, ethnic differences were evident: 69 percent of Hispanic Democrats favored Clinton, compared with 56 percent of Anglo Democrats. Ethnicity was less a factor among partisan supporters of the Republican candidates: 64 percent of Anglo Republicans and 61 percent of Anglo Hispanics favored Bush and Quayle.

The Independents' favorites were Perot and Stockdale, who received 33 percent support compared with 28 percent for Bush and Quayle and 22 percent for Clinton and Gore. With partisan attachments absent, ethnic differences were magnified. One-third of Hispanic Independents favored Clinton and Gore, compared with 19 percent of Anglo Independents.

Although ethnicity was obviously a factor correlated with presidential preference, it was even more evident in congressional races in which Hispanic candidates were running. In the 1st Congressional District, the Hispanic challenger, Robert Aragón, had a slight margin among all Hispanic voters—47 percent to 44 percent—over incumbent Republican Steve Schiff. Among Anglos, 73 percent favored Schiff and only 21 percent preferred Aragón. Among his own Democratic partisans, Aragón received majority support (58 percent) from Hispanics but only 39 percent from Anglos. On the other hand, incumbent Republican Schiff garnered majority support from both Anglo (88 percent) and Hispanic (63 percent) copartisans.

In the 2nd Congressional District, a Hispanic Democrat was also challenging an incumbent Republican. The ethnic factor was again evident—even more so perhaps—as Anglos favored incumbent Republican Joe Skeen 69 to 27 percent. Dan Sosa, Skeen's Democratic opponent, attracted a majority of Hispanic voters (58 percent) to incumbent Skeen's 29 percent. Skeen was the choice of both Anglo (82 percent) and Hispanic (78 percent) GOP identifiers as well as 57 percent of Anglo Democrats. Democratic challenger Sosa had majority support only among Hispanic Democrats (66 percent).

The 3rd Congressional District featured a popular incumbent, Democrat Bill Richardson, running against relatively unknown challengers. A few days before the election, Representative Richardson was drawing the support of 75 percent of the Hispanic voters as well as 58 percent of the Anglo voters in his district. Richardson enjoyed huge majorities of both ethnic groups of Democrats as well as a plurality of Hispanic Republicans. Only Anglo Republicans gave plurality support to his opponent, Gregg Bemis.

The results of the election confirmed the preference expressed in the preelection survey. Once again, overall, New Mexico voted as the nation did for its presidential candidates. New Mexico voters cast 46 percent of their votes for the Clinton ticket, 37 percent for Bush, 17 percent for Ross Perot.

Exit polls conducted by Voter Research and Surveys, Inc. (1992), reported that Hispanic voters voted 60 percent for Clinton, 29 percent for Bush, and 11 percent for Perot. Although continuing the traditional large majority level of support for Democratic presidential candidates by Hispanics, this was a decline of about 69 percent in Democratic support among Hispanics from the 1988 election (Sierra 1992). Of course, one must consider that 11 percent of the total vote went to Perot. Among "whites," New Mexicans' vote was 38 percent for Clinton, 43 percent for Bush, and 19 percent for Perot.

It is true that Hispanic (or Democratic) voters were instrumental in giving the state's electoral votes to Clinton. A majority of Hispanic voters preferred Clinton and Gore, while the largest plurality of Anglo voters favored Bush and Quayle. The traditional pattern of Hispanic Democratic voting for presidential candidates in New Mexico seemed to have been little affected by the long and costly campaign. Even though New Mexico received more attention than it had in many years, voting patterns in general and Hispanic voting patterns specifically did not seem to reflect that heightened interest.

Turnout among New Mexican Hispanics was 51.3 percent of those eligible (U.S. Bureau of the Census 1993). This proportion equals the average turnout over the previous three presidential elections. Among "white" voters, the turnout in 1992 was 3.7 percent higher than the average in the presidential elections of 1980, 1984, and 1988.

Although the state underwent considerable redistricting following the 1990 census, the new district boundaries had little effect on Hispanics as a group. For example, they made no difference in the proportion of Hispanics in the state legislature. After the 1988 general elections, 41 of New Mexico's 112 state legislators were Hispanic. Subsequent to the 1992 redistricting and presidential elections, 42 Hispanics took their legislative seats in Santa Fe to compose 38 percent of the legislature.

Conclusion

What, then, was the role of Hispanics in the 1992 general election in New Mexico? It could be summed up by observing that it was the role that has conventionally been played by Hispanics in the state's politics. Hispanics were an integral part of the process. Probably more so than in any other state they were incorporated into the campaign and the election of 1992. Hispanics also were less distinctive, at least publicly, as an electoral bloc, than in other places. In spite of the strategic intentions of the national organizations, the local evidence of major campaign efforts to target Hispanics, as Hispanics, in effect seemed to take for granted their traditional patterns of support or to attract them through appeals that transcended ethnicity.

State Democratic party leaders felt that they did focus on Hispanics, but as major players in Democratic party politics more than as a distinctive ethnic voting bloc. Any special efforts directed at Hispanics were primarily because they were traditionally strong supporters of Democratic candidates, and this election was perceived as being a close race. In reflecting on the campaign, the party chair surmised that "there probably was not as much effort as there should have been" in directing the campaign specifically to Hispanics as Hispanics. In spite of this, the Democratic presidential candidate still received 60 percent of the Hispanic vote, about in the middle of the 50 to 70 percent vote range of Hispanic support for Democrats over the past several general elections (Sierra 1992).

Republican party leaders were frustrated at their inability to get out their message to Hispanics and to convert enough to deliver the state for their candidate. One problem they perceived was that the media largely shut the gate on their party's activities and efforts by not printing prepared press releases or reporting events. Perhaps even more important, the feeling was that the overwhelming focus on the economy obliterated all other messages, and that these economic concerns "affected Hispanics and Anglos in the same way" (Archuleta 1993).

Several Hispanics ran for office with mixed success. At the congressional level, in two of the three districts, Hispanic Democratic challengers, having won their party's primary, ran against incumbent Anglo Republicans. Both lost. In the 3rd Congressional District, a Hispanic incumbent Democrat won. There were virtually no changes in the proportion of Hispanic members in state-level elected offices, including the state legislature.

In New Mexico the campaign itself featured a minimal focus by both parties on the Hispanic vote as a distinctive ethnic voting bloc. There were a few pointed appearances and appeals by political visitors to the state. There were some campaign materials produced in Spanish and targeted to Hispanic voters produced by the parties. The Democrats focused on solidifying the traditional Hispanic-Democratic participation rate, including getting out the vote in largely Hispanic-Democratic areas. The Republicans, who would have had to make much more specifically ethnic appeals and hope that ethnicity would override partisanship, struggled unsuccessfully to make inroads against tradition. Few, if any, of the state and local politicos felt that an explicitly ethnic strategy would have a significant positive effect.

Some 60 percent of the Hispanic voters voted for Democratic presidential candidate Bill Clinton. Independent candidate Ross Perot drew less support from the Hispanic community than from the non-Hispanic voters. In the congressional races, the Hispanic candidates, regardless of party affiliation, attracted a majority of the Hispanic electorate's support. It should be noted that the preferences of Anglos were proportionately even stronger for the Anglo candidates.

So, although New Mexico in some ways appeared to be given more attention in the 1992 presidential election than it had for decades, nothing much seemed to alter or be altered by the Hispanic vote. Once again, as earlier, New Mexican Hispanics' role in the general election contests for national offices could be characterized as "prominent but not pivotal" (Sierra 1992). In moderate to conservative New Mexico, the state's political culture, so fragmented and resistant to anything but incremental change, preserved and maintained traditional patterns of participation, both among Hispanics and non-Hispanics.

Note

1. I would like to express my thanks and appreciation to Margaret Banek, Enrique Cardiel, Sandra García, Marcy Henry, Virginia Ortiz, Gil St. Clair, and Zia Research Associates for their contributions to this chapter.

References

Archuleta, David. 1993. Interview with the author (August 13).
Asher, E. 1992. "S. Valley Greets Veep with Skepticism, Cops." *Albuquerque Tribune* (May 5).
"Brown Wins Praise of Hispanic Group Ignored by Clinton." 1992. *Santa Fe New Mexican* (May 21, B7).
García, F. Chris. 1974. "Manitos and Chicanos in New Mexico Politics." In F. Chris García, ed., *La Causa Política: A Chicano Politics Reader*, pp. 271–280. Notre Dame: University of Notre Dame Press.
García, F. Chris, and Robert D. Wrinkle. 1971. "New Mexico: Urban Politics in a State of Varied Political Cultures." In Robert D. Wrinkle, ed., *Politics in the Urban Southwest*, pp. 35–49. Albuquerque: Division of Government Research, Institute for Social Research and Development, University of New Mexico.
Hain, Paul L., and José Z. García. 1981. "Voting, Elections and Parties." In F. Chris García and Paul L. Hain, eds., *New Mexico Government*, pp. 218–239. Albuquerque: University of New Mexico Press.
Linthicum, Leslie. 1992. "Quayle Lends an Ear to Albuquerque." *Albuquerque Journal* (May 5).
Martínez, Ray. 1992. Interview with the author (October 10).
Moreno, Ed. 1992. "Canceled Meeting Angers Hispanics." *Albuquerque Journal* (May 20).
Nelson, Kate. 1992a. "N.M. Demo Caucus Blasted." *Albuquerque Tribune* (March 20).
―――. 1992b. "Clinton Musters N.M. Troops." *Albuquerque Tribune* (May 19).
―――. 1992c. "Time-Squeezed Clinton Scatters Promises to Crowd." *Albuquerque Tribune* (May 20).
―――. 1992d. "Herky, Jerky Campaign Touches Down." *Albuquerque Tribune* (May 21).
―――. 1992e. "Clinton Folk Scurry to Curry Favor with Hispanics." *Albuquerque Tribune* (June 4).

Powell, Ray. 1993. Interview with the author (August 18).
Robertson, John. 1992a. "Clinton Tops Democratic Poll." *Albuquerque Journal* (March 22).
———. 1992b. "Candidate's Visit Hoopla Gives Party High Hopes." *Albuquerque Journal* (May 19).
———. 1992c. "Campaign Keeps Distance Between Clinton, Reporters." *Albuquerque Journal* (May 20).
———. 1992d. "Brown Stands Firm Against Trade Pact." *Albuquerque Journal* (May 21).
Rodríguez, Robert. 1992. "Hispanics Ready to Take Stand." *Albuquerque Journal* (May 23).
Sierra, Christine Marie. 1992. "Hispanos in the 1988 General Election in New Mexico." In Rodolfo O. de la Garza and Louis DeSipio, eds., *From Rhetoric to Reality: Latino Politics in the 1988 Elections*, pp. 43–68. Boulder, Colo.: Westview Press.
U.S. Bureau of the Census. 1993. *Voting and Registration in the Election of November 1992*. Current Population Reports, Series P-20, No. 466. Washington, D.C.: U.S. Government Printing Office.
Vigil, Maurilio E. 1979. "Hispanos and the Governorship in New Mexico." *New Mexico Highlands University Journal* 1 (May): 4–13.
———. 1978. *Chicano Politics*. Washington, D.C.: University Press of America.
Voter Research and Surveys, Inc. 1992. Unpublished results of exit polls conducted by Voter Research and Surveys, Inc. commissioned by KOAT-TV, ABC affiliate in Albuquerque, New Mexico.
Yeager, John. 1992. "Democratic Delegates Chosen for Convention." *Albuquerque Journal* (June 14).
Zia Research Associates, Inc. 1992a. "Action 7/Zia Poll." Unpublished results of survey of New Mexico registered voters, May 27–June 1, conducted for KOAT-TV for the June 2, 1992, primary election. Albuquerque.
———. 1992b. "Action 7/Zia Poll." Survey of New Mexico registered voters, October 29–November 1, conducted for KOAT-TV for the November 3 election. Albuquerque.

3

An Essential Vote: Latinos and the 1992 Elections in Colorado

Rodney E. Hero

Colorado's Latino population of approximately 420,000 (13 percent) may not initially appear large in comparison with that of other states. However, Colorado has the highest rate of adult citizenship among Latinos (over 90 percent in 1990) of any of the nine states with substantial Latino population (NALEO 1992: 7). As a result, Latinos compose as great or larger a segment of the Colorado electorate (about 10 percent of eligible voters) as do Latino voters in such states as California, Arizona, and Florida (NALEO 1992: 2).

Despite these potentially significant numbers, the votes of Colorado Latinos have not been critical in previous presidential elections or in other statewide elections (Saiz 1992). The 1992 election may well have been different, although it is difficult to determine conclusively. At a minimum, the Latino vote was essential in the state's presidential race and appears to have been quite significant in at least two other races as well.

In 1992, Democratic presidential candidate Bill Clinton gained Colorado's eight electoral college votes by winning 40.1 percent of the popular vote, to 35.9 percent for incumbent George Bush and 23.3 percent for independent candidate H. Ross Perot. The Clinton margin over Bush was 66,831 votes. This was the first time since 1964, the year of the Johnson landslide, that the Democratic presidential nominee had carried the state. In the intervening years Colorado, like most of the Rocky Mountain states, commonly provided comfortable margins for Republican presidential candidates. Given early estimates and the size of Republican victories in Colorado from 1968 to 1988, and because most presidential races in those years were not especially close at the national level, various preconditions for the Latino vote to be significant were not present (Guerra 1992; NALEO 1992: 19).

In 1992, Colorado was seen as a swing state in the presidential election (*Denver Post* [September 16, 1992: 6A]), thus enhancing the potential importance of the Latino vote in this race. The Latino vote also appears to have substantially influenced outcomes in other phases of the 1992 electoral process. This chapter assesses the extent and nature of the Latino impact on the 1992 Colorado elections and seeks to provide a broader perspective on these issues.

Prior to addressing the substantive matters of Latino voting patterns, some methodological caveats must be offered. The distribution and concentration of the Latino population in Colorado, along with the absence of readily available data on this group, makes any simple or definitive assessment of its impact in statewide elections very difficult, as is underscored by the data in Table 3.1. For instance, the largest *number* of Latinos, over 107,000, is in the city and county of Denver; yet Hispanics compose only 19 percent of the population there. On the other hand, the two counties with the largest *proportion* of Hispanics—Costilla (77 percent) and Conejos (60 percent)—are small counties, with fewer than 4,000 and 8,000 residents, respectively. Pueblo is the only county among the top ten in both the proportion and the number of Latinos. And, while the Latino population is somewhat concentrated within the counties just noted, there is also considerable dispersion.

How, then, might the impact of the Latino vote best be examined? This analysis focuses on, first, the areas with the highest numbers of Latinos. This includes three counties: Adams, Denver, and Pueblo. My second focus is areas with the largest proportion of Latinos. These include two counties: Conejos and Costilla, the only Colorado counties in which Hispanics are a majority of the population. These counties, the metropolitan Denver area (Denver and Adams), and southern Colorado (Pueblo, Conejos, and Costilla),

TABLE 3.1 The Distribution of Latinos in Colorado, Most Heavily Hispanic Counties

County	% Latino	County	No. of Latinos
Costilla	77	Denver	107,382
Conejos	60	Adams	49,179
Saguache	46	Pueblo	44,090
Las Animas	44	El Paso	34,473
Huerfano	40	Jefferson	30,791
Rio Grande	40	Weld	27,502
Alamosa	39	Arapahoe	21,743
Pueblo	36	Boulder	15,195
Otero	35	Larimer	12,227
Bent	27	Mesa	7,563

Source: Latin America Research and Service Agency (1992a: 1).

represent the two largest concentrations of Latinos in the state. Collectively, about 50 percent of the state's Latino population resides in these five counties.

Examining only county-level data is inadequate, however, because Latinos compose a third or less of the population in three of the five counties. This poses problems for accuracy and generalization. Therefore, I examine the precincts with the highest and the lowest proportion of Latinos in all five counties to provide a better portrayal of Latino voting patterns and, as data permit, voter turnout. This precinct-level focus lessens somewhat, but does not remove, the accuracy and generalization problems. It should also be emphasized that the proportion of Latinos in the most heavily Latino precincts varies considerably from county to county, and in no instance approaches 100 percent. In Denver and Pueblo counties, for example, Latinos as a percentage of registered voters in 1992 were about 68 percent in the five most heavily Latino precincts; in Adams County Latinos accounted for only 40 percent of registered voters in the most heavily Latino precincts (see notes to Tables 3.2 through 3.6).

Background

Socioeconomic status conditions levels of political participation and activity (Verba and Nie 1972). As is well known, the socioeconomic status of Latinos is substantially lower than that of the general population. This is also the case in Colorado; by most indicators of socioeconomic well-being, Latinos lag much behind the state's Anglo, and often the black, population (Hero 1992: 104).

In terms of ethnic identification, 67 percent of Colorado's Latinos identify their ethnic background as "Mexican" origin, 2 percent as either Puerto Rican or Cuban, and 31 percent as "other Hispanic" (*LARASA Today* [Summer 1992: 1]; de la Garza et al. 1992: 39-40). Many of those who identify as "other Hispanic" are from southern Colorado and tend to think of themselves as being of "Spanish" background because they trace their heritage to early Spanish, pre-Mexican, settlers.

Party Affiliation among Colorado Latinos

Individual party affiliation is a strong predictor of voting behavior. It is, thus, important to note the party affiliation patterns of Latinos. The state's population in general is almost equally split between Republicans, Democrats, and unaffiliateds, with Republicans holding a slight plurality (McIver and Stone 1992: 64-65). In the state as a whole, my estimate (based on various data) is that over 60 percent, and perhaps as many as 70 percent, of registered Latinos are Democrats, about 16 percent are Republicans, and the remainder are unaffiliated. Latinos, therefore, are about twice as likely as the general population to register as Democrats, and only half as likely to register as Republicans. This also suggests that Latinos can be highly influential in Democratic party primaries.

Tables 3.2 through 3.6 indicate the pattern of party affiliation for the precincts with the highest proportion of Latinos and for the precincts with the lowest proportion of Latinos for each of the counties examined. The heavily Latino precincts clearly have higher percentages of Democrats, particularly noteworthy in that these counties have higher Democratic party affiliation to begin with than the statewide average.

The 1992 Primaries

The 1992 Presidential Primary

On March 3, 1992, Colorado held its first presidential primary ever (Loevy 1993). On the Democratic side there were five major candidates on the ballot: former California Governor Jerry Brown, Arkansas Governor Bill Clinton, former Massachusetts Senator Paul Tsongas, and Senators Robert Kerrey of Nebraska and Tom Harkin of Iowa. Prominent Latinos were split in their endorsements of the major Democratic candidates. Clinton supporters included state senate Minority Leader Larry Trujillo of Pueblo and House Democratic member Tony Hernández of Denver. Kerrey backers included state Senator Bob Martínez of Adams County and Pueblo County Clerk Chris Muñoz (*Denver Post* [March 2, 1992: 7A]).

Tsongas, who had done surprisingly well in the earlier primaries held in other states, led in the early polling. However, Brown, who made a major effort in the state, won the primary, with almost 29 percent of the vote, edging out Clinton, who received 27 percent, and Tsongas, with 25.4 percent. Kerrey, who campaigned extensively, received only 12 percent, and dropped out of the race shortly after the Colorado primary (Loevy 1993).

While data limitations (i.e., differences in the configurations of precincts in different elections) make determining Latino voting patterns or turnout in the Democratic presidential primary difficult, several points can be suggested. In the two counties with the highest *proportion* of Latinos included in this study, Clinton received over twice the proportion of the vote he received statewide. Specifically, Clinton won 65.2 percent in Conejos and 76.3 percent in Costilla. Conejos and Costilla are sparsely populated counties and the actual numbers are, thus, quite small; but the extraordinary level of support for Clinton among Latinos suggested by these patterns should not be dismissed. Indeed, my interviews indicate that the Latino vote was key to Clinton's close second-place finish and was thus instrumental in providing momentum to his eventually successful pursuit of his party's nomination. It also boded well for his ability to attract Latino voters in the general election.

TABLE 3.2   Latino Voting Patterns in Denver County, 1992

	5 Precincts with Highest % Latinos		5 Precincts with Lowest % Latinos	
	Mean (%)	(S.D.)	Mean (%)	(S.D.)
Party affiliation				
Democratic	70.1	(3.2)	45.9	(20.2)
Republican	9.1	(1.5)	33.3	(20.4)
Unaffiliated	20.8		23.8	
U.S. Senate Democratic primary				
Campbell	65.8	(6.5)	25.2	(6.8)
Heath	14.6	(5.1)	22.2	(8.9)
Lamm	17.7	(2.4)	51.2	(13.9)
(Turnout)	25.1	(13.2)	54.4	(11.6)
General election				
President				
Clinton (D)	72.0	(5.1)	32.6	(14.6)
Bush (R)	11.2	(2.2)	51.0	(17.5)
Perot (I)	11.2	(4.1)	11.5	(4.2)
(Turnout)	61.3	(6.2)	72.7	(5.5)
U.S. Senate				
Campbell (D)	75.0	(2.5)	51.7	(15.6)
Considine (R)	11.0	(2.7)	36.5	(14.7)
Initiatives				
"Tax limitation"				
% yes	50.1		38.3	
% drop-off in turnout*	24.7		13.5	
"No protected status for gays"				
% yes	35.3		45.3	
% drop-off in turnout	21.8		9.8	
"Sales tax for education"				
% yes	60.4		47.8	
% drop-off in turnout	18.9		12.8	
"Education vouchers"				
% yes	35.2		26.6	
% drop-off in turnout	21.8		16.4	
Average % of Latinos registered in these districts	68.9	(3.4)	1.0	(0.1)

* Percentage of those who voted in presidential race who did not vote on the initiative. Thus, percentage voting "yes" on initiatives is based on percentage of votes actually cast. Otherwise, percentages are computed based on total turnout.
Source: Author's calculations based on unpublished data obtained from Voter Contact Services (Colorado Springs) and from the *Denver Post* [November 4, 1992].

TABLE 3.3 Latino Voting Patterns in Adams County, 1992

	5 Precincts with Highest % Latinos		5 Precincts with Lowest % Latinos	
	Mean (%)	(S.D.)	Mean (%)	(S.D.)
Party affiliation				
Democratic	56.1	(3.0)	33.1	(6.5)
Republican	16.1	(1.4)	37.9	(11.0)
Unaffiliated	27.8		29.0	
U.S. Senate Democratic primary				
Campbell	57.9	(6.5)	46.8	(3.9)
Heath	18.2	(5.2)	16.8	(2.8)
Lamm	23.9	(5.2)	37.3	(4.0)
(Turnout)	Na		Na	
General election				
President				
Clinton (D)	56.2	(2.6)	30.3	(3.7)
Bush (R)	20.8	(1.5)	38.1	(4.6)
Perot (I)	21.7	(1.2)	24.4	(9.4)
(Turnout)	Na		Na	
U.S. Senate				
Campbell (D)	74.8	(2.4)	48.3	(3.5)
Considine (R)	25.2	(2.4)	51.7	(3.5)
Initiatives				
"Tax limitation"				
% yes	62.5		62.9	
% drop-off in turnout*	Na		Na	
"No protected status for gays"				
% yes	47.5		61.8	
% drop-off in turnout	Na		Na	
"Sales tax for education"				
% yes	49.3		38.6	
% drop-off in turnout	Na		Na	
"Education vouchers"				
% yes	47.2		36.8	
% drop-off in turnout	Na		Na	
Average % of Latinos registered in these districts	39.8	(7.7)	1.8	(0.7)

* Percentage of those who voted in presidential race who did not vote on the initiative. Thus, percentage voting "yes" on initiatives is based on percentage of votes actually cast. Otherwise, percentages are computed based on total turnout.
Na = Not available.
Source: See Table 3.2.

TABLE 3.4 Latino Voting Patterns in Pueblo County, 1992

	5 Precincts with Highest % Latinos		5 Precincts with Lowest % Latinos	
	Mean (%)	(S.D.)	Mean (%)	(S.D.)
Party affiliation				
Democratic	76.0	(2.3)	46.1	(9.4)
Republican	8.0	(0.8)	29.7	(7.6)
Unaffiliated	16.0		24.2	
U.S. Senate Democratic primary				
Campbell	85.0	(2.7)	78.8	(2.5)
Heath	5.3	(1.3)	7.0	(2.0)
Lamm	5.8	(1.5)	12.9	(1.8)
(Turnout)	37.9	(2.8)	46.1	(4.3)
General election				
President				
Clinton (D)	67.6	(1.8)	33.3	(2.1)
Bush (R)	12.1	(1.0)	40.8	(2.9)
Perot (I)	11.6	(1.6)	24.1	(2.8)
(Turnout)	67.0	(2.1)	71.2	(2.8)
U.S. Senate				
Campbell (D)	75.1	(0.7)	45.7	(5.3)
Considine (R)	16.2	(1.6)	48.8	(4.4)
Initiatives				
"Tax limitation"				
% yes	58.2		65.4	
% drop-off in turnout*	12.3		5.5	
"No protected status for gays"				
% yes	45.4		69.4	
% drop-off in turnout	11.2		2.2	
"Sales tax for education"				
% yes	44.8		28.3	
% drop-off in turnout	10.3		2.5	
"Education vouchers"				
% yes	48.5		37.6	
% drop-off in turnout	10.8		3.4	
Average % of Latinos registered in these districts	67.0	(4.1)	5.2	(0.7)

* Percentage of those who voted in presidential race who did not vote on the initiative. Thus, percentage voting "yes" on initiatives is based on percentage of votes actually cast. Otherwise, percentages are computed based on total turnout.
Source: See Table 3.2.

TABLE 3.5 Latino Voting Patterns in Conejos County, 1992

	5 Precincts with Highest % Latinos		5 Precincts with Lowest % Latinos	
	Mean (%)	(S.D.)	Mean (%)	(S.D.)
Party affiliation				
Democratic	66.9	(6.1)	47.5	(5.4)
Republican	27.1	(4.6)	46.3	(6.3)
Unaffiliated	6.0		6.2	
U.S. Senate Democratic primary				
Campbell	82.0	(4.9)	84.5	(3.9)
Heath	5.5	(1.3)	6.6	(2.1)
Lamm	12.4	(3.7)	8.9	(2.9)
(Turnout)	Na		Na	
General election				
President				
Clinton (D)	59.4	(10.5)	38.0	(6.1)
Bush (R)	23.3	(6.4)	42.6	(8.3)
Perot (I)	15.1	(2.8)	18.5	(2.6)
(Turnout)	Na		Na	
U.S. Senate				
Campbell (D)	72.8	(7.2)	61.9	(3.3)
Considine (R)	20.4	(4.9)	35.0	(4.1)
Initiatives				
"Tax limitation"				
% yes	48.3		51.0	
% drop-off in turnout*	Na		Na	
"No protected status for gays"				
% yes	52.1		63.4	
% drop-off in turnout	Na		Na	
"Sales tax for education"				
% yes	49.2		44.3	
% drop-off in turnout	Na		Na	
"Education vouchers"				
% yes	27.9		23.4	
% drop-off in turnout	Na		Na	
Average % of Latinos registered in these districts	75.1	(10.3)	42.4	(9.7)

* Percentage of those who voted in presidential race who did not vote on the initiative. Thus, percentage voting "yes" on initiatives is based on percentage of votes actually cast. Otherwise, percentages are computed based on total turnout.
Na = Not available.
Source: See Table 3.2.

TABLE 3.6 Latino Voting Patterns in Costilla County, 1992

	5 Precincts with Highest % Latinos		5 Precincts with Lowest % Latinos	
	Mean (%)	(S.D.)	Mean (%)	(S.D.)
Party affiliation				
Democratic	93.9	(0.0)	77.9	(0.0)
Republican	3.8	(0.0)	13.7	(0.0)
Unaffiliated	2.3		8.4	
U.S. Senate Democratic primary				
Campbell	81.1	(0.9)	78.0	(11.7)
Heath	10.6	(1.9)	9.4	(4.4)
Lamm	8.4	(2.7)	12.7	(9.9)
(Turnout)	Na		Na	
General election				
President				
Clinton (D)	80.5	(3.5)	62.7	(13.9)
Bush (R)	13.2	(0.7)	25.4	(5.7)
Perot (I)	6.3	(2.9)	16.6	(6.9)
(Turnout)	Na		Na	
U.S. Senate				
Campbell (D)	89.6	(1.8)	72.9	(6.8)
Considine (R)	10.4	(1.8)	27.1	(6.8)
Initiatives				
"Tax limitation"				
% yes	46.7		51.6	
% drop-off in turnout*	Na		Na	
"No protected status for gays"				
% yes	40.0		54.3	
% drop-off in turnout	Na		Na	
"Sales tax for education"				
% yes	64.6		57.1	
% drop-off in turnout	Na		Na	
"Education vouchers"				
% yes	Na		Na	
Average % of Latinos registered in these districts	89.4	(0.0)	56.0	(0.1)

* Percentage of those who voted in presidential race who did not vote on the initiative. Thus, percentage voting "yes" on initiatives is based on percentage of votes actually cast. Otherwise, percentages are computed based on total turnout.
Na = Not available.
Source: See Table 3.2.

The Republican presidential primary was probably little affected by Latinos, given low Latino Republican affiliation and because the incumbent, President Bush, was sure to win. However, challenger Patrick Buchanan's almost 30 percent of the vote indicated some weakness in the president's Republican support in the state.

Of the sixty-two Colorado delegates to the Democratic National Convention, seven (or 11.3 percent) were Latinos. While this percentage approximates the Latino proportion of the state's population, Latinos compose about 20 percent of those affiliated as Democrats in the state. The Latino delegates to the Democratic National Convention were distributed as follows: three for Clinton, two for Brown, one for Tsongas, and one uncommitted. Of the thirty-seven delegates to the Republican National Convention, one, Gloria Gonzales Roemer, was Hispanic. Gonzales Roemer, who had been the Republican candidate for U.S. House District 1 in 1990 (and was defeated by Patricia Schroeder) gave a speech at the convention seconding the nomination of the president and went on to serve as the chair of the Colorado Bush/Quayle campaign.

The Democratic U.S. Senate Primary

The 1992 Democratic U.S. Senate primary is important in assessing Latino voter influence because of potential Latino influence in state Democratic primaries. That influence is probably magnified in this case because this was an open seat and because Latino leaders took a strong position on this race.

After Democratic incumbent Tim Wirth announced that he would not seek re-election, three major candidates for the party's nomination emerged: Representative Ben Nighthorse Campbell, the only Native American member of the U.S. Congress, who represented the House district that includes most of southern Colorado and the western slope (including the three heavily Latino counties of Conejos, Costilla, and Pueblo); former three-term governor Richard Lamm (who had last held elected office in 1986); and Josie Heath, a former Boulder county commissioner and the Democratic party's unsuccessful U.S. Senate nominee in 1990. Lamm and Heath faced opposition from the Latino community.

A number of Latino public officials and other political activists publicly stated their opposition to Lamm for having supported the Official English measure, which was enacted in Colorado through an initiative in 1988. Lamm was also criticized for comments about the detrimental impact of illegal immigration. Other groups, particularly the elderly, chastised him for his "duty to die" statements.

Many Latino Democrats also felt there was reason to oppose Heath. In 1990, she had defeated a Latino, Carlos Lucero of Alamosa (in southern Colorado), in the Democratic U.S. Senate primary. After that defeat, an embittered Lucero refused to formally endorse Heath because he felt he had been treated unfairly by her during the primary campaign.

In short, there were ample grounds for Latinos to vote for Campbell. These included his minority (Native American) background; his moderate (some would say, conservative) voting record—a record that seems is not altogether inconsistent with the positions of Latinos and many other voters in southern Colorado and elsewhere in the state; and his status as the representative from southern Colorado, with its considerable Latino population.

Statewide, Lamm was the early favorite in this race (*Denver Post* [May 13, 1992: 1B-2B]). Over time, however, Campbell gained strength and eventually won the Senate primary that was held August 11, with 45 percent of the vote, to 36 percent for Lamm and 18 percent for Heath.

Latino support for Campbell in the Democratic primary was substantially higher than that of non-Latinos. In the counties examined here that were part of Campbell's House district—Pueblo, Conejos, and Costilla—the vote in the heavily Latino precincts approximated or exceeded that in the least-Latino precincts (see Tables 3.2 through 3.6). In most instances, the support for Campbell was near 80 percent. In Denver, not part of Campbell's House district, his vote was 40 percent higher in the predominantly Latino precincts than in the predominantly Anglo precincts.

The Latino margins were probably essential for Campbell's victory in the Democratic primary. However, it is unclear whether Latino votes were the decisive ones. As indicated in Tables 3.2 and 3.4, Latino turnout in Denver's heavily Hispanic precincts was only about half that of the non-Latino precincts, and in Pueblo there was also somewhat lower turnout among Latinos than among non-Latinos in the Democratic Senate primary.

The 1992 General Election

The 1992 Presidential Election Campaign

There were early indications that Colorado would be a strongly contested state in 1992. As noted earlier, Colorado had been a solidly Republican state in the 1970s and the 1980s. In 1988, for example, Bush won the state with 53 percent of the vote to 47 percent for Michael Dukakis.

From the start, however, it appeared that Clinton would reverse this pattern of Republican dominance. In one poll conducted immediately after the Democratic National Convention in July, Clinton led Bush in Colorado by 25 percentage points. By August, however, just after the Republican convention, Clinton's lead over Bush was down to 8 points in one poll (*Denver Post* [Sept. 16, 1992: 6A]). Through all of October, Clinton led Bush by an average of 6 points (39 to 33 percent) in a series of polls by the *Rocky Mountain News* and by 13 points (42 to 29 percent) in another poll by the

Denver Post; Perot support averaged 17 and 20 percent in the two polls, respectively, over this period. But neither poll presented specific data on Latino preferences.

A University of Colorado at Boulder poll did delineate Latinos and was concluded a few days before the election. In this poll, which focused on those registered and intending to vote, 65 percent of Latinos indicated that they would vote for Clinton, 22 percent for Bush, and 13 percent for Perot. (The total number of respondents in the sample was 257, with 23 persons, or 8.9 percent of the sample, identified as "Hispanic" [McIver 1992].)

Early in the 1992 election year, Clinton made an effort to court, and apparently made an impression on, Latinos in Colorado. Several Latino Democrats were involved in the Clinton/Gore campaign. Further, Clinton included Latinos in important positions in his national campaign and met with prominent Latino Democrats from Colorado, such as Federico Peña and Polly Baca, early in 1992.

During the general election campaign, the approach of the Clinton/Gore campaign in Colorado was, evidently, similar in most respects to that in other "Latino states." There was not a distinct "Hispanic" message; rather, general issues, such as the economy, particularly employment, and health care were stressed. These issues were seen as especially salient for Latinos because of their general socioeconomic conditions and concerns.

While there was not a specific Latino message, the campaign relied on specific Latino and Latina messengers. As described by a central figure in the Clinton/Gore campaign, Federico Peña, the former two-term mayor of Denver, was the "face" of the Adelante con Clinton! campaign in Colorado; Peña made a dozen or so appearances in behalf of the ticket. Former San Antonio mayor Henry Cisneros made several appearances in Colorado for the Democratic ticket in such southern Colorado areas as Pueblo and Trinidad and in west Denver, all heavily Latino areas. Los Angeles County Supervisor Gloria Molina, Representative Bill Richardson, and actor Esai Morales also visited the state to support the ticket and to encourage voter turnout among Latinos.

Furthermore, several Clinton/Gore offices were set up in Latino areas of Denver, Pueblo, and Adams counties and specific funds were provided for get-out-the-vote (GOTV) efforts and advertising in Spanish-language media. Advertisements also appeared in Spanish/English newspapers such as *La Voz* in Denver. Significant latitude was given to Latino Democrats in the state in determining how best to reach and influence Latino voters. In short, the Clinton/Gore campaign emphasized general campaign themes, but sought to ensure that the themes effectively reached the Latino electorate.

The Bush/Quayle campaign also tended to stress a general message but, at the same time, made specific appeals to Latino voters. The Republicans tried to emphasize voting for "the person, not the party," and also sought to appeal to Hispanics with "small business" backgrounds. Those campaigning in behalf of Bush were encouraged to focus on several "talking points on Hispanic issues." These points included the following general claims, supplemented with specific assertions:

1. President Bush has a solid record of Hispanic appointments.
2. Republicans foster economic growth for Hispanics.
3. New exporting opportunities create jobs for Americans.
4. Education is the key to greater opportunity.
5. President Bush recognizes the value of home ownership.
6. President Bush sees an urgency in rejuvenating cities.
7. President Bush understands the need for health care.
8. Clinton's record is weak on issues important to Hispanics.

Regarding the last point, the Bush literature claimed, among other things, that Clinton had signed "an 'English Only' law in Arkansas in 1987, while President Bush ha[d] repeatedly opposed such measures" and that "after 12 years under Bill Clinton, Arkansas is one of only two states without a civil rights law, and one of only nine states without a law banning housing discrimination." These points were also made in advertisements in Spanish/English newspapers in Denver and in Colorado Springs.

Beyond the efforts noted, however, the Colorado Bush/Quayle campaign did not heavily target its message to the Latino community. Unlike in 1988, there was no specific Viva Bush! initiative in Colorado in 1992. And while some Spanish-language radio advertising was used and there was some assistance provided to voter registration programs, the Republicans did not undertake specific Latino registration drives or get-out-the-vote activities.

Campaign appearances by the candidates and their spouses indicate the perceived importance of Colorado in the election and the ostensibly different approaches to the Latino electorate in the state. Clinton and his running mate, Albert Gore, made several separate and one joint appearance. While most appearances were in the state's largest media area, the Denver metropolitan area, visits were also made to Pueblo. The last stop of the Clinton campaign was Denver's airport, the morning of the election. Clinton's and Gore's visits were coordinated to include appearances with local officials and candidates, including Latinos, and particularly with U.S. Senate candidate Ben Nighthorse Campbell. Hillary Rodham Clinton came to the state twice, Tipper Gore, once.

President Bush came to Colorado several times, visiting Colorado Springs, a Republican stronghold, Denver, and Arapahoe County. According to one observer, Arapahoe County (which has a Latino population of 4 percent, or about twenty-one thousand) is the base of Hispanic Republicans in the state. The vice-president made campaign appearances in Colorado Springs, Denver, Durango, and Grand Junction; the latter two cities are in extreme western Colorado (and have very small Latino populations).

Latino Votes and the 1992 Colorado Presidential Election

I present the analysis from the selected counties in Tables 3.2 through 3.6. Clearly, the vote for Clinton in the most heavily Latino precincts was well above—generally 20 to 40 percent above—that in the least Latino precincts. In most instances, the vote for Clinton in the heavily Latino areas was 20 percent or more above his statewide vote of 40 percent. However impressive these margins for Clinton may be, they are not very different from the Colorado (or national) Latino vote for the Democratic presidential nominee in 1988. The Bush vote was significantly below his statewide average of 36 percent. Generally, the Perot vote was about half as high in the heavily Latino precincts as it was statewide.

The Denver and Pueblo tables also provide turnout data for registered voters. In Denver, turnout in the heavily Latino precincts was 61 percent, about 10 points below that in the least Latino precincts; in Pueblo, the 67 percent turnout was about 4 points below that in the least Latino precincts. Unfortunately, similar data were not readily available for the other counties.

It is difficult to know whether the patterns in Denver and Pueblo reflect general patterns for Colorado Latinos. But, based on the selected precincts in these two counties, it appears that Latino turnout among those registered in 1992 was well above the 47 percent among registered Latinos in the state as a whole in 1988 (LARASA 1992).

Statewide Races

The U.S. Senate

In a five-candidate U.S. Senate race, where abortion and reform of Congress specifically and of government generally were the most hotly debated issues, Democratic nominee Ben Nighthorse Campbell defeated Republican Terry Considine by over 140,000 votes. The margin of victory for the pro-choice Campbell was large enough that Latino votes were not critical to the outcome. Tables 3.2 through 3.6 indicate very high levels of support for Campbell in the heavily Latino precincts. At a minimum, Latino support appears to have been central to the decisiveness of Campbell's victory. Indeed, in postelection comments Campbell mentioned the importance of the "minority" vote (*Denver Post* [November 4, 1992: 8A]).

Ballot Initiatives

In addition to the presidential and U.S. Senate races, Coloradans voted on a number of other matters in 1992, including ten ballot initiatives. It seems fair to say that none of these had explicit or primary salience for Latinos. The general dearth of research on Latinos, including information on voting patterns and turnout in non-candidate-based or issue elections, however, makes consideration of several of these initiatives worthwhile.

The tables provide evidence of Latino voting on four initiatives. The first—tax limitation—limits tax increases by state and local governments to the rate of population and inflation growth, unless a popular vote allows otherwise; it passed with 53.4 percent of the statewide vote. The second—protected status for gays—prohibits "the state of Colorado and any of its political subdivisions from adopting or enforcing any law or policy which provides that homosexual, lesbian, or bisexual orientation or conduct, or relationships constitutes or entitles a person to claim any minority or protected status, quota preferences, or discrimination." This measure also passed; votes supporting no protected status outnumbered the opposition, 53.4 to 46.6 percent statewide. The final two initiatives dealt with education. The first called for an increase of 1 percent in the state sales tax to fund public schools and would have required public school districts to set plans for achieving educational standards. The state's governor, Roy Romer (a Democrat), was a central and highly visible force behind having this measure placed on the ballot. This initiative was defeated 54.4 to 45.6 percent. The second education-related initiative would have required that state funds for kindergarten, elementary, and secondary education be apportioned among students in the form of vouchers. This measure was soundly defeated statewide, 66.8 to 33.2 percent. How did Latinos vote on these initiatives?

Statewide, Latinos showed a slightly higher likelihood of supporting tax limitation than did non-Latino voters. This pattern was strongest in Denver. However, in Denver's heavily Latino precincts, support for this measure was slightly below the statewide pattern. In both Pueblo and Adams counties, voters in the most heavily Latino precincts cast a majority of votes in favor of tax limitation; in both cases, support for tax limitation was above the statewide average.

In Conejos and Costilla counties, even the two least Latino precincts have a substantial portion of Latinos—42 and 56 percent, respectively. In the most heavily Latino precincts, support for the tax limitation initiative was only slightly less solid than in the precincts with lower proportions of Latinos. In all the precincts considered in these two counties, support for the tax limitation measure was slightly below the statewide average.

The general pattern of Latino support for this tax limitation measure is not easily summarized. The evidence does not clearly or strongly support the perception or impression that Latinos support greater taxing and spending more than does the general public (Welch and Hibbing 1988). Rather, Latinos in each of the counties were almost as likely, and in Denver were more likely, to support this tax limitation measure as were non-Latinos within their respective counties. Moreover, the data presented do not account for differences in socioeconomic status; if the lower socioeconomic status of Latinos were accounted for, the patterns indicated might well change.

Along with general tax limitation, the initiative preventing a protected status for gays and lesbians was the most hotly debated initiative; it has subsequently been a focus of national attention. A "yes" vote on this measure was seen as the more conservative or less tolerant view; a "no" vote was seen as the more liberal position. Some observers speculated that Latinos were more likely to vote "yes" on this measure because of certain cultural proclivities, that is that Latino machismo or other attitudes would lead to opposition to tolerance for homosexual orientation (de la Garza et al. 1992: 82). Others perceived that Latinos might support the measure because a "no" vote might give homosexual status equal footing with ethnic or racial minority status, and thereby undermine the claims of Latinos to special status.

On the other hand, some perceived, and most Latino officials and politicians argued, that the issue should be seen as one of protection of minorities and of prohibiting discrimination; from this perspective a "no" vote was preferred. What does the evidence indicate?

The view perceived as consistent with opposing discrimination and with the position urged by most Latino elites prevailed; higher proportions of Latinos voted "no" in all five counties. In the heavily Latino precincts in the five counties, the proportion of "yes" votes is consistently below the statewide average, in some cases dramatically so. Overall, however, the data offer no support for the machismo or cultural interpretations.

As discussed earlier, Latino support for tax limitation appears similar to that of the general population. However, on the initiative to increase the state sales tax, to allocate new revenues to education, and to require education reforms, Latino support seemed somewhat higher than the support from non-Latino counterparts within the counties examined. And in the heavily Latino precincts in all five counties, Latino support for the measure was at, and in two instances (Denver and Costilla), well above the average level of support statewide.

The ostensibly higher than average Latino support for this initiative may simply be due to lower Latino educational achievement and a perceived need to provide more education funding to address that concern (the data do not allow a direct test of that). But the sales tax is a regressive tax. Thus, a vote supporting the tax increase, albeit for education, is a vote that falls disproportionately on lower-income groups.

Education vouchers were defeated soundly. The heavily Latino precincts (within the four counties for which data are shown) tended to be somewhat more supportive of vouchers than their non-Latino counterparts. In no case, however, did a majority vote in favor of vouchers in the heavily Latino precincts. Nonetheless, in the aggregate it seems that Latinos were more supportive of vouchers, if only slightly so, than the statewide average.

Summary of Initiative Voting

Latino voting patterns on these initiatives—in themselves and compared with non-Latino patterns—do not permit simple and easy characterization. Latino voting on these initiatives was varied and did not entirely follow simple impressions or stereotypes; that is itself an important finding (de la Garza et al. 1992).

A final point concerning the initiatives deserves attention. For the two counties in which turnout rates among registered voters can be examined, Denver and Pueblo, the drop-off in voting from the presidential race to the initiatives (i.e., the incidence of voting in the former race but not in the latter ones) is rather high. Drop-off is especially high in the heavily Latino precincts; in several instances, the drop-off in the most heavily versus the least heavily Latino precincts is more than 2 to 1. Thus, the initiative electorate is less descriptively representative of Latinos than is the electorate in candidate-based elections, which themselves already underrepresent disadvantaged populations.

Conclusion

Latino votes were an important part of the 1992 Clinton victory in Colorado. Latinos voted much more heavily for the Democratic nominee than did non-Latinos, but not significantly more so than they had in recent presidential elections. Were they *decisive*? Table 3.7 provides data that allow speculation, based on various assumptions and scenarios, about the precise significance of Latino votes in the 1992 presidential election. Table 3.7 indicates, for example, that Latinos could well have provided the margin of the Clinton victory in the state and almost certainly overcame the slight pro-Bush bias among non-Hispanic white voters.

Voter Research and Surveys exit polls indicated that the white vote favored President Bush by a margin of 39 percent to 38 percent. In the survey, whites made up 83 percent of the Colorado presidential vote. To overcome this deficit, Latinos, who made up about 10 percent of the state's electorate, and other nonwhite voters had to overcome a deficit of approximately eleven thousand votes as well as provide the victory margin of sixty-seven thousand votes. Although there are no data on the voting patterns of Colorado's small black and Asian populations (6 and 1 percent of the voters,

TABLE 3.7 Latinos and the 1992 Colorado Presidential Vote

Clinton margin over Bush:	66,831	
Latinos in Colorado	424,302	
Estimated no. of Latino citizens in Colorado	403,100[a]	
Estimated no. of Voting-age Colorado Latino Citizens		
Assuming 65% are voting age	262,015	
Assuming 70% are voting age	282,170	
Registration among Voting-age Colorado Latino Citizens[a]		
Estimated no. of Adult Citizens	262,015	282,170
Assuming 60% registration	157,209	169,302
Assuming 65% registration	170,310	183,411
Assuming 70% registration	183,411	197,519

Estimates of Latino Voters Based on Various Assumptions of Total Numbers, Citizenship Rates, Voting Age, and Registration[a]

	% Turnout among the Registered	
	90%	95%
157,209	141,488	149,349
169,302	152,372	160,837
170,310	153,279	161,795
183,411	165,070	174,240
197,519	177,767	187,643

Estimated Votes for Clinton Based on Various Levels of Support[b]

Latino	Clinton Share of Latino Vote		
Vote	55%	65%	75%
141,488	77,818	91,967	106,116
149,349	82,142	97,077	112,012
152,372	83,805	99,042	114,279
153,279	84,303	99,631	114,959
160,837	88,460	104,544	*120,628*
161,795	88,987	105,167	*121,346*
165,070	90,789	107,296	*123,803*
174,240	95,832	113,256	*130,680*
177,767	97,772	115,549	*133,325*
187,643	103,204	121,968	*140,732*

Notes: All scenarios provide Clinton with sufficient *net* Latino votes to overcome 11,000-vote deficit among non-Hispanic white voters. Italicized scenarios provide Clinton with sufficient *net* Latino votes to overcome 11,000-vote deficit among whites and provide the 66,831 margin of victory.

[a] U.S. Bureau of the Census (1993: 110) indicates that 95 percent of Colorado Latino adults are U.S. citizens, 66.5 percent of adult citizens are registered, and that 94 percent of registered Latinos turned out to vote.

[b] Range derived from previous Colorado elections and exit poll data from 1992. Voter Research and Surveys (1992) found that Clinton received 78 percent of the Colorado Latino Vote.

respectively), the various estimates in Table 3.7 demonstrate that the *net* effect of the Latino vote based on all of the assumptions used was to provide these eleven thousand votes. Only under much more narrow assumptions, however, did the net impact of the Latino vote provide the nearly seventy-eight thousand votes that reversed the preferences of white voters and assured the victory margin. For the votes of Latinos to have provided the Clinton victory margin over and above the votes Latinos cast for President Bush, Latino registration and turnout would have had to be at the high end of the range of possible rates.

However critical Latino votes may have been, they might have been yet more important. Turnout among registered Latinos was lower than among other voters, and eligible Latinos are substantially less likely to register in the first place (LARASA 1992). Latino votes probably affected the outcome of the Democratic presidential primary and the U.S. Democratic Senate primary as well. Latino voting on ballot initiatives is somewhat more complex than might be expected. And Latino turnout in initiative elections is below that in candidate-based elections. Better understanding of voting and turnout patterns will require attention to other factors known to affect political behavior, such as socioeconomic status and party affiliation.

The seldom-studied Colorado Latino electorate is an important one whose voting (and turnout) behavior in some ways is consistent with, and in others departs from, expectations (de la Garza et al. 1992). The patterns and impact of that vote are likely to become increasingly salient and increasingly worthy of scholarly attention.

References

de la Garza, Rodolfo O.; Louis DeSipio; F. Chris García; John A. García; and Angelo Falcón. 1992. *Latino Voices: Mexican, Puerto Rican, and Cuban Perspectives on American Politics.* Boulder, Colo.: Westview Press.

Guerra, Fernando. 1992. "Conditions Not Met: California Elections and the Latino Community." In Rodolfo O. de la Garza and Louis DeSipio, eds., *From Rhetoric to Reality: Latino Politics in the 1988 Elections,* pp. 99–107. Boulder, Colo.: Westview Press.

Hero, Rodney E. 1992. *Latinos and the U.S. Political System: Two-tiered Pluralism.* Philadelphia: Temple University Press.

Latin America Research and Service Agency (LARASA). 1992. "Voter Registration and Reapportionment in Colorado." *LARASA Report* (February).

Loevy, Robert D. 1993. "Colorado's First Ever Presidential Primary." Paper presented at the 1993 Annual Meeting of the Western Political Science Association, Pasadena, California.

McIver, John P. 1992. "The Colorado Poll." Boulder: University of Colorado.

McIver, John P., and Walter J. Stone. 1992. "Stability and Change in Colorado Politics." In Maureen Moakley, ed., *Party Realignment and State Politics,* pp. 56–73. Columbus: Ohio State University Press.

National Association of Latino Elected Officials (NALEO). 1992. *The Latino Vote in 1992*. Washington, D.C.: NALEO Educational Fund.

Saiz, Martin. 1992. "Cohesion, Mobilization, and Latino Political Influence: Colorado in 1988." In Rodolfo O. de la Garza and Louis DeSipio, eds., *From Rhetoric to Reality: Latino Politics in the 1988 Elections*, pp. 69–76. Boulder, Colo.: Westview Press.

U.S. Bureau of the Census. 1993. "Table 4A. Reported Voting and Registration, by Race, Hispanic Origin, and Age, for States: November 1992." Unpublished. Washington, D.C.: Bureau of the Census.

Verba, Sidney, and Norman Nie. 1972. *Participation in America: Political Democracy and Social Equality*. New York: Harper and Row.

Voter Research and Surveys. 1992. Unpublished exit polls, Colorado.

Welch, Susan, and John Hibbing. 1988. "Hispanic Representation in the U.S. Congress." In F. Chris García, ed., *Latinos and the Political System*, pp. 291–299. Notre Dame, Ind.: University of Notre Dame Press.

4

Promise and Missed Opportunity: The 1992 Latino Vote in Arizona

Manuel Avalos

By early 1992, the strong support President Bush had enjoyed in 1991 was eroding nationally. Even the Arizona electorate, which had cast a majority of its votes for Republican presidential candidates since 1948, seemed on the verge of defecting in 1992. Public opinion polls in Arizona taken before and after the primary elections indicated that the presidential election could be one of the closest in over three decades. The election also generated a high level of voter interest. One week before the election, Arizona voters had requested over seventy thousand early voting ballots from Maricopa County election officials. This unprecedented interest in early voting led election officials to predict a 70 percent voter turnout.

The ballot was the longest in the state's recent history. Arizonans voted on fourteen statewide propositions (many of which were controversial), thirty-seven superior court judgeships, a new congressional seat, and other statewide offices. The 1992 preelection trends also raised conjecture among pollsters and some Latino organizations that, for the first time in decades, Arizona's Latinos might emerge as an important swing vote in the presidential election. The very narrow margin between Bush and Clinton in polls the week before the election and expectations for high turnout fueled speculation that the Latino vote could tilt the election in Clinton's favor.

If Latinos were to play a role in the presidential race, partisanship would dictate that their importance would be as supporters of the Clinton candidacy—75 percent of Latinos registered to vote in Arizona are Democrats. The key factor in determining the Latino impact, however, is voter turnout, particularly in Maricopa County. The National Association of Latino Elected Officials (NALEO) estimated that a 7 percent increase in the Latino vote could effect a 1 percent shift in the statewide vote (NALEO 1992).

In the end, however, the Latino voice was muted. Arizona's voter participation rates were markedly higher in the 1992 presidential election, but in other fundamental respects the race in Arizona did not alter electoral precedent. The majority of Arizonans cast their ballots for the Republican candidate, and Latino voters did not function as a swing vote. Before analyzing the outcome of the presidential election in Arizona, I examine the factors that limited Latino impact on the 1992 election in Arizona.

Demographic and Economic Characteristics of the Latino Population in Arizona

Arizona has one of the fastest-growing populations in the United States. The state's population increased by more than a quarter between 1980 and 1990 (25.8 percent). The growth of the state's Latino population exceeds even this high rate (35.9 percent). Latinos compose 18.8 percent of the state's population, an increase of 2.6 percent since 1980. Arizona has the eighth-largest Latino population (668,338) and ranks fourth nationally in Latino concentration (i.e., in the proportion of Latinos in the population). Most of Arizona's Latino population (about 90 percent) is of Mexican origin (U.S. Bureau of the Census [hereafter Census] 1991b).

Most of the Latino population in Arizona resides in the two largest counties—Maricopa (50.2 percent) and Pima (23.7 percent) (Census 1992). Maricopa (with 57.9 percent of the state population) and Pima (18.2 percent) also have the two largest cities in the state, Phoenix and Tucson. Over 90 percent of the Latino population lives in urban areas.

Although Arizona continues to be one of the fastest-growing states, almost every economic indicator indicates a decline in the state's economy during the last decade. The economy slumped particularly badly in the last half of the 1980s.

The Center for Business Research at Arizona State University reports that Arizona's 1990 average annual wage per job ($21,268) was 8 percent below the national average of $23,142. Economists attribute this persistently low wage level to Arizona's industrial base. In the 1980s, relative to other states, the low-wage sector absorbed the largest growth in new jobs in Arizona. Historically, Arizona's industrial mix has tilted toward low-wage jobs and away from traditionally high-wage manufacturing jobs. By 1990, Arizona's industrial mix ranked tenth-lowest nationally. While this decline in wages followed a nationwide trend, the industrial shift that occurred in the late 1980s was more pronounced in Arizona (Rex 1991).

The economic downturn has affected all Arizona citizens, but Latinos and other minority groups have borne the effects of the recession more heavily than have others. Statistics reveal a sobering fact: Arizona Latinos are worse off today than they were a decade ago. In 1989, the average Latino household earned $26,332 per year—almost $11,000 less than the average non-Hispanic white household ($37,219) (see Table 4.1). This gap in household income between Latinos and non-Hispanic whites in 1979 was approximately $7,400. In absolute dollars, Latino households were earning on average $1,291 less per year in 1989 than in 1979.

A comparison of poverty rates measured in the 1980s also indicates a decline in Latino economic conditions. The share of Latinos living in poverty increased at a significantly higher rate over the decade than that of any other minority group in the state. By 1989, over one-fourth of the Latino population (28.3 percent) was living below the poverty line, compared with 11.3 percent of the non-Hispanic white population. Over one-third of AFDC households in Arizona were Latino in 1989 (Arizona Department of Economic Security 1989).

Economic decline in Latino households in Arizona may be related to educational factors, specifically, the quality of educational opportunities and low academic attainment rates. An examination of data on educational attainment in Arizona reveals that in 1990 almost one-third (30.0 percent) of the Latino population aged twenty-five years and older had less than a ninth-grade education. The corresponding figure for the non-Hispanic white population was less than 6.4 percent. It is also notable that primarily urban-based Latinos in Arizona fared as poorly—and in some cases, more poorly—in educational attainment as the predominantly rural Native American population (Arizona Department of Economic Security 1989).

Over 90 percent of the Latino population in Arizona is urban, and its low level of educational attainment may be the consequence of the qualitative crisis facing the urban schools in minority districts. Latinos in Arizona have traditionally held the highest dropout rates (approximately 50 percent) in the state. The worst school districts, ranked by academic performance, serve a predominantly minority population.

TABLE 4.1 Mean Household Income, by Race and Ethnicity, for Arizona and Major Counties, 1979, 1989

Race/Ethnicity	Arizona 1979*	Arizona 1989	Maricopa County 1989	Pima County 1989
White	$35,019	$37,219	$40,415	$34,908
Black	$24,631	$26,635	$27,442	$27,831
Latino	$27,623	$26,332	$28,276	$25,866
Native American	$21,029	$18,607	$24,801	$18,107

Source: U.S. Bureau of the Census 1992.
* Expressed in 1989 dollars; inflation was 70.8 percent between 1979 and 1989.

Summary

Economic conditions in Arizona steadily declined in the 1980s, particularly in the latter part of the decade. The poor performance of the state's economy depressed per capita income and the average annual wage per job in Arizona. The state's economic woes have touched most Arizonans, but some minority groups have felt the sting of the recession more keenly than others. Latinos, in general, were worse off in 1990 than they were in 1980. Latino households earn less today, when income is adjusted for inflation, than they did a decade ago; Latino poverty rates have steadily increased; more than one-third of the AFDC families in Arizona are Latino; and levels of educational attainment are extremely low across the Latino population.

The Latino Electorate

During the 1980s, the Latino population grew substantially in the United States. While the national electorate grew by less than 10 percent, the Latino electorate grew by over 50 percent. Today approximately one out of twenty-two voters in the nation is Latino (NALEO 1992). The Latino population in Arizona increased more quickly than any race or ethnic group in the state (up 35.9 percent from 1980 to 1990). Latinos now represent 18.8 percent of the state's population and approximately 16 percent of the voting-age population. This increase in overall population, however, has not translated into a sizable share of the state's electorate; only 8 percent of Arizona's registered voters are Latino.

In a state in which overall party registration favors Republicans (45.1 percent) over Democrats (42.5 percent), Latinos show a marked preference for registering as Democrats (75 percent). Yet, low registration and voter turnout and the low percentage of U.S. citizens among Latinos have lessened the potential of the Latino electorate to function as a swing vote in presidential elections.

The largest single factor contributing to low Latino electoral participation in Arizona—as well as in the rest of the nation—is the high percentage of non-U.S. citizens within the Latino population. Nationwide, the number of Latino noncitizens doubled from 2.6 million in 1980 to 5.9 million in 1992 (Census 1993a). Since 1980, the noncitizen segment of the Latino population has grown by 127 percent, more than twice as fast as the adult Latino U.S. citizen population (58 percent) (Census 1982, 1993a). In 1992, 40.2 percent of Latino adults nationwide were not U.S. citizens; in Arizona, the rate of Latino noncitizenship was 26.2 percent (Census 1993b). Hence, despite increasing rates of emigration from Mexico and other Latin American countries into Arizona, low naturalization rates limit the impact of the Latino vote.

Mobilization of the Latino electorate in Arizona depends heavily on factors such as voter registration, voter turnout, and citizenship. Latino turnout in Arizona has generally been lower than that of the non-Latino population. In 1990, only 41.8 percent of Latinos eligible to vote were registered to vote. In the statewide gubernatorial election in 1990, only 32.2 percent of Latino registered voters actually cast a ballot (Census 1991a).

Local and Statewide Factors Affecting the Latino Vote in the 1992 Presidential Election

While these relatively low rates of electoral participation result in part from the economic condition and demographic characteristics of the Latino population, they are also shaped by statewide and local political issues and events. The most significant of these for the 1992 campaign were the creation of the new 6th Congressional District in Arizona through reapportionment; a 2nd Congressional District race that offered the possible re-election of the first Latino to ever serve Arizona in the U.S. Congress (Ed Pastor); the introduction of a new early voting procedure to replace the old absentee voting system; and a set of fourteen statewide initiatives that included voting on the establishment of a Martin Luther King holiday (rejected in the 1990 statewide election); and a vote to enact the most inflexible state antiabortion law in the United States.

Controversies over reapportionment of state legislative and U.S. congressional districts have been a feature of Arizona politics since the mid-1960s. Several times in the last three decades federal district courts and the U.S. Supreme Court have intervened to settle unsuccessful attempts by the Arizona state legislature to reapportion its U.S. congressional districts. Reapportionment following the 1990 census proved to be no less controversial than in past decades. This time the debate centered on two major issues: the creation of the new 6th Congressional District and the attempt by Latino legislators and Latino community-based organizations (CBOs) to establish single-member House of Representative districts (SMDs).

Reapportionment in the 1990s marked Latinos' introduction as key agents in the state's redistricting process. Many Latino community groups, including the Arizona Community Forum, the Mexican American Legal Defense and Education Fund (MALDEF), the Southwest Voter Registration and Education Project, and the Arizona Hispanic Chamber of Commerce, played a significant role.

Single-Member Districts

One of the two major controversies emerging from the 1990 reapportionment process that affected the Latino population directly was the issue of single member versus at-large elections to the state house of representatives. The sixty members of the Arizona House of Representatives are drawn from thirty legislative districts. House candidates run at-large.[1] A change to single-member house districts would require a constitutional amendment by voters or a court order. The Arizona Community Forum proposed the creation of sixty SMDs to replace Arizona's thirty two-member at-large districts. The argument made on behalf of the Latino community was that SMDs would enhance the ability of minority groups to elect a candidate.

The main advocate for single-member districts in the Arizona legislature was Representative Rubén Ortega, a Latino Democrat from Sierra Vista (a rural community in southeastern Arizona). He argued that the single-member district plan would increase Hispanic registration and give smaller communities a bigger voice in the state legislature (Ortega 1992). Ortega has also argued publicly that he believes that single-member districts could increase the number of minorities in the house of representatives from eleven members to sixteen members.[2]

Ortega believed that the U.S. Department of Justice would not initiate the move to require the state of Arizona to change the state constitution. Thus, with the assistance of the Hispanic Community Forum, he submitted two bills to amend the state constitution to install sixty single-member districts for the state house of representatives. Under the Ortega proposal the number of "majority-minority" districts—that is, those dominated by ethnic minorities—would have increased from five to eight, and the number of districts with a Latino majority would have increased from six to ten. Native Americans would have gained a third district in which they constituted a majority, and one additional district would have become a high-minority-influence district.

The state GOP leadership never considered the two bills seriously, and the Democratic party was unenthusiastic about the proposals. Many members of the Hispanic Caucus of the state legislature and the Hispanic Community Forum voiced their disappointment with the state Democratic party's lack of support for single-member districts. Interestingly, disappointment over this failure led to a variety of Hispanic-focused political activities. Edward Valenzuela, the state chair of the Hispanic Community Forum, noted that the state Democratic party's inattentiveness to Hispanic concerns had prompted Latino political leaders and organizations to concentrate their efforts on increasing Latino voter registration. Indeed, the failure of the single-member district plan has drawn several Latino CBOs together in a collaborative effort to establish a Phoenix office of the Southwest Voter Registration and Education Project. The objective of the collaboration was to increase Latino voter registration by the 1994 elections and to revive the campaign for a single-member district plan for the state house of representatives. As José Solárez, community empowerment chair for the Phoenix chapter of the Arizona Community Forum, stated, "Our people don't vote because they feel used, abused by some *politicos*. Single member districts could be the instrument to turn around Hispanic voter apathy" (Nowakowski 1992: 5).

Reapportionment

The increase in the population from 2.7 million in 1980 to over 3.6 million in 1990 entitled Arizona to a sixth congressional district. The Arizona house and senate responded with congressional redistricting plans, but failed to agree on a single plan. Consequently, a panel of three federal court judges convened in late February 1992 to determine the boundaries of Arizona's congressional districts.

The panel included one Democrat and two Republicans: District Judge Alfredo Márquez of Tucson; District Judge Stephen McNamee of Phoenix; and Ninth Circuit Court of Appeals Judge Charles Wiggins of Reno, Nevada. The court allowed three groups to submit additional redistricting plans: the Hispanic Chamber of Commerce and Arizona Community Forum appeared on behalf of the Latino community; several Native American tribes spoke for Native Americans; and Congressman Ed Pastor participated on behalf of his congressional district (the 2nd).

Districts 2 and 6 were the hub of the controversy over congressional redistricting. The critical question in this debate was the number of majority-minority districts emerging from reapportionment. The Democratic plan created two majority-minority districts; the Republican plan had only one.

Under the Democratic plan, Pastor's District 2 would have lost some of its heavily Latino precincts in South Phoenix; these would have been absorbed into the 6th district. The composition of District 2, however, would have remained about 60 percent minority (mostly Latino). The 6th District would have encompassed some Latino precincts in South Phoenix taken from District 2 and the Apache, Navajo, and Hopi reservations. This proposed new district would have swept west just north of Flagstaff and then jutted out to include the Hualapai and Havasupai reservations. The resulting district would have contained a 50 percent minority population, predominantly Native American. Under the Democratic plan, Districts 2 and 6 would have had 59 and 56 percent Democratic majorities, respectively. Additionally, District 5 in the southeastern corner of the state would have remained a partisan swing district.

In contrast, the Republican plan would have created only one majority-minority district (District 2) with a 70 percent minority population. The new District 6 would have included the Navajos, Hopis, and Apaches, but excluded much of metropolitan Phoenix's Native American population and the Hualapais and the Havasupais. Consequently, the district's minority count would have been around 34 percent. Under this plan, District 6 served as a partisan swing district.

On April 30, 1992, the federal judges rendered their decision detailing a redistricting plan that incorporated elements of the Democratic and Republican models as well as their own modifications (*Arizonans for Fair Representation et al. v. J. Fife Symington et al.* 1992). The applicable constitutional standard of "one person, one vote" guaranteed citizens an equal voice in the selection of a representative. Adhering to the principle, the judges found that the redistricting plans fulfilled this criterion. The Voting Rights Act (VRA) of 1965 prohibits denying protected minorities an equal opportunity to elect representatives of their choice. The court emphasized that the purpose of the VRA was to prohibit the dilution of minority groups' voting strength. Using VRA criteria, the court rejected the submitted redistricting plans and drew up its own districts. The court's plan favored the Native American intervenors, who had claimed widespread discrimination. The judges also stressed the importance of employing neutral criteria in drawing district boundaries that would preserve communities of interest, provide geographical and contiguous districts, and avoid unnecessary or invidious outdistricting of incumbents.

This judicial plan created a Democratic and Latino majority within District 2. Both the Republicans and the Democrats favored this result, but they disagreed over how many Latinos should be placed in the district. The court's decision made the district 50.46 percent Latino (the Republicans had asked for a 56 percent Latino majority; the Democrats had asked for 51 percent).

As redrawn, District 2 is 61.8 percent Democrat and 27.6 percent Republican. The court refused Representative Pastor's request to make the district even more Hispanic by including the heavily Hispanic towns of El Mirage and Surprise.

The court rejected the Democrats' proposed majority coalition of Native Americans and Latinos within the new District 6. Instead, the court decision evenly distributed Latinos outside District 2 throughout the other five districts, giving Democrats only a slight edge over Republicans in District 6. Consequently, Native Americans now hold a critical swing vote in that district, when they have a strong voter turnout.

The court also honored the Hopi Nation's request to be moved from the new District 6 into Republican Representative Bob Stump's District 3. The Hopis had argued that a single federal representative could not represent both the Hopi and the Navajo nations in their decades-long land dispute. The court plan placed the Navajo Nation in District 6.

The redistricting plan solidified a Latino majority-minority district for Ed Pastor in District 2, but the plan fell short of the Democratic goal to make the new District 6 a district in which Latinos rather than Native Americans could play a prominent role.

Thus, the reapportionment solidified Latino incumbent Ed Pastor's base of support. The majority of Pastor's electoral strength is found in the heavily populated Latino precincts within Maricopa County. No other district has both Democratic and Latino majorities.

Pastor easily won the Democratic primary and faced a relatively unknown Republican, Don Shooter, and Libertarian candidate Dan Detaranto in the general election. Pastor won handily with 66 percent of the vote. Voter turnout (63.3 percent), however, fell well below the statewide voter turnout of 77.2 percent. From the beginning of Pastor's campaign, it was apparent that a competitive election would not develop. It is likely that this factor deterred many Latinos from participating on election day.

Changes in Election Procedures

Two changes in election procedures eased the registration and voting process for Arizonans in the 1992 election. Effective January 1, 1992, Arizona introduced voter registration by mail. This change made it possible to mail in registration forms, which were readily available in most public libraries, driver's license offices, city or town clerk's offices, and many other locations. The deadline for registering for the state and local primary elections was August 10, 1992, October 5, 1992, for the general election. Prior to enactment of the new law, only officially deputized registrars registered voters.

The new law fulfilled its objective: voter registration increased significantly. Although it is not certain that the increase was due solely to changes in registration procedures, voter registration also rose among minority populations.

A second procedural amendment that could potentially affect voter turnout is the change from what was formerly called "absentee" voting to what is now called "early" voting. The early voting procedure in Arizona allows voters to request ballots as many as ninety-three days prior to state primary, general, and special elections. Early voters can cast their ballots as many as thirty-three days prior to the Friday before the election. As I have suggested, more than seventy thousand voters in Maricopa County requested early ballots for the 1992 general election, breaking previous records. Maricopa County voting officials expected to receive one hundred thousand early ballots by election day (Padgett 1992).

The impact of these changes in electoral procedures on Latino voter registration and voter turnout defies precise measurement. While there is no evidence that Latino voters relied on these rule changes to vote, Latino organizations could rely on a more procedurally open environment to mobilize Latino voters in future elections.

Statewide Initiatives

As mentioned earlier, the 1992 general election presented Arizonans with the longest ballot in recent history. Fourteen statewide propositions (initiatives) increased the complexity of the election for voters. Many of these initiatives received extensive media coverage and generated strong public debate. Proposition 100 (the "Evan Mecham" proposition, as it was facetiously nicknamed) proposed a change from a majority election (50 percent plus one) for governor to a plurality election to eliminate the possibility of third-party or independent candidates forcing races into runoffs. Proposition 107 proposed term limitations for Arizona's members of the U.S. Congress.

Probably the most hotly debated issue was Proposition 110, which proposed changes in Arizona law that would have made abortions illegal except in the case of a life-threatening situation to the mother. The proposed law would have enacted the strictest antiabortion law in the country. Finally, Proposition 300 marked the second attempt by the state to institute a Martin Luther King holiday.

Despite the considerable controversy generated by these initiatives, they did not seem to spark particular interest among Latino voters. For example, public opinion polls on the Martin Luther King proposition indicated that there was a rather unenthusiastic response to the issue among Latinos. While these propositions probably increased statewide voter turnout, there is no clear evidence that they had a direct impact on Latino voter turnout in the 1992 election.

The 1992 Presidential Election

Latino Participation in the Nomination Process

It is difficult to examine the extent of Latino involvement in the presidential nomination process in Arizona. Arizona's nominating conventions are procedurally complicated. We can, however, see that there were clear differences in Latino representation within state Democratic and Republican delegations. Latino membership in the Democratic party's delegation was directly proportional to the state's Latino population (18.8 percent). Eight of the forty-three delegates were Latino.

Only three of the thirty-seven-member Republican party delegation, on the other hand, were Latino. John Reyna, chair of the state Republican Hispanic Committee, sought eight Latino delegates, which would have matched the proportion of the state's Latino population. He was unsuccessful. In a newspaper interview, Reyna bemoaned the fact that the Republican party's campaign strategies focused on white middle-class voters. He was also critical of the party platform's acquiescence to Patrick Buchanan's demand for a more secure border between Mexico and the United States. Reyna stated, "We just tore down the Berlin Wall. Why are we talking about building a concrete wall along the 1,200 mile border between the U.S. and Mexico? It doesn't make sense" (Murphy 1992: 2).

Reyna stated that it was a constant struggle to get the GOP hierarchy to keep its doors open to minorities. Yet, he added, "we don't want any window dressing, we don't want any patronization. We want a meaningful and full participation in the political process" (Murphy 1992: 2).

These levels of representation in the state delegations to party conventions reinforce data on partisan registration and partisanship among Arizona Latino state legislators and members of Congress to suggest that Latinos play a much more significant role within the state Democratic party than in the Republican party. It is also evident, however, that the Latino voice in both parties is muted by a lack of proportional representation in elective office and in party positions.

The Latino Vote and the General Election

As mentioned earlier, public opinion polls taken during the last month preceding the general election indicated that Clinton and Bush were running in almost a dead heat. In early October, public opinion polls showed that Clinton held a six-point lead, but Bush closed the gap over the last month of the campaign. The general election produced one of the highest statewide voter turnouts in the state's history (77.6 percent). In the final statewide tally, Bush edged out Clinton 37.7 percent to 35.8 percent in the closest presidential election in Arizona since the 1964 Nixon-Kennedy race.

In the 1992 election, the predominantly Democratic Latino electorate did not materialize as a swing vote. The narrow margin separating Bush and Clinton reflected primarily the impact of the Perot campaign. Perot siphoned off a significant number of Republican supporters and received 23.3 percent of the statewide vote (in the 1988 election Bush received 60 percent of the popular vote in Arizona). Latino Democrats were not able to build the Democratic vote sufficiently to overtake the weakened Republican party.

Extremely low voter turnout was the major reason why the predominantly Democratic Latino electorate was not able to affect the outcome of the presidential election. An examination of statewide voter turnout by congressional district indicates that Ed Pastor's heavily Latino district (District 2) had the lowest voter turnout (63.3 percent) of any congressional district and was almost 15 percentage points lower than the statewide average. While no statewide voting data by race or ethnicity are available to examine Latino voting and turnout patterns, I used census data of population characteristics (percentage of Latinos living within precincts) and precinct voting data for the November election to indirectly analyze the impact of the Latino vote within Maricopa County.

Table 4.2 reports voter turnout and vote counts for the presidential election for the thirty precincts in Maricopa County with a Latino population of at least 60 percent. Voter turnout ranges from a low of 43.4 to a high of 73.7 percent, with an average voter turnout of only 57.7 percent for the thirty precincts. This figure was well below the statewide voter turnout average of 77.6 percent. If one looks at percentages rather than raw numbers, Clinton received his greatest support within Maricopa County in heavily Latino populated precincts. His support averaged 57.6 percent of the vote in these thirty precincts compared with 21 percent for Bush and only 11.4 percent for Perot. Overall, Bush won Maricopa County with 40.1 percent of the vote; 32.1 percent voted for Clinton; and Perot received 24.8 percent of the vote. From this analysis it is clear that, had the Latino voter turnout in Maricopa County equaled the statewide average turnout of 77 percent, the presidential race would have been much closer in what has been a secure Republican state.

Conclusion

Elsewhere in this volume Fernando Guerra and Luis Fraga identify a number of conditions necessary for the creation of an effective Latino electorate in California. Many of their conclusions are also applicable to Arizona's Latino electorate.

Clearly, a number of Guerra and Fraga's contextual conditions (that is, those outside the effective control of the Latino community) were not present in the 1992 presidential election. Their absence prevented the Latino electorate in Arizona from having much impact on the election. In state and local elections Latino turnout depends heavily on the competitiveness of races involving Latino candidates. While reapportionment created a Latino congressional district with a 50 percent Latino and 62 percent Democratic majority, it did so at the expense of creating a competitive voting district. Representative Ed Pastor did not face serious opposition in the 1992 general election, and it appears that Latinos were thus not motivated to turn out to vote.

A second contextual condition missing in Arizona relates to the absence of a Latino power structure within the state Democratic and Republican parties. Historically, Latinos have not been involved in the Republican party; it does not appear that this situation will change in the near future. Latinos have traditionally supported the state's Democratic party but have not built a significant power base within the party or the state legislature. The predominantly Anglo Democratic leadership has not encouraged active Latino political participation

A third contextual condition missing in Arizona involves electoral opportunities. Reapportionment created a safe Latino district but deliber-

TABLE 4.2 Voter Turnout for Presidential Election in Maricopa County Precincts with High Latino Population

Precinct	Latino Population %	Voter Turnout %	Bush %	Clinton %	Perot %
S. Mountain	60.0	53.9	15.7	65.9	13.2
Sky Harbor	60.6	48.2	21.5	48.1	24.6
Harrison	61.6	61.6	15.3	66.1	11.8
Glendale 2	62.1	73.7	45.0	28.0	23.9
Hope	63.7	62.1	20.8	57.4	18.3
Sullivan	64.6	59.5	18.9	51.1	25.1
Cash	65.2	81.5	23.3	59.3	14.8
Isaac	65.6	59.5	23.3	51.1	21.8
Surprise	67.3	59.9	21.1	58.6	15.9
Almeria	68.4	63.5	19.8	59.0	17.6
Broadway	68.8	58.7	20.2	61.2	16.0
Jackson	69.9	50.4	19.9	62.9	8.6
Sunland	69.9	57.0	25.2	52.1	17.5
Rio Vista	70.3	54.6	27.1	48.1	18.6
Latham	71.7	61.7	24.6	53.1	18.7
Southern	71.7	55.1	17.2	63.5	16.1
Tolleson	71.9	64.5	25.2	52.5	19.1
Lassen	72.1	58.7	20.2	60.5	15.7
Precinct Ave.	72.2	57.7	21.0	57.6	16.7
Guadalupe 1	72.4	52.1	11.9	74.4	9.8
Edison	72.8	49.2	20.9	55.8	17.9
Guadalupe 2	73.8	43.4	13.4	70.2	12.5
Hayden High	76.9	61.6	18.9	50.7	16.6
Garfield	77.2	56.2	19.9	56.9	19.5
McKinley	78.6	49.2	24.6	54.6	16.4
Cashion	82.8	56.8	19.5	62.0	15.1
El Mirage	83.1	52.3	19.0	61.9	14.5
Parkview	89.7	51.8	14.3	68.2	10.8
Glendale 21	89.8	60.1	21.3	58.3	16.5
Hilton	89.9	56.4	18.5	65.7	11.4

Source: U.S. Bureau of the Census 1992; Maricopa County Elections Department 1993.

ately lessened Latino political influence in the five other congressional districts in the state. The reapportionment plan effectively packed almost all the Latinos into one noncompetitive congressional district while creating two competitive districts in non-Latino-populated areas.

Guerra and Fraga also discuss the importance of factors within the control of the Latino electorate, which are necessary to build an effective Latino electorate. The favorable conditions missing in the 1992 election were effective registration drives and voter mobilization and community political development. The greatest obstacles to the emergence of an effective Latino electorate in Arizona are the absence of political leadership within the Mexican American community and the dearth of resources available to encourage voter mobilization (voter registration and turnout). Thus, although their vote was unified, there was no concerted effort to increase overall Latino turnout levels.

This discussion raises the question of why Arizona Latinos have not developed a leadership structure that can translate increasing numbers of adults into voters on election day. A partial answer can be found in the fact that Arizona's Latino community has always been marginalized and factionalized politically. Further, the Latino political leadership in the state is dominated by an "old guard," a condition that seems to have had a deadening effect on Latino political mobilization. In contrast to California, very few young, rising Latino political activists are on the Arizona horizon, especially in Maricopa County (and, for the most part, in Pima County). Without an injection of new blood running for office, a development that could vitalize political activity, the Latino community will continue to be politically marginalized.

While many Latino community organizations and Latino state legislators are keenly aware of the importance of voter registration and mobilization, they are severely hampered by a lack of political party funds at both the state and national levels, particularly within the Democratic party. National party funds are almost never available for these activities because of the state's historically poor record of support for Democratic presidential candidates. More than one Latino state legislator has indicated to me that the national party writes off the state in presidential elections, and Latino political activists are forced to raise money on their own to support voter registration drives and to mobilize voters. While Latino candidates have utilized organizations like the Southwest Voter Registration and Education Project to help with voter registration drives, this chronic lack of funds and volunteers make effective mobilization difficult to achieve. As one legislator explained, it is very cheap to simply register people to vote, but it is very labor intensive and expensive to deliver people to the polls.

Even when Latinos do turn out to vote in Arizona, they do not vote as a bloc. It is hard to determine exactly what the voting threshold would have to be in order for the Latino vote to have a major effect on the outcome of a presidential election. It appears that the Latino electorate gravitates toward Democratic candidates. But because of low voter turnout among this electorate, it has been estimated that it would take a 7 percent increase in the

Latino vote to create a 1 percent shift in the outcome of a statewide election (NALEO 1992). Without a tremendous increase in both voter registration and voter turnout, there is not much opportunity for the Latino electorate to have an impact on presidential races in a state that has voted overwhelmingly Republican in every presidential election since 1948.

In retrospect, the 1992 election presented a missed opportunity for the Latino electorate to have an unprecedented impact on a national election within Arizona. Latinos' persistent patterns of low voter turnout and state Democratic party indifference to the Latino voter have stifled this opportunity. Arizona Latinos have yet to present themselves as a politically engaged and potent force in state politics.

Notes

1. Thirty states have exclusive single-member district elections and fifteen states have varied forms of single-member district elections. Arizona, Alaska, New Jersey, North Dakota, and South Dakota are the only states that have only at-large elections for state house of representative elections.

2. The Latino legislative caucus consists of five members in the Arizona House of Representatives and four members in the state senate.

References

Arizona Department of Economic Security. 1989. *Governor's Office for Children— State of the Child.* Phoenix.
Arizonans for Fair Representation et al. vs. J. Fife Symington et al. 1992. "Memorandum of Decision and Order." April 30.
Maricopa County Elections Department. 1993. General election data.
Murphy, Mike. 1992. "Hispanics Knock at GOP Door." *Phoenix Gazette* (August 30).
National Association of Latino Elected and Appointed Officials (NALEO). 1992. *The Latino Vote in 1992.* NALEO Background Paper 19. Washington, D.C.: NALEO Educational Fund.
Nowakowski, Martin. 1992. "Arizona Redistricting and Reapportionment in the 1990s." Arizona State West University, Typescript.
Ortega, Rubén. 1992. Interview with the author. March 12.
Padgett, Mike. 1992. "Punching In Early." *Phoenix Gazette* (October 27).
Rex, Tom R. 1991. "The Economy of Arizona and Its Counties: Industrial Composition and Growth." Center for Business Research, College of Business, Arizona State University.
U.S. Bureau of Census. 1982. *Voting and Registration in the Election of November 1980.* Current Population Reports Series P-20, No. 370. Washington, D.C.: U.S. Government Printing Office.
———. 1991a. *Voting and Registration in the Election of November 1990.* Current Population Reports Series P-20, No. 453. Washington, D.C.: U.S. Government Printing Office.

———— 1991b. "Race and Hispanic Origin." *1990 Census Profile 2* (June). Washington, D.C.: U.S. Government Printing Office.

———— 1992. Summary Tape File 3A. Washington, D.C.: U.S. Bureau of the Census.

———— 1993a. *Voting and Registration in the Election of November 1992.* Current Population Reports Series P-20, No. 466. Washington, D.C.: U.S. Government Printing Office.

————. 1993b. "Table 4A. Reported Voting and Registration, by Race, Hispanic Origin, and Age, for States: November 1992." Washington, D.C.: U.S. Bureau of the Census.

PART THREE

The Must-Wins: Key States with Large Long-Term Latino Electorates

	Texas 1992	California 1992
Population	17,656,000	30,867,000
Latino population	4,718,000	8,286,000
% Latino of total population	26.7	26.8
Voting population	6,817,000	11,789,000
Latino voters	927,000	1,135,000
% Latino of voting population	13.6	9.6
Latino adult noncitizens	764,000	2,975,000
Electoral votes	32	54

5

Unrealized Expectations: Latinos and the 1992 Elections in Texas

Valerie J. Martínez

The 1992 elections provided numerous opportunities for political gains among Texas Hispanics. The more obvious opportunities included doubling the number of Latinos ever elected to statewide office; electing the first Latina at the statewide level; increasing the size of Latino delegations to the U.S. House of Representatives, the Texas House, and the Texas Senate; and delivering the Latino votes necessary for the Democratic presidential candidate to win the state. Despite these many opportunities, the only electoral gains to come from these opportunities, however, were one additional Latino member of Congress and seven additional Latino state legislators.

What is the significance of these electoral results? Were the expectations for Hispanic political gains unrealistic, or were Latinos unable to reach attainable goals? The answers are found by examining the role of Texas Latinos in the various stages of the 1992 elections. The dynamics of the various campaigns are likely to be as important as the political actions of the Latino community in answering these important questions (Guerra 1992).

In this chapter, I briefly review the factors that contributed to the optimism of Latino leaders and political observers for significant Texas Latino advances in the 1992 elections. Following this review, I analyze the process and outcomes of specific elections, including the presidential contest, two statewide races, and other salient congressional and state legislative races. For each election except the state legislative contests, I discuss the primary campaign and then the general election. The final section of the chapter synthesizes these findings in an effort to examine why Latinos did not meet the expectations they set for themselves and that others set for them.

Latino Optimism

The political expectations of Texas's Latino leaders were high in the months leading to the 1992 elections (García 1992; Hinojosa 1992; A. Rodríguez 1992). The increase in population and the distribution of eligible Latino voters were two sources of optimism. The Latino population is conservatively estimated at 25.5 percent of the total state population, up from 21 percent in 1980 (U.S. Bureau of Census [hereafter Census] 1991a). Except for Asians, who make up less than 2 percent of the state population, Latinos are the fastest-growing Texas subgroup according to the 1990 census.

The 1990 census located 4,339,905 residents of Hispanic origin in the state of Texas. The population is greatly dispersed, with sizable concentrations of Latinos living in every area of the state except for the Panhandle region. Table 5.1 provides some indication of the distribution and concentration of the Latino population. The largest number of Latinos live in the Houston metropolitan area in Harris County, more than 2.8 million, but they represent only 23 percent of the county population. Other counties with large numbers of Latino residents include Bexar (encompassing the San Antonio metropolitan area), El Paso, Hidalgo, and Dallas. Interestingly, Hispanics are the majority population (more than 50 percent) in only two of these counties, Hidalgo and El Paso. Yet, 38 percent of Texas Latinos live in Harris County and these four counties.

The greatest concentration of Latino residents is located in Starr County (97 percent). The other counties with the highest percentage of Latinos are Webb, Maverick, Jim Hogg, and Zavala. All of these counties are located in the southern region of Texas, beside or near the Rio Grande River. The Latino residents in these five counties, however, collectively compose only 5 percent of the total Hispanic population in the state.

There are numerous counties with fewer than one hundred Hispanic residents, but the five counties with the smallest number of Hispanics are Loving, Roberts, King, Armstrong, and Delta. Tyler, Lamar, Sabine, Newton, Cass, and Delta are predominantly Anglo, with less than 2 percent Latino residents.

Although the relative youth of the Latino population and number of noncitizens reduces the ranks of Texas Latinos eligible to vote, Latinos still compose 19 percent of the adult citizens in the state. Obviously, not all of those who are eligible will register. Approximately 15 percent, or 1,273,981 of the 8,439,874 people on the Texas registration roll in 1992, had Hispanic surnames, up from 14 percent in 1990 and 13 percent in 1988 (Texas Legislative Council 1992).

While the Republican party has tried to make inroads in the Hispanic vote with a message of shared conservative values regarding family and other social issues, there has been no increase in the level of Republican

TABLE 5.1   Distribution of Latinos in Texas, by County

County	Total Population	Latino Population	% Latino
Counties with highest number of Latinos			
Harris	2,818,199	644,935	23
Bexar	1,185,394	589,180	50
El Paso	591,610	411,619	70
Hidalgo	383,545	326,972	85
Dallas	1,852,810	315,630	17
Counties with highest percentage of Latinos			
Starr	40,518	39,390	97
Webb	133,239	125,069	94
Maverick	36,378	34,024	93
Jim Hogg	5,109	4,659	91
Zavala	12,162	10,875	89
Counties with lowest number of Latinos			
Loving	107	14	13
Roberts	1,025	34	3
King	354	53	15
Armstrong	2,021	55	3
Delta	4,857	67	1
Counties with lowest percentage of Latinos			
Tyler	16,646	177	1.0
Lamar	43,949	475	1.0
Sabine	9,586	111	1.1
Newton	13,569	153	1.1
Cass	29,982	373	1.2

Note: Delta County is the county with the sixth-lowest percentage of Latinos (1.3).
Source: U.S. Bureau of the Census 1991b: 109–112.

identification among Texas Latinos since 1986; fewer than 10 percent of those voting in 1992 identified with the Republican party. Identification with the Democratic party has declined from 1990, but about two thirds (67 percent) identified with the Democrats in 1992. A growing number of Latino voters refused to identify with either major party (*Southwest Voter Research Notes* 1992b). What does this indicate?

The growth in the Latino electorate and its historically high affiliation with the Democratic party caused several political observers to express a belief that Latinos would provide the margin of victory for Democratic candidates in Texas (Eskenazi 1992; Hernández 1992; Richards 1992; L. Rodríguez 1992). The prospect of being "key players in the Texas Democratic game plan for victory" also fueled Latino optimism (Richards 1992).

Redistricting was a final reason for Latino confidence going into the elections. The 1990 census determined that Texas would get three new congressional districts. The strength in Latino numbers and the support of the U.S. Justice Department enabled Latino leaders to press for better representation in the design of the districts. Responding to such pressures, two of the new congressional districts were created with majority Latino populations. State legislative districts were also redrawn with the intention of being more representative of minority concentrations in urban areas. At least six districts were specifically redrawn to produce Hispanic majority populations.

Thus, through redistricting, Latinos significantly improved their chances for electoral victory, especially in certain regions. Houston was a particular focus of these efforts. House District 145 and Senate District 15 were redrawn to include 60 percent Latino populations. Houston also was the site of one of the new Latino congressional districts.

The Presidential Contest

The Primary

With the exception of Arkansas Governor Bill Clinton, no presidential candidate made much of an effort to court the Latino vote during the primary campaigns. Clinton was the first Democratic presidential candidate to establish an organizational presence in Texas when he opened a regional office in San Antonio in October 1991. He was the only candidate in either party to make multiple trips to Austin, San Antonio, and South Texas in the early months of the primary contest. During that time, he made a concerted effort to recruit Latinos who were active in local politics to work in his campaign (A. Rodríguez 1993).

Clinton's early strategy paid off with the endorsement of a major Latino political organization. The Texas Mexican American Democrats (MAD) held their screening and endorsement convention in Laredo in February 1992. Shortly after Clinton addressed the convention, the 300 delegates, representing 1,950 association members, overwhelmingly voted to endorse his candidacy. A two-thirds vote was required for the endorsement; Clinton received 97 percent of the delegates' votes.

Clinton also received the personal commitments of several key Latino leaders. Besides Roberto Alonzo, chairman of the Texas Mexican American Democrats, Clinton enlisted the support of Henry Cisneros, former mayor of San Antonio, Regina Montoya, president of the Democratic Forum of Dallas, and others.

The only other Democratic candidate to make overtures to the Latino community was California Governor Jerry Brown. He campaigned in South Texas accompanied by United Farmworkers' leader César Chávez in the weeks leading up to the primary election. He arrived too late to secure critical endorsements because most of the Latino leadership was already committed to Clinton. Brown's appeal for grass-roots support also appeared to make little difference in the outcome of the election.

Brown received only 9 percent of the Latino vote in the Democratic primary. Former Massachusetts senator Paul Tsongas, who waged a very limited campaign in Texas, garnered 19 percent. A large Latino majority (64 percent) voted for Clinton (*Southwest Voter Research Notes* 1992a). The Latino percentages were very similar to the statewide Democratic tally: 66 percent for Clinton, 19 percent for Tsongas, and 8 percent for Brown. Thus, it does not appear that Latino votes were decisive in Clinton's primary victory. Moreover, the divided popular vote among Latinos was in sharp contrast to the united endorsement given to Clinton by MAD and other state Latino leaders. Thus, the vote indicates that the strength of support for Clinton among Latino elites did not accurately reflect his popularity among Latino Democrats in general.

Latino turnout for the primary was reportedly higher than that of the general population, 27 percent to 19 percent, respectively. Exit polls also found that Hispanic women voted at a higher rate than did Hispanic men. Interestingly, except among those with college degrees or with annual incomes of sixty thousand dollars or more, Clinton was the majority choice of all categories of Texas Latinos regardless of gender, age, income, education, or ideology (*Southwest Voter Research Notes* 1992a).

Education, the economy, and jobs were most frequently mentioned by Latino voters when asked which issue mattered most in making their selection for president. Those voting for Clinton were more likely to cite the economy or jobs as the most important issue (*Southwest Voter Research Notes* 1992a).

The Party Conventions

Following the primary, Clinton continued the strategy that emphasized early contact in courting the Latino vote. In July 1992, he spoke at the League of United Latino American Citizens' (LULAC) National Convention in San Antonio. His remarks emphasized education reform—a top priority of LULAC—and he pledged to appoint Hispanics to key cabinet posts and federal judgeships. After his speech Clinton met privately with LULAC officials and Latino political leaders. Significantly, he was the only 1992 presidential candidate to speak to LULAC.

The pivotal role Texas Latinos were expected to play in the presidential election was evident in their prominence at the 1992 Democratic National Convention. There were forty-seven Latino delegates from Texas at the convention, up from thirty-nine in 1988. Thirteen of the delegates served on standing committees: five on the Platform Committee, four on the Rules

Committee, and four on the Credentials Committee. Texas attorney general Dan Morales also cochaired the Credentials Committee. In 1988, there were only three Texas Latinos on the Platform Committee, three on Rules, and three on Credentials. In 1988, no Latinos from the Lone Star State were asked to speak at the convention. In 1992, there were three speakers: Morales, Railroad Commissioner Lena Guerrero, and U.S. Representative Kika de la Garza (*Official Proceedings* 1988, 1992).

The General Election

After the convention, Clinton seemed to step away from minority populations. Whether he wanted to distance himself from special interests or was concentrating on attracting Anglo Democrats who had previously supported Bush, Clinton did not personally campaign for Texas Latino support after the convention until a few days before the election.

Latino leaders in the state, especially Henry Cisneros, took up his campaign among the Latino community (Casey 1992; Evans and Novak 1992). In early September, MAD and other Latino groups under the auspices of the Adelante con Clinton! organization launched a combination voter registration and get-out-the-early-vote drive that targeted Latinos in thirty-three Texas counties. Although much of the financial support for these activities was expected to come from local sources, the Clinton campaign provided critical start-up funds and promised to provide more money as needed.

After a widely publicized beginning, the funding from the Clinton campaign was withdrawn before the drive was completed (Alonzo 1993). The deemphasis of Adelante con Clinton! was part of a broader strategy in the Clinton campaign not to spend campaign money in states, such as Texas, that were perceived of as likely to support President Bush. In order to assure that the Bush campaign would have to commit its resources, however, Clinton continued to visit Texas throughout the campaign. Thus, he made several campaign visits in late October and included South Texas and Dallas among his last three campaign stops.

At the same time that Clinton's campaign was cutting back its Hispanic outreach, Bush's forces were gearing up for a major grass-roots mobilization targeting Texas Latinos. Starting in October the Viva Bush! campaign conducted a fifteen hundred-mile bus trip from Austin to South Texas. The caravan of Bush campaigners made numerous stops along a route specifically drawn through majority Hispanic communities. Among the bus riders at various times were First Lady Barbara Bush, her Hispanic grandson, George P. Bush, his mother, Columba Bush, and most of the Latinos who served in the Bush administration.

Although there is no direct evidence to use in evaluating the impact of campaign activities, the sizable difference in the proportion of Latinos who voted early in 1992 (33 percent) and those who voted early in 1988 (25 percent) is worth noting. A more salient indicator of the effectiveness of presidential campaign efforts to mobilize Hispanic voters could be the 6 percent increase in the overall Latino turnout for the general presidential election, from 46 percent in 1988 to 52 percent in 1992 (*Southwest Voter Research Notes* 1992*b*).

The three-way presidential contest for Texas's thirty-two electoral votes developed into a tight race between Democratic challenger Bill Clinton and Republican incumbent George Bush. With Anglo support sharply divided, some still felt a high Latino turnout could tip the vote in favor of Clinton (Eskenazi 1992). Forty-six percent of the registered Latinos in Texas turned out to vote in the 1988 presidential election. Harry Pachon, director of the National Association of Latino Elected and Appointed Officials (NALEO), predicted that an increase of "only 4 percent of the statewide Latino vote [would] shift the overall Texas vote by 1 percent in the November [1992] elections" (L. Rodríguez 1992). His prediction, however, was based on the assumption that turnout among non-Latino voters would be the same or very close to the level of turnout posted in the 1988 presidential election.

Latinos did turn out in record numbers on election day (52 percent), but so did Texans in general, and the numbers that voted for Clinton were not enough to defeat Bush. Seventy-three percent of Texas's registered voters cast ballots in the 1992 presidential election, a 7 percent increase from the 1988 election and the highest proportion since 1968. Figures provided by the Texas secretary of state and the Southwest Voter Research Institute indicate that Hispanics composed approximately 11 percent of the voting electorate in the 1992 presidential contest.

Although the turnout among Texas Latinos increased, their support for the Democratic ticket declined. In 1988, 85 percent of the Hispanic vote went to Democrats Dukakis and Bentsen. According to estimates based on the Southwest Voter Research Institute's exit poll of 1,511 Hispanic voters on election day and 389 Hispanics who voted early, only 70 percent of Hispanics voted for the Clinton/Gore ticket, with Bush/Quayle and Perot/Stockdale splitting the other 30 percent (*Southwest Voter Research Institute* 1992*b*). Even with more than two-thirds of the Latino vote, Clinton and Gore received only 37 percent of the overall Texas vote, compared with 40 percent for Bush and Quayle and 22 percent for Perot and Stockdale. One percent voted for other candidates (Texas Secretary of State 1992*a*).

The Bush margin of victory over Clinton in Texas was 214,256 votes. Assuming the Southwest Voter Research Institute's estimate of 663,013 Texas Latinos voters is roughly accurate, even if 100 percent of the Latino voters had cast ballots for the Democratic ticket, Bush still would have defeated Clinton by a margin of more than 15,000 votes. Thus, the expected pivotal role of Latinos in the outcome of the presidential election in Texas did not materialize.

An analysis of voter distribution and turnout indicates that Clinton received the greatest proportion of votes cast in counties with the highest percentage of Latinos as well as in those with the lowest percentage of Latinos (see Table 5.2). The proportions voting for Clinton were significantly higher, however, in the Latino-dominant counties—especially in Starr County, which has the highest concentration of Latinos. He also received the greatest proportion of votes cast in counties with the highest numbers of Latinos, except in Harris and Dallas counties, where Latinos compose less than 25 percent of the population. Unfortunately for Clinton, Harris County had the largest number of voters on election day (942,947) and Dallas County had the second-highest amount (661,252).

The significant finding of the analysis relates to the differences in voter turnout, that is, the percentage of registered voters who cast ballots in the presidential election. The turnout in each of the predominantly Latino counties was at least 9 percent lower than in any of the predominantly

TABLE 5.2 Voter Distribution and Turnout for 1992 Presidential and Vice-Presidential Candidates, by County

County	Clinton/ Gore %	Bush/ Quayle %	Perot/ Stockdale %	Other %	Turnout %
Counties with highest percentage of Latinos					
Starr	83	13	4	<1	54
Webb	58	31	10	<1	48
Maverick	61	27	10	1	55
Jim Hogg	72	23	5	<1	56
Zavala	79	15	6	<1	54
Counties with lowest percentage of Latinos					
Tyler	47	32	21	<1	68
Lamar	39	36	25	<1	69
Sabine	49	32	19	<1	70
Newton	59	22	19	<1	65
Cass	47	34	18	1	67
Delta	43	30	27	0	70
Counties with highest number of Latinos					
Harris	38	43	18	1	72
Bexar	42	41	17	<1	71
El Paso	50	35	15	<1	64
Hidalgo	58	30	11	1	58
Dallas	35	39	26	<1	75

Source: Texas Secretary of State 1992a: 1–6.

Anglo counties. The trends in levels of voting were similar in the counties with high numbers of Latinos; turnout levels decreased as the proportion of Latino residents increased. Overall, the analysis illustrates the positive relationship between the percentage of Latinos residing in a county and the proportion of votes that Clinton received, but it also shows the limited impact of Latino support for Clinton because of the low level of Latino turnout relative to Anglo turnout.

While the failure of Hispanics to deliver enough votes to produce a Clinton victory in Texas was a disappointment to many Latinos, the hard work of Hispanic leaders was not overlooked by the newly elected president. Clinton selected two Texas Latinos for important jobs in Washington: Henry Cisneros was appointed U.S. secretary of health and human services, and Regina Montoya became Clinton's coordinator of intergovernmental affairs.

Statewide Races

There were two viable Latino candidates for statewide office in the 1992 primary contests. Pete Benavides sought to secure his place on the state's highest criminal court—the Court of Criminal Appeals. Lena Guerrero was seeking a full term on the powerful three-member Railroad Commission, which regulates oil, gas, and transportation. Both had been appointed by Governor Ann Richards. Had Guerrero and Benavides been victorious, they would have been the third and fourth Latinos elected to statewide office in Texas in the modern era. Guerrero also would have been the first Hispanic woman (Latina) to win office in Texas at the statewide level.

Justice on the Court of Criminal Appeals

Fortunato "Pete" Benavides had twelve years of judicial experience when Richards appointed him to the Court of Criminal Appeals in April 1991. He was serving his second term on the 13th Court of Appeals in Corpus Christi at the time of his appointment.

A conservative judge with high ratings from the Texas Bar Association, Benavides was unopposed in the Democratic primary. In the general election, he faced Republican justice Larry Meyers from the 2nd Court of Appeals in Fort Worth.

While other judicial races were grabbing the newspaper headlines with charges of ethics violations, the race between Benavides and Meyers received little media attention. Benavides was well known in South Texas, but was never able to establish any grass-roots support in other regions of the state (A. Rodríguez 1993). He lost to Meyers by a narrow margin, 49 percent to 51 percent.

Voter turnout for the Benavides-Meyers contest (64 percent) was considerably lower than the state turnout for the presidential race (73 percent). Yet, even in defeat, Benavides received more votes than Bill Clinton (2,677,996 to Clinton's 2,281,815). Thus, it is difficult to judge whether Clinton could have helped Benavides had he committed more personal attention and financial resources to his Texas campaign (Texas Secretary of States 1992b).

Benavides received strong support from Latino voters (89 percent of their vote), but he still lost the election by over fifty-four thousand votes. His defeat points up the fact that even solid support from the Latino community is not likely to be decisive in a statewide race unless the non-Latino vote is fairly evenly split between the two candidates or Latino turnout is higher than non-Latino turnout. In Benavides's case, the non-Latino vote was not evenly divided: he received 44 percent of the non-Latino vote to Meyers's 55 percent. Further, Latino turnout was lower than non-Latino turnout.

Table 5.3 indicates that the voter distribution and turnout levels in counties with the highest percentage of Latinos, the lowest percentage of Latinos, and the highest numbers of Latinos follow a pattern similar to that

TABLE 5.3   Voter Distribution and Turnout for Judge, Court of Criminal Appeals, Place 3, by County

County	Pete Benavides %	Larry Meyers %	Turnout %
Counties with highest percentage of Latinos			
Starr	92	8	48
Webb	79	21	45
Maverick	82	18	48
Jim Hogg	85	15	44
Zavala	87	13	48
Counties with lowest percentage of Latinos			
Tyler	62	38	58
Lamar	59	41	62
Sabine	62	38	56
Newton	74	26	57
Cass	62	37	56
Delta	64	35	56
Counties with highest number of Latinos			
Harris	50	50	62
Bexar	52	48	62
El Paso	60	40	59
Hidalgo	69	31	50
Dallas	47	53	65

Source: Texas Secretary of State 1992b: 74-79.

identified in the presidential contest. Benavides received the greatest proportion of votes cast in all of the counties considered, with the exception of Harris and Dallas, but he garnered a larger share of the votes in counties with higher percentages of Latinos citizens. Turnout in the Latino-dominated counties was significantly lower than in Anglo-dominated counties.

Railroad Commissioner

Lena Guerrero was a three-term state representative from Austin when Governor Ann Richards appointed her to the Railroad Commission in January 1991. Her appointment received national media attention as she was the first woman and first minority to serve on the commission in its one hundred-year history.

Considered a rising star by the Democratic National Committee and the National Women's Political Caucus, Guerrero was able to amass a sizable financial base for her campaign from nationwide contributions (Newman 1992). She collected more than one million dollars in early contributions and still had about eight hundred thousand dollars eight days before the primary (Guerrero 1992).

Guerrero's most visible supporter was her mentor, Governor Richards. The governor accompanied her on several occasions to campaign functions throughout the state. Guerrero's strategy during the primary did not appear to include courting the Latino support. She was already well known within the Latino community, so she focused her efforts on other counties with high Democratic concentrations. Guerrero did, however, attend the Mexican American Democrats Convention in Laredo. She and Richards spoke to the assembled delegates. The association responded with its endorsement.

Guerrero soundly defeated her opponent, receiving 58 percent of the total votes cast in the Democratic primary. She ran much stronger among Latino Democrats, capturing 88 percent of their votes (*Southwest Voter Research Notes* 1992a).

Lena Guerrero's general election chances looked extremely promising through early September of 1992. Her Republican opponent, Barry Williamson, was a political newcomer with close ties to the Texas oil industry. Guerrero's tough campaign was already hurting his credibility when revelations from the *Dallas Morning News* began to surface about her misrepresenting her educational background. By the end of September, Guerrero admitted allowing "misperceptions, embellishments, and errors of fact" concerning her academic record and resigned her position on the Railroad Commission. While vowing to continue in the race for her seat, most observers agreed with political consultant Bill Miller's assessment of her chances, "I would have to say a win by Lena would be one of the greatest political comebacks in Texas history" (Hoppe 1992).

With the House of Representatives banking scandal still fresh in the minds of voters and a widespread disgust with politicians of every stripe, 1992 was a particularly bad year to have integrity problems. Not surprisingly, Guerrero was soundly defeated by Williamson, by a margin of 54 percent to 39 percent (7 percent went to a third-party candidate). About the only noteworthy finding regarding Guerrero's defeat is that Latinos remained strongly supportive of her, giving her 80 percent of their vote (*Southwest Voter Research Notes* 1992b).

Congressional Contests

As was previously noted, three new congressional districts were added in Texas after the 1990 census. Two of the new districts, Districts 28 and 29, were created with majority Latino populations. Assuming Latinos retained the seats currently held by incumbents Henry González, Solomon Ortiz, Kika de la Garza, and Albert Bustamante, the new districts were expected to increase the number of Latino representatives in the Texas congressional delegation from four to six.

Frank Tejeda, a Democrat, was the only declared candidate for District 28 in the primary contest. A popular, highly rated legislator, Tejeda served ten years in the state house and six years in the state senate before running for Congress. During his time in Austin, he acquired the reputation of having conservative, probusiness views coupled with a streak of social activism. He built strong ties to the Hispanic and business communities around San Antonio as he worked effectively to pass bills that built housing for veterans, increased protection for crime victims, and assisted minority and woman-owned businesses. He also successfully led the effort to revise the state's worker compensation law to reduce the employer's share of costs of injuries without dramatically changing the benefits paid to workers.

The Hispanic majority district was reportedly tailor-made for Tejeda because he assisted in the drafting of the district to have the bulk of its population residing in Bexar County, which he represented in Austin (*Congressional Quarterly* 1993: 137). Unchallenged in the primary, Tejeda faced only Libertarian David Slatter in the general election. With no major-party opposition, he hardly had to campaign and was able to find the time to organize and lead a National Veterans Task Force for Clinton (Tejeda is a former marine and decorated Vietnam veteran). Tejeda captured 87 percent of the votes cast and easily defeated Slatter.

Latinos were not successful, however, in winning the Democratic or Republican nominations in the other newly created congressional district. Former state representative Gene Green narrowly defeated Houston councilmember Ben Reyes in the Democratic runoff election. Clark Ervin, an African American, defeated Freddy Ríos in the Republican primary.

With Latinos composing fewer than 3 percent of Republican voters in the district, Ríos's loss to Ervin can hardly be explained as the failure of Latinos to turn out for a Latino candidate. Moreover, ethnicity was probably not a factor in outcome of the contest. Ervin's victory is more likely attributable to voters' perception that he was better qualified (Ervin is a former White House aide; Ríos is a small-business owner) and to the fact that Ervin had considerably more money to spend on the contest.

On the Democratic side, however, the saga of District 29 illustrates how generalized political power does not automatically translate into electoral victory. Indeed, if one were looking for the opportunity to increase Latino representation in Congress prior to the 1992 elections, the 29th would fit the bill admirably. As an open seat, there would be no well-heeled, well-recognized incumbent to unseat. Demographically, the district looked extremely attractive to Latino activists, with its 60 percent Latino, 10 percent African American, and 30 percent Anglo breakdown and a solid blue-collar, staunchly Democratic voting profile (Grandolfo 1992*a*).

The long-term opportunity for Latino political power represented by this district was underscored by University of Houston political scientist Richard Murray, who noted before the general election, "It's a prize. It's not just a two year term here; it is a seat that probably can be held by the winner for a long time" (Grandolfo 1992*c*). The eventual defeat of the Latino candidate for the Democratic nomination serves as a case study of how the dynamics of a particular campaign can ultimately overshadow favorable demographics and the hard-fought gains of redistricting. This is not to suggest that the creation of a new Latino district failed to mobilize Latinos into greater political activity, but that greater activity must be relatively unified to be decisive. In this case it was not.

Real people, not idealized ethnic profiles, run for political office; for Latinos in the 29th Congressional District of Texas, the person who emerged as the Latino standard-bearer, Ben Reyes, was not the perfect candidate. Reyes came into the primary with high negatives in opinion polls. He had filed for personal bankruptcy in 1991 and had pleaded no contest to misdemeanor theft and election code violations.

Nevertheless, Reyes was not without his supporters. As a former four-term state representative and a twelve-year member of the Houston City Council, Reyes had built an impressive army of volunteers for his campaign run, and he was clearly the favorite going into the Democratic primary. Perhaps Reyes's eventual undoing can be traced to the particularly strong set of candidates who lined up to take a shot at the open congressional seat.

His opponent in the runoff election, Gene Green, was a twenty-year veteran of the state house who apparently did not want for campaign funds. The fact that Green even made it into a runoff can be attributed in part to vote splitting between Latino candidates. The final vote tallies showed Reyes with 34 percent of the vote to Green's 28 percent, Chief Municipal Judge Sylvia García finished a strong third, with 21 percent, and longtime Reyes rival (and former protégé) Al Luna garnered a respectable 15 percent. Clearly, had Reyes received even half of the votes given to the other two Latino candidates in addition to his 34 percent, he would have won the primary without a runoff (Grandolfo 1992b).

Another factor that would have an impact on the runoff election especially was that, even with Latino candidates finishing one, three, and four, this predominantly Hispanic district turned out in extremely low numbers—about 5 percent of registered Democrats actually voted. While exit polls indicated a higher turnout of Latino voters than in previous congressional primaries, this may have been due more to Anglo uninterest than to Latino activism. Indeed, even with a higher Latino percentage of the total turnout, Anglos still accounted for most of the vote (Grandolfo 1992b, 1992c).

The task facing Reyes in the runoff election with Green was clear: mobilize enough of the support garnered by the other two Latino candidates without actively mobilizing the more participatory Anglo voters against him. At the outset this would not appear to have been a difficult task, but events would prove otherwise. There existed considerable long-standing animosity among Reyes, Luna, and García, especially between Luna and Reyes, as was clearly demonstrated immediately following the primary. Reyes talked of registering three thousand new voters and bringing in Henry Cisneros to help heal the rift within the community. Luna's campaign manager, Marc Campos, responded by declaring, "The reason for the divisiveness among the Hispanic Community is Ben Reyes. It all seems to center on his style of leadership" (Grandolfo 1992b). Sylvia García expressed similar misgivings about Reyes's strategy: "He wants an Hispanic from out of town to come bring Houston Hispanics together?" (Grandolfo 1992b).

A month later, on April 15, Reyes lost the bitterly fought runoff election to Green by 186 votes. While Reyes would successfully contest the runoff (some Republicans who had voted in the Republican primary illegally crossed-over and voted in the Democratic runoff), he would eventually lose the second runoff by an even larger margin, 1,132 votes. In both runoff elections Reyes was unable to effectively mobilize enough support within the Latino community to prevail. Low voter turnout proved decisive, as the second runoff still attracted only 6.7 percent of registered Democrats, an abysmal number given the controversy generated over a four-and-one-half-month period in which the stakes for the Latino community could not have been more clearly defined (Friedman 1992).

Although 55 percent of the district's voting-age population is Latino, nearly 60 percent of its registered voters are Anglo. The bulk of the Anglo voters live in an area of the district known as "Redneck Alley," where Green grew up and that he had represented in the state legislature since 1973 (*Congressional Quarterly* 1993). With overwhelming Anglo support, Green easily defeated Ervin in the general election.

What does Reyes's loss signify? On the surface, it could be said that the Latino community was unmoved by the opportunity to fill a new seat designed to offer a high likelihood of electing a Latino, and that ethnicity failed to translate into real political gain. Ethnicity is not a simple causal agent, however, but must be mediated through the intervening variables of candidate characteristics, the unity of the Latino community behind the candidate, and the strength of the opponent. In retrospect, the Reyes candidacy failed on each of these counts.

In the other congressional races with Latino candidates, Albert Bustamante was the only Latino incumbent nationwide to lose his bid for re-election. He lost his seat to political newcomer Henry Bonilla. Bonilla thus became the only Republican Latino in the Texas delegation to the House of Representatives and the only Republican Mexican American in Congress. The remaining Latino incumbents were easily re-elected and, with the addition of Frank Tejeda, the Texas Latino delegation to Congress increased by one.

State Legislative Contests

With the boost from redistricting, a record number of Latinos vied for seats in the state legislature in 1992. Between 1984 and 1990, the highest number of Latinos (if we use Hispanic surnames as a guide) to ever have run for legislative office was thirty-five, in 1988. There were thirty-eight house candidates and ten senate candidates with Hispanic surnames on the combined Republican and Democrat primary ballots in 1992 (Texas Secretary of State 1992c).

Latino majorities did not necessarily guarantee Latino victories. In Senate District 15, the Houston district that was designed to raise the likelihood of electing a Latino, State Representative Román Martínez was defeated by State Senator John Whitmire in the Democratic runoff, 47 percent to 52 percent.

Statewide, thirty-nine Latinos won the right to compete for six other senate seats and twenty-nine house seats in the general elections. Latinos finished strong in those contests, winning the remaining senate seats and twenty-six of twenty-nine house seats. All of the winners were Democrats. In only three instances were Latino candidates defeated by non-Latino candidates. Before the 1992 elections, there were twenty Latinos in the house and five in the senate. Overall, Latinos increased their representation in the Texas legislature by seven (*Southwest Voter Research Notes* 1992b).

Conclusion

The high expectations of Texas Latinos (based on growth in numbers, their perceived importance to Democratic victories, and the creation of additional Latino majority districts through redistricting) going into the 1992 elections were understandable but, in the end, unrealistic. While the growth in Latino population provided the raw material for greater political influence via increasing the pool of potential voters and strengthening the constitutional argument for greater representation based on population, the raw numbers were not adequately transformed into a critical mass of Latino voters. In the general election for president and other statewide races, Hispanics composed only 11 percent of the total voting population. The Benavides defeat illustrates the disheartening truth that, even with a united Latino electorate, the number of Hispanic voters was not large enough to decide the outcome of the election.

Furthermore, the Latino electorate was not as united in its voting preferences as it has been historically in Texas. The decline in Democratic identification and the increased number of Republican Latino candidates are two reasons that can be offered to explain the fissures in the bloc of Latino support for Democratic candidates.

The defeat of Latino candidates (Reyes and Martínez) in Latino majority districts indicates that redistricting, although it raises the odds of electing Latino candidates, was not a panacea for increasing their representation in government. The quality and number of candidates and their ability to mobilize Latino support—especially at the ballot box—appeared to be as important as the ethnicity of the candidate.

The limited size of the Texas Latino voting electorate is an ongoing problem that must be addressed effectively if Latinos are ever to realize their potential influence. New methods of reaching out to the potential Texas Latino voter that go beyond conventional voter registration and get-out-the-vote efforts must be developed, adequately funded, and implemented (de la Garza 1992).

The sizable increase in the number of Hispanic legislators is the most significant outcome of the 1992 elections. Its long-term importance to Latino interests should not be minimized. The thirty-two Latinos elected to the state legislature provide a critical mass of influence that cannot be ignored by non-Latino politicians. To the extent the Hispanic legislative caucus is successful in coordinating its legislative efforts and presenting a unified front to the governor and other legislators, the caucus will ensure the placement of Latino policy concerns on the institutional agenda. If the twenty-six Latinos in the state house can be persuaded to operate as a voting bloc, they should be able to play a decisive role in the passage or rejection of controversial legislation.

References

Alonzo, Roberto. 1993. Interview with the author. March 17.
Casey, Rick. 1992. "Cisneros, Clinton Good for Each Other." *San Antonio Light* (August 9).
de la Garza, Rodolfo O. 1992. "From Rhetoric to Reality: Latinos and the 1988 Elections in Review." In Rodolfo O. de la Garza and Louis DeSipio, eds. *From Rhetoric to Reality: Latino Politics in the 1988 Elections*, pp. 171–180. Boulder, Colo.: Westview.
Evans, Rowland, and Robert Novak. 1992. "Bush's Texas Shuffle." *Washington Post* (September 18).
Eskenazi, Stuart. 1992. "Support from Blacks, Hispanics Can Make or Break Candidate." *Austin American-Statesman* (August 23).
Friedman, Steve. 1992. "Green Wins District 29 Slugfest." *Houston Post* (July 29).
García, Domingo. 1992. Interview with the author. March 17.
Grandolfo, Jane. 1992a. "GOP Hopeful Likes Reyes-Green Fight." *Houston Post* (May 20).
———. 1992b. "Hispanic Vote Key in 29th District." *Houston Post* (March 12).
———. 1992c. "Reyes, Green Face Runoff for District 29 Seat." *Houston Post* (March 11).
Guerra, Fernando J. 1992. "Conditions Not Met: California Elections and the Latino Community." In Rodolfo O. de la Garza and Louis DeSipio, eds., *From Rhetoric to Reality: Latino Politics in the 1988 Elections*, pp. 99–110. Boulder, Colo.: Westview.
Guerrero, Lena. 1992. "Candidate/Officeholder Sworn Report of Contributions and Expenditures in Compliance with Title 15, Texas Election Code." July 15.
Hernández, Roger E. 1992. "Running on Empty." *Hispanic* (January/February).
Hinojosa, Mike. 1992. Interview with the author. January 21.
Hoppe, Christy. 1992. "Guerrero Quits Rail Panel, Asks Voters' Forgiveness." *Dallas Morning News* (September 25).
Newman, Jody. 1992. Interview with the author. January 5.
Official Proceedings of the 1992 Democratic National Convention. 1992. Washington, D.C.: Democratic National Committee.
Official Proceedings of the 1988 Democratic National Convention. 1988. Washington, D.C.: Democratic National Committee.
Richards, Ann. 1992. Speech to Mexican American Screening and Nomination Convention. Laredo, Texas. Typescript (January 11).
Rodríguez, Abraham. 1992. Interview with the author. February 3.
———. 1993. Interview with the author. January 20.
Rodríguez, Lori. 1992 "Hispanics Cast Lot with Clinton." *Houston Chronicle* (March 12).
Southwest Voter Research Notes. 1992a. San Antonio, Tex.: Southwest Voter Research Institute (March).
———. 1992b. "Special Edition: 1992 Presidential Election in Texas." San Antonio, Tex.: Southwest Voter Research Institute (November).
Texas Legislative Council. 1992. "1992 Election Profile." Typescript. Austin: Texas Legislative Council.

Texas Secretary of State. 1992a. *General Election Returns/County by County Totals Report, President/Vice President.*

———. 1992b. *General Election Returns/County by County Totals Report, Judge Court of Criminal Appeals, Place 3.*

———. 1992c. "Primary Election/Listing of Candidates" March 27. Typescript. Austin, Tex.: Office of the Secretary of State.

U.S. Bureau of Census. 1991a. "Public Law 94-171 Redistricting Data." Washington, D.C.: U.S. Government Printing Office.

———. 1991b. *Summary of Population and Housing Characteristics: Texas.* Washington, D.C.: U.S. Government Printing Office.

6

Theory, Reality, and Perpetual Potential: Latinos in the 1992 California Elections

Fernando Guerra and Luis Ricardo Fraga

The 1992 presidential election in California is over. William Jefferson Clinton, governor of Arkansas, has won, and all of California's fifty-four electoral votes are cast in his favor. As usual, the Latino vote in California has not been a significant factor in a presidential election. Had no Latino voted, the final results for president and most other statewide races would have remained the same.

Bill Clinton won the presidential election in California by a margin of 1,473,304 votes over his closest rival, George Bush. Clinton received 47 percent of the total vote, to 32 percent for Bush and 21 percent for Ross Perot. The Field Poll estimates that 10 percent of the California statewide electorate in 1992 was Latino (Field Institute 1993: 4). This represents approximately 1,030,417 Latino voters. Exit poll results from the Southwest Voter Research Institute place support levels among Latino voters for major presidential candidates at 71 percent for Clinton, 14 percent for Bush, and 15 percent for Perot (*Southwest Voter Research Notes* [December 1992]). Even this estimate, which is higher than that for other polls, indicates that just 750,000 Latino votes contributed to Clinton's victory margin. If we exclude all Latino voters from the California electorate, Clinton would have received 44 percent of the "Latino-excluded" California vote, Bush, 34 percent, and Ross Perot, 21 percent. Thus, if none of California's 1992 Latino voters had been allowed to participate, this would not have made any difference in the outcome of the presidential election.

This characterization of the Latino role in the 1992 election is sobering. California Latinos represented 25.8 percent of the statewide population in 1990, a noticeable increase from 19.2 percent in 1980. As a result, a number of commentators on California politics and many Latino leaders saw 1992 as representing an opportunity for Latinos to be major players in statewide elections. These predictions proved false in the presidential election and in two U.S. Senate races.

This does not mean that the 1992 elections were insignificant to Latino interests. Southern California sent four Latinos to the U.S. House of Representatives, a net increase of one, and seven members to the state assembly, a net increase of three. Of these, one of the house members and four of the state assembly members were women.

Conditions for an Effective Statewide Latino Electorate

Using the California experience, we offer the following model of conditions that must be met for Latinos to influence any statewide election. We subdivide these conditions into two categories. The first, contextual conditions, is linked in that each represents factors outside Latinos' effective control. The second category, strategic conditions, is linked in that these conditions are largely within effective control of Latino leaders, organizations, electorates, and communities generally. These two sets of conditions can be cumulative in their overall impact: the greater the number of conditions met, the greater the likely impact of the Latino vote. We do not attempt to rank order the individual conditions by the magnitude of contribution to the effectiveness of the vote. We do, however, view those conditions discussed first as primary and more significant to the immediate campaign.

Contextual Conditions

The first contextual condition is *competitive elections*. The more competitive an election, the more significant each voting bloc becomes, including Latino voters. To the extent that statewide elections are historically competitive between the two major parties, each party should develop strategies early in a campaign to capture the Latino vote (Fraga 1992). To the extent that any election is expected to be highly competitive, the Latino vote should be sought more highly, and if the election is competitive, the Latino vote should be more significant to the outcome. Competitive elections serve to explain the planned and targeted resources parties and candidates devote to gaining Latino votes.

The more significant the Latino vote becomes because of the competitiveness of a particular election, however, the more significant the votes of other groups also become. How a campaign mobilizes Latino votes without, in turn, losing other votes becomes an important decision. Thus, our second contextual condition is the *minimization of white backlash* by a campaign attempting to maximize the Latino vote. The greater the white backlash and resultant vote polarization, the lower the likelihood that Latino voters will be significant to the outcome of a statewide election. Because Latinos in California are a small segment of the electorate, as they are in many other states, their influence in statewide outcomes will be small if they are confronted with substantial white opposition.

White backlash may be minimized in at least two ways—one directed to the general electorate and one directed internally to the Latino community. First, candidates can reduce the use of race baiting, racial code words, or more general race-based campaigning that identifies Latinos, and perhaps other people of color, as major sources of social problems. Second, candidates can minimize appeals targeted to Latino and other communities of color. Through this method, Latino interests are included within a larger set of interests, and those interests are defined and discussed using nonethnic terms. This method can be characterized as making an appeal to an "informed public interest." Latinos may hear a message specific to Latinos, but other segments of the population, particularly whites, also hear a message that, if not specific to their interests, is at least not threatening or is neutral. Appeals to enhance economic growth or to promote law and order are examples of this method. A more specific example during the 1992 elections was candidate Clinton's often-repeated phrase that he would have an administration "which would look like America." There was little that whites could disagree with in this statement, yet Latinos and other minorities saw it as including their interests.

The third contextual condition is the presence of *electoral opportunities*. The more opportunities there are for Latino voters to elect candidates of first choice, the more likely it is that Latino voters will be a focus of campaign efforts and therefore the more likely it will be that they can be mobilized to participate (Guerra 1992). It is the political system that largely structures these opportunities through four means: (1) decennial apportionment and redistricting; (2) redistricting through the Voting Rights Act (VRA); (3) seats open because of resignations; or (4) seats open because of term limits. We do not mean to imply that the system promotes these opportunities absent the active participation of Latino advocates. It is, however, the case that advocates do not determine opportunities; they push other decisionmakers within the system to allow these opportunities.

The fourth condition is the presence of *ballot issues of particular concern to Latino voters*. The greater the number of these issues, the greater the likely turnout of Latino voters. These ballot issues may be of special concern to Latino voters because they address needs specific to many Latinos, such as English-only provisions or bilingual education. As well, they may be of special salience to non-Latinos because of their overall significance to all voters. Examples might include tax issues and issues related to economic growth.

Strategic Conditions

Although the contextual conditions provide opportunities for Latino voters to be significant in determining the outcome of a statewide election, our strategic conditions focus on the efforts that Latino voters and their leaders can pursue to take full advantage of those opportunities. We have six conditions that can be grouped into two voter-focused conditions and four elite-focused conditions.

Voter-focused Conditions. The first voter-focused strategic condition is a *unified vote* by the Latino community. A unified Latino vote has two aspects: (1) the degree to which Latinos vote as a bloc, where partisan preference differs in comparison to the non-Latino vote; and (2) the degree to which the partisan preferences of Latino voters in a particular election are distinct from those in previous elections, that is, the extent to which the pattern of Latinos' traditional partisan support changes in a given election (DeSipio and de la Garza 1992). In the case of California, the first condition is frequently met. Latinos vote overwhelmingly Democratic while the state as a whole votes Republican. The second condition is rarely met. California races for president and governor in the 1980s and the 1990s were all won by Republicans, although Latinos supported the Democratic nominee by an average difference score of twenty-six points. That is, on average, Latinos supported the Democrat 63 percent to 37 percent for the Republican in a two-candidate race, with the Republican still winning the election. Thus, the Latino vote is clearly cohesive, but stable and thus, insignificant to electoral outcomes.

If a unified Latino vote is to swing an election, bloc voting must manifest itself as it has traditionally done and then change from its traditional partisan support of twenty-six points for the Democratic nominee. Each five-point shift in the Latino vote equals a one-point shift in the statewide California vote (Pachon et al. 1992).

Thus, the Latino vote could remain unimportant if Latinos' traditional level of partisan support remained the same and the Democratic candidate won. In 1992 what led to a Democratic victory was not the Latino vote doing anything distinctive, but some other bloc of voters manifesting some unusual or distinctive behavior. Thus, for the Latino vote to have been part of this movement of non-Latino voters, it would have had to move to even greater support for the Democratic candidate. The Latino vote at its average level of support can thus provide the margin of victory for a Democratic candidate only when other electorates move toward the Democrats.

This phenomenon could also work in favor of a Republican candidate in a close election if the Latino vote moves at least five points in favor of the Republican nominee. In this situation, the Republican nominee would not have to receive a majority of the Latino vote, but only enough to swing one or two percentage points in the overall vote by shifting five to ten points away from Latinos' traditional Democratic support. Thus, a close election with a 51 to 49 percent Republican victory and Latinos supporting the Democratic candidate with 53 percent or less of the vote could be interpreted as Latinos having swung the election to the Republicans, even though a bare majority of Latinos supported the Democratic nominee. It would obviously take a special Republican candidate, message, or strategy to have Latinos buck the norm in an election in which whites and African Americans maintained their traditional Democratic support.

Another scenario offers the potential for Latino impact. Traditional partisan support could remain stationary, but higher turnout could increase the number of Latino voters. Latinos would then be a higher proportion of the electorate. Thus, our second voter-focused strategic condition is *effective voter mobilization to ensure turnout* of Latinos registered to vote. These efforts can be organized through campaigns, parties, or other organizations. The mobilization can occur through targeting of direct mailings, phone calls, or door-to-door canvassing. In California, such efforts have increasingly been used with precise messages to specific groups like Latinos. Such messages can even be transmitted in Spanish. The more likely the voter, the more he or she will be the target of such efforts. This creates a catch-22. For Latinos to become likely voters a campaign must target them; for campaigns to target Latinos, they must be likely voters. Latino political leaders need to help break this vicious cycle by mobilizing Latinos to vote when traditional campaign mobilization is absent.

The numbers associated with these two voter-focused strategic conditions are what make the Latino vote insignificant in most statewide elections in California, yet potentially critical. What is important to a major party statewide campaign is how many Latinos are going to vote, measured as a percentage of the total electorate, and how they are going to vote, measured from their traditional twenty-six-point support of the Democratic candidate over the Republican. Given the limited resources of a campaign and its relatively short-term perspective, neither the Democratic nor the Republican nominee will take the time or spend the resources required to change these conditions. It is incumbent on the Latino leadership, organizations, and community to change. The next subgroup of conditions focuses on such changes.

Elite-focused Conditions. Effective voter registration and naturalization drives are the first elite-driven strategic condition. These efforts must be ongoing and not tied to election cycles or particular campaigns. They may heat up during election cycles when more resources are available, but the infrastructure (personnel, offices, techniques) and effort must be sustained through the four-year presidential election cycle.

Although Latinos in California are almost 27 percent of the general population, they compose only 15 percent of adults eligible to vote and only

12 percent of the registered voters in the state (Field Institute 1993: 4). In 1988, the Current Population Survey estimated that 59 percent of Latino U.S. citizens aged eighteen and above were registered to vote in California, compared with 80 percent of Anglos, 78 percent of African Americans, and 67 percent of others (*California Latino/Latina Demographic Data Book* 1990: 63). These figures indicate that the Latino community includes a very sizable number of potential new voters, not only those not registered to vote, but also potential citizens. Over 950,000 Californians, most of them Latino, who applied for permanent residency status under the legalization provisions of the Immigration Reform and Control Act of 1986, become eligible for citizenship between 1993 and 1995 (U.S. Immigration and Naturalization Service 1992: Table 23). They supplement the 1.25 to 1.75 million Latino legal permanent residents in California who are currently eligible to naturalize. If Latino-targeted voter registration and naturalization campaigns are successful, the significance of the Latino vote could be enhanced.

The second elite-focused condition is *substantive advocacy*. This condition occurs when Latino political elites and activists identify, articulate, and advocate issues at nominating conventions, party meetings, and campaign strategy sessions. The higher the level of advocacy, the more likely that this advocacy will be successful and that Latino voters will be seen as an important campaign focus. There will always be Latino leaders advocating for more resources targeted to the Latino community. The point is that Latinos need to hold substantive or important positions within the campaign when making these arguments. Latino political leaders, including Latino candidates making explicit appeals to Latino voters, need to be strategically placed to influence decisions. The greater the number of such candidates, the greater the likely Latino voter turnout, and thus the greater the potential effectiveness of Latino voters. The presence of viable Latino candidates on the statewide ballot can do much to enhance the salience of all statewide elections for Latino voters. Their presence at the local level can also contribute to enhancing the viability of all elections. Latino candidates running in races that are highly competitive, and where Latino voters are identified and publicized during the campaign as critical to a Latino candidates' chance of success, should enhance mobilization and thus effectiveness.

The third elite-focused strategic condition is *unity and intensity of endorsement by Latino political elites, organizations, and media*. Like cohesion among Latino voters, more cohesive endorsement of the candidates or ballot issues by authoritative or respected segments of the Latino community can enhance the significance that any individual candidate will have for Latino voters. If elites, organizations, or media have a history of being able to deliver sizable numbers of votes, this elite cohesion can be even more useful in enhancing the effectiveness of Latino voters.

The fourth elite-driven strategic condition is *community organizational development and coordination*. The greater the number of community-based organizations that are not candidate- or campaign-specific, but that focus on electoral participation, the more likely it is that Latino voters will be wooed for support. Organizations of this sort can be based on voter mobilization or on the development of issue positions. That is, they can focus on enhancing turnout or on developing an agenda of issues that concern Latino voters. These organizations must coordinate activities to reduce replication in the same geographic region and to prevent competing campaigns from splitting and potentially neutralizing the effort.

In California, a coordination of sorts has occurred among the major Latino organizations that are concerned with long-term issues related to Latino electoral participation. The National Association of Latino Elected Officials focuses on naturalization drives, the Southwest Voter Registration and Education Project, on voter registration, and the Mexican American Legal Defense and Education Fund (MALDEF), on legal remedies to electoral obstacles. The National Council of La Raza (NCLR) and the League of United Latin American Citizens are not strong in California and play only a minor role in elections. The Latino Issues Forum, based in San Francisco, plays a role similar to NCLR's national role, and there are emerging policy centers such as the Tomás Rivera Center and the Alta California Policy Center to complement the various university centers. In addition, two strong caucuses are emerging, which will focus on the election or, at a minimum, the re-election of Latinos: the Latino Caucus of the California State Legislature, and the Latino Caucus of the League of California Cities.

To summarize, these four contextual and six strategic conditions should serve to enhance the effectiveness of the statewide Latino vote. Again, their contribution to a model of maximum effectiveness is cumulative. The greater the presence of these conditions, the greater the effectiveness of the Latino vote.

This model serves three purposes: first, it can predict the effectiveness of the statewide Latino vote before an election; second, it can explain the effectiveness of the vote during an election; finally, it should provide direction to those interested in trying to develop new or to modify existing approaches to enhancing the influence of Latino voters. In our view, our model has productive, explanatory, and prescriptive validity.

The 1992 Election in California

The conditions necessary for an effective Latino vote did not manifest themselves statewide in the 1992 California election. There was not a competitive election at the top of the ticket, no special appeal to Latinos was made, and no significant ballot issues for the Latino community appeared.

The only contextual condition present was the number of electoral opportunities.

As previously mentioned, Bill Clinton easily won California. The state was unofficially conceded by the Bush campaign before Labor Day as it shifted resources elsewhere. Within the context of previous California elections, this was an extraordinary event; Republicans had been competitive in all but one of the presidential elections for the past fifty years. The cause of this political earthquake was the shifting support of every ethnic group. This shift was not, as one would expect, from a candidate of one major party to that of another, but away from both major candidates to the independent candidacy of Ross Perot. What won the election for Clinton in California was not attracting more voters than Dukakis had (he actually received a smaller percentage of the total vote than had Dukakis) but maintaining the same base of white voters while Bush lost some of his.

As indicated in Table 6.1, all populations moved away from the two major candidates, except for whites and, according to one set of polls,[1] Latinos. Clinton actually received greater support from whites than had Dukakis while receiving moderately less support from blacks and, according to another set of polls, significantly less support from Latinos. Bush, on the other hand, received less support from all three groups, especially whites.

While fewer Latinos supported Clinton than had backed Dukakis, the difference in their support for the Democratic nominee over the Republican

TABLE 6.1 Support for Major Party Candidates, by Race and Ethnicity, 1988 and 1992

Group	1988 Dukakis %	1992 Clinton A %	1992 Clinton B %	Difference 1988–1992
White	42	43	42	+1/0
Black	86	80	83	−6/−3
Latino	65	51	65	−14/0
	Bush	Bush		
White	56	33	35	−23/−21
Black	13	12	9	−1/−4
Latino	34	27	23	−7/−11

Sources: Field Institute 1988; Los Angeles Times (November 5, 1992): A14; New York Times (November 5, 1992): B5.
Key: A = Los Angeles Times exit poll of California voters.
    B = New York Times exit poll of California voters.

candidate in 1992 was, depending on the source, between twenty-four and forty-two percentage points, the low end of which was near the average twenty-six-point difference score that manifested itself from 1980 to 1990. Thus, one could say that a unified Latino vote did materialize in which Latinos supported Clinton over the Republican nominee in their usual manner. However, the 1992 election was anything but usual. The candidacy of Ross Perot muddied the waters to such an extent that it could be argued that the second necessary aspect to a distinctive Latino vote, that they move toward the winner, may or may not have materialized. While movement toward the winner may not have been required in a three-person race, certainly maintaining previous levels of support, as whites did, would have included Latinos in the winning coalition.

What led to one poll's finding a decline of Latino support for the Democratic nominee from 1988 to 1992? The Perot candidacy had an impact in two ways. First, it provided an alternative for all voters, including Latinos. Second, it made California an easy victory for Clinton, so that no outreach was necessary. In fact, the Clinton campaign deliberately did not reach out to the Latino voters of California for fear of alienating the white voters. While no overt backlash from whites occurred, the fear kept the Clinton campaign from mobilizing the Latino vote. Latinos were not given a specific reason to vote for Clinton, no special get-out-the-vote effort or registration drive was coordinated, no prominent Latinos from California were placed on the national or even state campaign staff to advocate for a Latino campaign in the state. While there was a unified endorsement of Clinton by Latino officeholders, it occurred out of obligation to party and without any sense of excitement or intensity. Los Angeles County Supervisor Gloria Molina was an honorary cochair of the California campaign in part because the campaign believed her appeal to white voters made her safe. She was not, however, asked to carry out any important task. In short, no Latino campaign was run by Clinton because the election was not competitive and for fear of a backlash.

Electoral Opportunities

While many of the necessary conditions did not materialize for an effective Latino vote, one salvaged the 1992 election for the California Latino community or, more specifically, the Los Angeles County Latino community. Many new electoral opportunities for Latinos presented themselves for the first time in ten years. A decade before, Latinos had increased their representation from one U.S. representative to three while maintaining their representation at three state senate seats and four state assembly seats. This did not change throughout the eighties. No potential, growth, or influence seats shifted from an Anglo to a Latino official after the elections immediately following reapportionment, as had been predicted by some and promised by others. Latinos waited another ten years and again depended on reapportionment for the opportunity to expand representation.

Latinos Elected to the U.S. Congress

The 1992 reapportionment created a congressional seat in the heart of the East Side of Los Angeles, which pushed the three seats already held by Latinos farther east. With one exception, this was not a major concern for the existing districts with Latino officeholders, since the Latino population had continued to move east throughout the 1980s. The one exception was the new 30th Congressional District. While the district maintained a large Latino population, only about one-third of the voters were Latino (see Table 6.2). This concern was mitigated by the expectation that longtime incumbent Edward Roybal would run in the newly drawn district. His old seat had been split into the new 30th and the 33rd. He decided to run for the 30th for several reasons: first was residency; second, he enjoyed high name recognition in the new district and had previously won elected office to districts that were not majority Latino; finally, his daughter, Lucille Roybal-Allard, then in the state assembly, would declare in the 33rd, the safer of the two districts. Incumbents Matthew Martínez and Esteban Torres would run for reelection in the other two districts. No other congressional districts in the state offered the opportunity for Latino representation.

At first, it appeared that none of the four candidates would be seriously challenged in the primary or general election. Thus, an opportunity to create competition within these districts and to mobilize the Latino vote seemed lost. Representative Martínez eventually faced a young activist Latino attorney. The challenger did not have the resources to make a serious challenge, however, though he did attract a lot of attention and close to one-third of the primary vote.

TABLE 6.2   Characteristics of Congressional Districts Won by Latinos, 1992, Los Angeles County

District	Victor	Latino Population %	Latino Voting Age Population %	Latino Registration %
30	Becerra	61	57	34
31	Martínez	59	54	42
33	Roybal-Allard	84	79	48
34	Torres	62	58	43
Average		67	62	42

Source: Vargas 1992.

The opportunity for competition finally presented itself when thirty-year incumbent Roybal announced that he would not after all seek re-election and endorsed his longtime chief of staff to replace him. By waiting until the last minute to announce, he prevented other candidates from preparing a challenge. Soon, however, one-term Assemblyperson Xavier Becerra announced his candidacy and Roybal's chief of staff withdrew to support Becerra. School Board Member Leticia Quezada also announced her candidacy and received the endorsement of several prominent Latino officials. This would be a competitive race with two well-known and well-financed Latino candidates.

Rumors then began that a white assemblymember from the northern part of the 30th would also enter the race. As she was an elected official with ties to other elected officials, including U.S. Representatives Henry Waxman and Howard Berman, Assemblyperson Friedman would have been a serious challenger. This situation inspired a fear that the two prominent Latino candidates would split the Latino vote, and the white candidate would win the primary election. In previous years, this scenario would have led the two Latinos to try to persuade each other to withdraw from the race. Instead, both candidates and their supporters turned their attention to the potential white challenger. It was communicated that no Latino elected official would endorse any candidate running statewide with ties to Assemblyperson Friedman or Representatives Waxman or Berman. Thus, the Latino elected elite used the potential of the Latino vote in a crowded Democratic primary race for U.S. Senate to prevent a challenge and to ensure a Latino versus Latino primary in the 30th Congressional District.

The Latino political elites argued that the conditions were ripe for the Latino vote to have an impact on a statewide race. Their strategy had four parts. First, they asserted that Latinos could compose as much as 15 percent of the statewide Democratic primary vote. Second, they noted that several statewide races were competitive, with prominent candidates. These races could turn on small cohesive votes. Third, they argued that there would be no backlash in appealing to Latino or other minority voters because of the liberal primary electorate and because of the liberal ideologies of the likely candidates. Finally, Latinos threatened to unite against, rather than for, a candidate. In this case, negative issues proved a greater mobilizer than positive issues. As a result, the Friedman candidacy never developed. Thus, the potential Latino statewide vote was utilized to ensure increased Latino representation at the legislative level.

Competitive State Legislative Races in the Los Angeles Area

While the congressional races on the East Side produced only one competitive race, the elections for state assembly produced five hotly contested campaigns among Latinos. Before 1992, Latinos held only four of the eighty assembly seats in California—three from Los Angeles County and one from San Diego. After the 1992 elections, Latinos held seven seats—six from Los Angeles County and one from San Bernardino County. The opportunities were created by vacancies and reapportionment. Of the three incumbents in Los Angeles County, two (Becerra and Roybal-Allard) ran for Congress, and one (Polanco) for re-election. Thus, 1992 presented the East Side with five vacant "Latino" assembly seats (see Table 6.3).

These came to be recognized as Latino seats for four reasons: (1) Latinos made up a large share of the population; (2) they composed more than one-third of the registered voters and close to half of the Democratic registered voters; (3) white voters in these districts were fractured into several communities; and (4) Latino elected officials, activists, and organizations quickly labeled these as Latino districts and off-limits to white candidates supported by other organizations or elected officials.

This final point needs elaboration. While Latino elites could not prevent whites from running, they made it clear to various Democratic constituencies, such as legislative leaders, elected officials, party activists, trade and professional organizations, and PACs, that there would be repercussions for support of non-Latino candidates in the Democratic primary election in any of these five districts. Thus, individual whites could run but they would not have organizational support, significant endorsements, or resources.

Two prominent Latino candidates emerged in each of the five vacant "Latino" districts. As a group, these ten candidates had impressive credentials, such as graduate and law degrees from prominent universities; experience as local officials, staff members, or community activists; and access to campaign professionals and resources. These ten candidates compared favorably to any other candidate across the state competing for a vacant seat.

TABLE 6.3 Characteristics of Vacant Assembly Districts Won by Latinos, 1992, Los Angeles County

District	Victor	Latino Population %	Latino Voting Age Population %	Latino Registration %
46	Caldera	70	65	35
49	Martínez	55	51	44
50	Escutia	89	86	55
57	Solís	64	59	40
58	Napolitano	62	58	44
Average		68	64	44

Source: Vargas 1992.

What drew this impressive group of candidates was that they knew that as Latinos they could now compete. Being a Latino was no longer a disadvantage. Ethnicity had been neutralized.

In addition, the split of endorsements and resources into two Latino electoral networks made these districts competitive. Once a Latino victory was assured by creating Latino districts and discouraging viable white candidates, Latinos could compete among themselves. The two networks, one led by Supervisor Molina and retiring U.S. Representative Roybal and the other by Assemblyperson Polanco, Councilmember Alatorre, and State Senator Torres, went head to head in the five vacant assembly districts and the congressional district vacated by Roybal. The Molina-supported candidates won the congressional seat and one assembly seat and the Polanco, Alatorre, Torres-supported candidates won the other four assembly seats.

While many in the Latino community have lamented the emergence of these Latino electoral networks and the splitting of the community into two camps as unhealthy, these two networks spurred electoral competition, which is a necessary condition for a healthy democracy. Moreover, in none of the many electoral competitions in which these two networks have met has the Latino vote been split and caused the election of a non-Latino. Interestingly, vote splitting leading to the election of a non-Latino was much more frequent before the emergence of the two Latino electoral networks.

The success of Latinos capitalizing on electoral opportunities at the local level seems to have very little connection with the success of Latinos in a statewide vote. The necessary conditions for Latino electoral success differ in the two environments. At the local or legislative level, the success of an effective vote means electing Latinos and not just influencing electoral results. More important, the two are disconnected because one plays itself out mostly during the primary and is almost dormant in the general while the other, the statewide vote, is important during both the primary and the general election.

Conclusion

The Latino vote remains ineffective statewide in California. The necessary conditions did not materialize in 1992 and will most likely not do so in the foreseeable future. On the other hand, Latinos continue to enjoy local and legislative success. It is also clear that the conditions that produce this success will continue to manifest themselves in additional jurisdictions, which will lead to even more Latino elected officials. It is ironic that this continued local success has little if any impact on the effectiveness of the statewide vote.

The conditions that produce local and legislative success cannot be reproduced statewide. Reapportionment, usually driven by the VRA or a potential suit under the act, creates the necessary environment for Latino success. The VRA cannot have an impact on the contextual conditions discussed above. It may create more electoral opportunities, as in 1992, but isolated from the absent contextual conditions, its impact on the statewide vote was minimal and maybe nonexistent in the general election.

It is clear that Latinos must empower themselves in the foreseeable future through local and legislative means. From an analysis of the 1992 election in California, it appears that strategies at the elite level may produce greater results than does mass behavior. That is, to influence campaigns, candidates, elected officials, and policy, Latinos should follow a strategy in which Latino elites develop a network to ensure local and legislative successes. It must be clear, however, that these successes are in large part due to the VRA, which is currently under attack and may soon be reinterpreted. A foundation built on mass voter behavior could survive executive, legislative, and even judicial attacks. While pursuing a short-term elite-based strategy through local and legislative means, Latinos must continue to work for the long-term conditions necessary for an effective statewide vote.

Note

1. Exit polling of the Latino community is an inexact science (de la Garza 1987). This is particularly evident in the exit polls for the 1992 presidential race (see Table 6.1). Polls conducted by two major polling organizations for the nation's two most prominent papers differed by fourteen percentage points in their findings concerning Latino support for Clinton. In their reporting on whites and blacks, they differed by one and three percentage points, respectively.

References

California Latino/Latina Demographic Data Book. 1990. Berkeley: University of California, California Policy Seminar.

de la Garza, Rodolfo, ed. 1987. *Ignored Voices: Public Opinion Polls and the Latino Community*. Austin, Tex.: Center for Mexican American Studies.

DeSipio, Louis, and Rodolfo O. de la Garza. 1992. "Will Latino Votes Equal Political Clout? Core Voters, Swing Voters, and the Potential Vote." Paper prepared for presentation at the American Political Science Association, Chicago.

Field Institute. 1988. "Voting in the 1988 General Election." *California Opinion Index* (December). San Francisco.

———. 1993. "Voting in the 1992 General Election." *California Opinion Index* (January). San Francisco.

Fraga, Luis Ricardo. 1992. "Prototype from the Midwest: Latinos in Illinois." In Rodolfo O. de la Garza and Louis DeSipio, eds., *From Rhetoric to Reality: Latino Politics in the 1988 Elections*, pp. 111–126. Boulder, Colo.: Westview Press.

Guerra, Fernando. 1992. "Conditions Not Met: California Elections and the Latino Community." In Rodolfo O. de la Garza and Louis DeSipio, eds., *From Rhetoric to Reality: Latino Politics in the 1988 Elections*, pp. 99–110. Boulder, Colo.: Westview Press.

Pachon, Harry P.; Louis DeSipio; Juan-Carlos Alegre; and Mark Magaña. 1992. *The Latino Vote in 1992*. NALEO Background Paper #19. Washington, D.C.: NALEO Educational Fund.

U.S. Immigration and Naturalization Service. 1992. *1991 Statistical Yearbook of the Immigration and Naturalization Service*. Springfield, Va.: National Technical Information Service.

Vargas, Arturo. 1992. "Memorandum to Redistricting Coalition Members and Interested Parties." January 22. Los Angeles: MALDEF.

PART FOUR

The New Kids on the Block: Key States with New and Potentially Influential Latino Electorates

	Illinois 1992	Florida 1992	New York 1992
Population	11,631,000	13,488,000	18,119,000
Latino population	978,000	1,726,000	2,284,000
% Latino of total population	8.4	12.8	12.6
Voting population	5,650,000	5,772,000	7,613,000
Latino voters	171,000	411,000	382,000
% Latino of voting population	3.0	7.1	5.0
Latino adult noncitizens	276,000	621,000	351,000
Electoral votes	22	25	33

7

Leverage Without Influence: Illinois Latino Politics in 1992

Roberto Rey

With twenty-two electoral votes, Illinois is a major player in presidential politics. Home to more than nine hundred thousand Latinos, the fifth-largest Hispanic population in the United States, it holds the promise of significant Latino influence in municipal and state politics and under certain conditions in presidential elections (Fraga 1992; Valadez 1994). An analysis of the Latino role in the state's 1992 election offers insights into the latent power inherent in the concentrations of Latinos in large, urban, nationally pivotal states as well as into the limits on the realization of that potential.

This chapter concentrates on Latino politics in the Chicago metropolitan area. The city's large and rapidly expanding Hispanic population constitutes 60.4 percent of the state's Latino population. This concentration assures that political developments within Chicago's Hispanic communities are more richly documented by the news media. Latino civic organizations are also more active and influential in Chicago than elsewhere in the state. More to the point, the 1992 elections produced large, immediate gains in Latino electoral representation within the city and set the stage for continued expansion, developments that merit detailed analysis. The presence within the city of a representative cross section of the largest Latino nationalities residing in the United States is also an added enticement to the analyst (Padilla 1985; "Chicago Area a Melting Pot Where Hispanic Cultures Merge" 1991). Thus, Chicago provides a unique test of the potential for and the nature of intra-Hispanic alliances, which will be necessary for the maximum realization of Hispanic power at the national level.

If their numbers offer the potential for political influence, the extent to which Illinois's Latinos are able to realize this potential is conditioned by their demographics. These demographic considerations determine the resources they bring to the electoral arena, the general characteristics of the electoral environment, and the peculiarities of specific races.

The Dynamics of Chicago and Illinois Politics

The electoral environment of Illinois's Hispanics is conditioned by three underlying cleavages. First, competition between the Democratic and the Republican parties dominates national, statewide, and, to a significant degree, some Cook County races. The second and third cleavages are unique to Chicago. Here, the divisions are between machine regulars and reformers and between the white and the African American communities. To a certain extent, the electoral blocs formed by the last two conflicts overlap, yet retain significant, unique differences in terms of the issues they address, sections of the electorate they appeal to, internal dynamics, and their repercussions for local, state, and national politics.

The conflict between machine regulars and reformers tends to reflect the white ethnic versus African American split, but the respective constituencies are not entirely identical. These two cleavages are primarily expressions of intra-Democratic party conflict, but they have significant impact on statewide and national electoral contests. These splits offer Chicago's Latinos more opportunities than would exist in a situation in which the only competitive dimension was interparty. Chicago's Latino community took advantage of these cleavages to play an important role in several local races and to win favorable treatment in state and municipal redistricting in 1992.

In his study of the 1988 election, Fraga (1992) notes that Illinois has been ranked in various studies as having one of the highest national levels of competition between the two major parties. Both parties have strong bases of support in specific regions within the state and compete vigorously in presidential, congressional, gubernatorial, and state legislative elections (Bibby et al. 1983). Fraga suggests that in the context of high interparty competition Latinos can potentially act as a swing vote in these races if they deliver their votes as a bloc and practice effective coalition building (1992: 122). The potential for Latinos to serve as a decisive swing vote in these contests has been neutralized in the past by political and demographic factors. Chief among these political factors are (1) the traditional Latino loyalty to the Democrats and the concomitant lack of interparty competition for their votes, and (2) the emergence in past decades of "Reagan Democrats" as the paramount focus of interparty competition in Illinois. The demographic limitations on Latino influence are not unique to Illinois. I discuss these further in the next section.

Demographic Factors Conditioning Latino Electoral Power

Illinois's Hispanic population grew by 42.3 percent between 1980 and 1990, easily surpassing the growth rates among whites and African Americans. However, a number of factors work to undercut the electoral clout of these 904,446 Hispanics. The most fundamental limit on Latino influence at the state level is their relatively small share of the state's population (7.9 percent). Because Hispanics are relatively young, their share of the voting-age population is an even lower 6.8 percent (Midwest Northeast Voter Registration and Education Project [hereafter MWNEVRP] 1991). The low citizenship rate among non-Puerto Rican Hispanics makes additional inroads into their voting power. The U.S. census calculates that, at the time of the November 1990 elections, 46 percent of the state's adult Hispanic population were not U.S. citizens, which drops Latinos' share of the potential electorate to approximately 3.1 percent (U.S. Bureau of the Census [hereafter Census] 1992).

Relatively lower socioeconomic standing reinforces the limits resulting from a young population and low citizenship rates. Table 7.1 compares key socioeconomic indicators for Latinos, whites, and African Americans living in Cook and its five collar counties (90.1 percent of Illinois's Hispanic population). In spite of modest improvements over the past decade, Latinos continue to lag considerably behind the white population. Their low educational attainment, which falls short of that of both the white and the African American populations, is particularly noteworthy, given the importance of an educated electorate for effective political mobilization (Wolfinger and Rosenstone 1980).

TABLE 7.1 Selected Socioeconomic Indicators for Latinos, Whites, and African Americans in Cook, Du Page, Kane, Lake, McHenry, and Will Counties

	Latino		White	African American
	1980 %	1990 %	1990 %	1990 %
High school graduates	35.6	44.0	81.1	65.9
Persons in poverty*	20.6	19.9	5.5	29.4
Unemployment rate	11.1	10.4	4.2	17.2
Homeowners	31.1	38.2	68.2	37.5

Source: Chicago Urban League, Latino Institute, and Northern Illinois University (1992).

* Poverty rates are for 1979 and 1989.

Latinos' concentration in the Chicago metropolitan area and its satellite communities partially offsets the limitation on Latino electoral power caused by their youth, citizenship status, and small share of the state's population. Cook County (encompassing Chicago and the suburb of Cicero) accounts for 76.8 percent of the state's Hispanic population. The other major concentrations are found in the cities located within thirty miles of Chicago—Aurora, Waukegan, and Joliet. Combined, these three cities account for 5.8 percent of the state's Hispanic population. As Table 7.2 indicates, the Latino share of these cities' populations makes them a presence to be reckoned with in their municipal politics. In the case of Chicago, it offers a base from which to influence state and national politics.

The growing importance of Latinos in Chicago's politics can be readily gleaned from Table 7.3. While the city's population decreased by 7 percent between 1980 and 1990 under the combined influence of white flight and a decline in the African American population, its Latino population increased by 23 percent. Mexican immigration is the engine driving this expansion. In

TABLE 7.2 Illinois Cities with Greatest Latino Population

	Chicago	Cicero	Aurora	Waukegan	Joliet
Total population	2,783,726	67,436	101,769	78,185	84,243
Latino population	545,852	24,931	24,497	18,363	10,659
% Latino	19.6	37.0	24.1	23.5	12.7

Source: MWNEVRP (1991).

TABLE 7.3 Population of the City of Chicago, by Race and Hispanic Origin

	1980		1990	
	No.	%	No.	%
Total population	3,005,078	100.0	2,783,726	100.0
White	1,512,411	50.3	1,265,953	45.5
African American	1,197,174	39.8	1,086,389	39.0
Hispanic	442,063	14.7	545,852	19.6
Mexican American	255,802	8.5	352,560	12.7
Puerto Rican	112,074	3.7	119,866	4.3
Cuban	11,513	0.4	10,044	0.4
Other Latino	42,674	1.4	63,382	2.3

Source: City of Chicago (1993), and Census (1991a).

1990, Mexicans composed 65 percent the city's Latino population, compared with 58 percent in 1980. Central Americans also registered large gains in this period, with the Guatemalan community, at 12,895, edging out Cubans as the city's third-largest Hispanic community.

The increase in the Latino population has laid the foundation for dramatic gains in electoral representation through redistricting: the creation of a Latino congressional district, the doubling of the Hispanic delegation in the state legislature, and the expansion of Hispanic supermajority wards from four to seven. The past fifteen years have seen consolidation and expansion of Hispanic settlements on the southwest side of Chicago and the rapid expansion of the Mexican American population on the northwest side of Chicago, where the majority of the city's Puerto Ricans live. This development has eroded the previous separation of the two major Latino nationalities, which saw Puerto Ricans on the north side of the city and Mexican Americans on the south side. The once predominantly Puerto Rican communities in Chicago's near northwest side now have approximately equal numbers of Mexican American and Puerto Rican residents. This appears to be only a transitional balance, however. Given the Mexican American population's faster growth rate, it will become the majority group on the city's north side in the coming decade.

In the long run, the development of a mixed Mexican American and Puerto Rican community on the city's northwest side is a powerful foundation for greater cooperation between the two groups. Daily contact and joint work in community groups and school functions in pursuit of common concerns such as bilingual education, city services, and gang control promote the development of a shared "Latino" identity (Padilla 1985). The rate of intermarriage among the groups is a material manifestation of this developing common Latino identity. Chicago Department of Planning statistics indicate that, in 1987, 10 percent of Puerto Rican marriages were to Mexican Americans (*Chicago Tribune* [February 27, 1991]). While offering an opportunity for greater cooperation, the mixed Latino neighborhoods could also give rise to friction and competition along nationality lines if established Puerto Rican-dominated organizations or elected leaders fail to adopt policies that include Mexican American concerns. Alliance formation is a simultaneously cooperative and conflictive process. Cooperation between Mexican Americans and Puerto Ricans around redistricting in order to secure a Latino congressional district followed by competition over who will fill the position exemplify the opportunities and dangers associated with the process.

Redistricting

If their growing numbers give Latinos the potential for greater influence at the polls, the successful realization of that potential depends on redistricting and increasing electoral participation. The success of Chicago Latinos laid the foundation for the substantial gains in state and local electoral representation realized in the 1992 elections. Contributing to this positive outcome was a favorable political environment, the unity of Latino leaders around a redistricting strategy, and the experience and resources resulting from previous redistricting struggles.

The municipal redistricting process in Chicago was dominated by a conflict pitting the regular Democrats under the leadership of Mayor Richard Daley, Jr. against a coalition of most of the city's African American aldermen and several white reformers. The conflict, centered on the number of black wards that would be created, was a continuation of the contest between elements of the coalition that had supported Harold Washington and his white ethnic machine opponents. Daley's redistricting strategy sought to avoid a splintering of his electoral coalition while sidestepping any highly visible contest that might unite and mobilize his opposition within the African American community. Secure in his leadership of white ethnics and with a generally compliant city council, he was willing to grant significant concessions to both Hispanic and African American aldermen at the expense of some white council allies in order to secure city council passage of a redistricting proposal and avoid a politically risky public referendum.

Daley's proposal increased Latino wards from the existing four to seven supermajority wards (i.e., wards with over 65 percent Hispanic population) and a Hispanic "influence" ward (with a 43 percent Hispanic population). The proposal gained him the votes of the four Hispanic aldermen. His offer to increase the number of African American wards to twenty-one supermajority wards (the city had eighteen supermajority black wards and two majority wards represented by white aldermen) was rejected by most black aldermen, who proposed an alternative map with twenty-two black and seven Hispanic supermajority wards (but no Hispanic influence ward). Lacking the required votes to approve the map in the city council, two proposals were submitted to a public referendum in the primary. The Daley map, supported by three Latino aldermen (the fourth remained neutral), was easily approved.[1]

For the African American-led coalition, the decision to force a referendum flowed primarily from dissatisfaction with the Daley offer, but it also involved considerations of the advantages the coalition might reap from a public referendum in anticipation of the 1995 mayoral elections. The Hispanic aldermen's alliance with the Daley camp on this issue was based on the strong ties of the three with the regular Democrats, the greater gains offered by the Daley map, and the calculation that, with greater financial and organizational resources, the mayor would likely win any referendum.

In the redistricting of state legislative and U.S. congressional districts by the Illinois General Assembly, an intense contest between the Democrats and the Republicans for control of the legislature offered a scenario analogous to the machine versus the African American and reformers' coalition in Chicago. The contest gave Hispanics greater leverage than they would have had under less competitive circumstances. Whereas in Chicago the votes of Latino aldermen on the council and of the Latino community in the ongoing conflict between the regular Democrats and the black-led opposition was the Latinos' source of leverage, the struggle in the statehouse involved different resources and tactics.

With considerably less electoral clout in Springfield than in Chicago (one state senator out of 59, two state representatives out of 118, and approximately 3 percent of the state's voting population), the main weapon the Latino leadership wielded was the threat to scuttle any map that did not meet the minority representation criteria the courts mandated under the Voting Rights Act. The Republican governor vetoed the initial Democratic proposal. In a coin toss, the Republicans won the right to draw the new districts. Given the close nature of the redistricting contest between the two parties, the Republicans were unwilling to have a map that would otherwise give them significant advantages over the Democrats put at risk over the issue of minority representation.

Latinos were able to exploit this situation because of the political and legal expertise that organizations and elected leaders had gained in the redistricting struggle of the 1980s. In addition, two other factors benefited Latinos: Latino elected officials participated directly in the redistricting process; and these Latino leaders set aside personal differences to support a common redistricting strategy. The sole Hispanic state senator was appointed to the Senate Elections and Reapportionment Committee, which put together the new legislative map. The Latino delegation in Springfield put out a clear, united message on what it wanted out of reapportionment in terms of the numbers and types of districts, and delegation members coordinated their efforts with groups such as the Mexican American Legal Defense and Education Fund, the Latino Institute, and the MWNEVRP (Midwest-Northeast Voter Registration Project). Each of these community organizations had legal and technical expertise as well as experience in previous reapportionment struggles. The absence of conflict between Latino aldermen over municipal redistricting facilitated Latino unity in Springfield.

Hispanic efforts in Springfield resulted in a doubling of Latino districts in the state senate (from one to two) and in the state house of representatives (from two to four), the creation of four Hispanic judicial districts,[2] and the creation of the first Hispanic congressional district in Illinois. However, the high degree of community unity that was crucial to these advances was strained in the subsequent races to fill some of the newly created spots—most notably in the elections for the newly created Latino 8th Congressional District.

Voter Registration Efforts

As I have indicated, the demographics of Chicago's Latinos assure a sharp drop-off between the raw population data used in redistricting and the number of Latino voters in the newly created districts. The recognition that Latinos did not constitute the majority of voters in many of the newly created districts necessitated the creation of the supermajority districts. Demographic considerations also shaped the electoral strategies of Latino candidates and community leaders. There was, for example, a concerted effort to increase Latino voter registration, and candidates developed their electoral strategies with an eye toward non-Hispanic (mainly white ethnic) voters.

A joint project of the Illinois Hispanic Democratic Council (a component of the state Democratic party) and the MWNEVRP was the principal voter registration effort targeting Latinos. The project relied primarily on the resources of Latino candidates and organizations. Neither the state nor the national Democratic party nor the presidential candidates invested significant resources in Latino voter registration. The Latino-led effort registered more than forty thousand new voters from the months leading up to the primary through the general election, over 75 percent of whom lived in the Chicago area (Rivera 1992).

These figures, however, overestimate the impact of Latino voter registration efforts. Senator Del Valle, whose office accounted for a large share of the project's new registrations (nineteen thousand between the primaries and the general elections), noted that 50 percent were Hispanics and the other 50 percent primarily African Americans. The significance of the numbers of registered Hispanics left after non-Hispanic voters are factored out is reduced even further when placed in the context of the extremely low registration rates among Hispanics vis-à-vis black and white voters. The U.S. census reported that for the 1990 election only 33 percent of the state's voting-age Hispanic population was registered to vote, compared with 72 percent of the black and 66 percent of the white populations (Census 1991*b*: 34).[3]

The Presidential Vote

Primary Election

By the time of the Illinois primary, the field of candidates for the Democratic nomination had narrowed to Clinton, Tsongas, and Brown. Illinois state politics is defined by three distinct regions: Chicago, Chicago's suburbs, and downstate. Table 7.4 gives a rough approximation of the importance of each region in any statewide Democratic primary race. Each region accounts for approximately one-third of the state Democratic electorate. Based on the census estimate of Latinos as approximately 3 percent of the state's electorate, the statewide Latino vote in the Democratic primary was approximately forty thousand. This number would be insufficient to swing any but the closest election. The 1992 Democratic primary was not to be that race.

The low salience of the Latino voted contributed to the insignificance of Latino issues in the Democratic primary. Above all, Clinton and the other Democratic party candidates sought to avoid accusations of pandering to special interests in order not to alienate Reagan Democrats. Neither Clinton nor Tsongas made minority issues a central component of their Illinois campaigns. Brown did try to capitalize on his friendship with César Chávez, but his efforts did not go beyond that symbolic level. Tsongas targeted his economic message at middle-income taxpayers, and Clinton focused on issues such as health care and education, which appealed to the traditional Democratic voter, regardless of ethnicity. His proposals were constructed to benefit both middle- and low-income voters. Consequently, specific Hispanic issues were not addressed by any of the candidates.

In seeking Latino support, the three Democratic candidates followed the requisite protocol, by soliciting the endorsements of local Latino political leaders and making a limited number of symbolic appearances at community events. They did not, however, make a special effort to mobilize the Latino electorate by allocating resources for voter registration, targeting campaign outreach at Latinos, or addressing the specific ways in which general issues (such as education) affect Latinos. "They took the Latino vote for granted based on the historical voting trend of Latinos" summarized the director of newly elected Representative Gutiérrez's district office (Rivera 1992).

The opportunity to cast a vote against Republicans for their record on the economy generated considerable grass-roots interest in voter registration. According to State Senator Del Valle, "in this respect the mood in the Latino community reflected the mood in the rest of the country; people wanted change" (Del Valle 1993).

TABLE 7.4   Vote Totals, by Region, Illinois 1992 Presidential Primary

	Clinton	Brown	Tsongas	Regional Total
Chicago	301,181	74,332	128,319	503,832
Chicago suburbs	182,203	80,846	164,661	427,710
Downstate	273,815	61,247	88,302	423,364
State total	757,199	216,425	381,282	1,354,906

Source: "Election '92" (1992a).

While the increased number of local races heightened interest in the elections, Latino leaders generally credited the presidential race as the main motivator of higher registration. Alderman García (1992) observed that, in spite of people's optimism about beating Bush, there was less participation at the grass-roots level in both the primary and the general elections than in either the Dukakis or the Mondale campaigns. The campaigns did not distribute much literature, few signs went up on windows, and the bulk of campaign resources went into print media and TV spots that contained no special emphasis on minority concerns.

The more populist cast of Clinton's program relative to Tsongas's, the endorsement of his candidacy by the regular Democratic organization and local Latino political leaders, and a better-financed campaign all contributed to a convincing victory in the primary. While Tsongas's focus on middle-class concerns made it a close race in the suburbs, Clinton piled up large margins in the city and among downstate voters. Within the city, Clinton's strongest support came from African American and Latino voters (see Table 7.5). Again, it is necessary to note that the high percentage of the vote Clinton received in the four predominantly Latino wards actually translates into relatively few votes.

An MWNEVRP exit poll provides a breakdown of the Latino primary vote by each of the major national-origin groups. As indicated in Table 7.6,

TABLE 7.5   1992 Chicago Presidential Primary Election, Vote by Ward Composition

Wards	Latino	White	Black*	Clinton	Brown	Tsongas
Latino (%)	74.6	14.3	10.1	68.8	12.3	18.8
No. of votes				13,107	2,351	3,588
African American (%)	3.3	5.7	90.1	80.4	9.6	10.0
No. of votes				140,996	16,759	17,535
White Ethnics (%)	14.1	75.2	4.4	47.4	18.1	34.6
No. of votes				83,140	31,729	60,645
Lakeshore (%)	10.0	68.3	14.8	35.5	19.8	44.8
No. of votes				23,042	12,830	29,067
Citywide (%)	17.4	45.3	37.2	59.9	14.8	25.3

Notes: *Population data do not add up to 100 percent because of the presence of other populations.
Source: Chicago Board of Election Commissioners (1992); "Election '92" (1992a): 22; Census (1992).
Population data are for persons eighteen years old and over.

there were no significant differences among the major Latino subgroups with regard to their support of the major candidates, with one exception—a higher preference for Tsongas among "other Latinos." Most differences could be accounted for by the poll's margin of error.

General Election

The general election campaign continued the pattern of minimal attention to the Hispanic (and African American) voter. In the late summer, following the convention, the Clinton campaign established Adelante con Clinton! to conduct outreach to the Hispanic community. According to several local leaders involved with it, however, Adelante con Clinton! was primarily a paper organization with very few resources to draw on. The general election's interparty competition, with its focus on gaining the votes of the Reagan Democrats (the key swing vote in the last three elections), diminished the importance of the Latino and African American electorates. Given minorities' lower voter turnout, both major parties focused their staff and resources to a greater degree than in the primaries on the contest for the white middle-class vote. This effort was particularly important in light of Ross Perot's bid for the support of these same voters—manifested in the much higher vote totals he received in the suburbs and downstate (see Table 7.7).

TABLE 7.6 Latino Vote in the Presidential Primary, by Ancestry

	Clinton %	Brown %	Tsongas %	Other %
Latinos	60.3	8.6	22.2	8.9
Mexican American	66.2	3.5	19.7	10.6
Puerto Rican	57.5	12.4	21.2	8.8
Cuban	58.3	12.5	20.8	8.3
Other Latino	48.8	14.6	36.6	0.0

Source: MWNEVRP (1992a).

TABLE 7.7 Illinois 1992 Presidential General Election, by Region

Region	Clinton	Bush	Perot	Total
Chicago	749,073	191,142	97,946	1,038,161
Chicago suburbs	774,036	833,964	378,742	1,986,742
Downstate	878,502	693,331	357,464	1,929,297
State totals	2,401,611	1,718,437	834,152	4,954,200

Source: "Election '92" (1992b).

The potential for Latino influence was further dampened when in mid-October the Bush campaign virtually conceded defeat in the state by withdrawing all campaign resources. The decision assured Clinton Illinois's electoral votes and diminished his need to reach out to any electorate, including Latinos. Thus, the competition for the disaffected white voters that focused on the suburbs and downstate, combined with the absence of active Republican competition in the state, effectively eliminated any possibility of a Latino or African American swing vote. It was consequently unnecessary for the Clinton campaign to undertake any major investment in the Latino vote beyond the basic get-out-the-vote effort. Clinton's campaign assumed the support of Latinos. Election night results justified that confidence.

Repeating the pattern established in the primary, African Americans and Latinos turned in the most lopsided vote for Clinton (see Table 7.8). Over 71 percent of Latinos voted for him. Although there was no poll of Chicago's Latino national-origin groups, an MWNEVRP phone poll of northeastern and central states indicated approximately equal rates of support (in the mid-seventies) for Clinton among Puerto Ricans and Mexican Americans and a split of the Cuban vote, with 63 percent voting for Bush and 30 percent for Clinton. The similarity in Mexican American and Puerto Rican voting patterns reflects similar socioeconomic characteristics. This gives them the capacity to vote as a bloc on a large number of issues. Cuban Americans' special preoccupation with U.S. foreign policy toward Castro, on the other hand, inclines them to vote Republican in national races. Given their small numbers in Illinois, the impact of their split vote on the Latino vote as a whole is insignificant.

The regional breakdown of the state's vote highlights the significance of the Chicago suburbs and downstate. Each outvoted the city by nearly 2 to 1. Political analysts highlighted the Reagan Democrats' return to the fold as an important element in Bush's defeat. A *Tribune* election day poll revealed that 65 percent of Democrats who had voted for Reagan, voted for Clinton in Illinois; only 16 percent gave their vote to Bush. Clinton's and senatorial candidate Carol Moseley-Braun's strength in the suburbs indicates a weakening Republican grip as more traditionally Democratic voters migrate from the city. It also indicates that traditionally Democratic voters will grow in importance as a key battleground in future elections and will continue to undermine the importance of Chicago and its minority voters.

Congressional Election

The minority status of Latino voters within the nominally Latino district was the dominant factor shaping the strategies and outcome of the race in the newly created 8th Congressional District. Although the district's popu-

TABLE 7.8 Chicago 1992 Presidential General Election, Vote by Ward Composition

Wards	Hispanic	White	Black*	Clinton	Bush	Perot
Latino (%)	74.6	14.3	10.1	71.4	19.5	9.1
No. of votes				28,882	7,910	3,685
African American (%)	3.3	5.7	90.1	93.6	3.7	2.8
No. of votes				365,946	143,369	10,795
White Ethnics (%)	14.1	75.2	4.4	52.2	31.9	15.9
No. of votes				161,068	98,513	49,233
Lakeshore (%)	10.0	68.3	14.8	64.1	25.2	10.7
No. of votes				92,758	36,503	15,535
Citywide (%)	17.4	45.3	37.2	71.9	18.6	9.5

Notes: * Population data do not add up to 100 percent because of the presence of other populations.
Source: "Election '92" (1992b); Census 1992.
Population data are for persons eighteen years old and over.

lation was 65 percent Hispanic, only 41 percent of its registered voters were Hispanic; 58 percent were non-Hispanic whites (*Chicago Tribune* [February 5, 1992]). The district's composition raised the specter of a white candidate's election. This possibility was increased when a white alderman with a strong ward organization joined three Latino candidates and a second white alderman in the primary bid for the congressional seat. A controversial deal between one of the Latino candidates and Mayor Daley reduced the possibility of a white victory, however.

In a last-minute break with a coalition of African American aldermen and the city's other Hispanic aldermen, Luis Gutiérrez cast a decisive vote against a strong affirmative action amendment to a key city contract. Alderman Gutiérrez's vote enabled Daley to avoid a veto, which would have battered his standing among the city's Hispanic and African American communities. In exchange, the mayor threw his support behind Gutiérrez's candidacy for Congress. In the following weeks, the two white aldermen and one of the Hispanic candidates (all regular Democrats) bowed out of the race under intense mayoral pressure. The race narrowed to a contest between Gutiérrez (of Puerto Rican origin) and Mexican American candidate Juan Soliz.

The mayor's endorsement and the regular Democratic organization's resources gave Gutiérrez a commanding lead over Soliz among white voters and a 2-to-1 advantage in campaign funds. A *Chicago Tribune* poll taken two weeks before the election found that 40 percent of white voters preferred Gutiérrez while only 14 percent indicated support for Soliz. Almost half of the non-Hispanic voters said that Daley's support made them more likely to vote for Gutiérrez (*Chicago Tribune* [March 5, 1992]).

In spite of Soliz's strong attacks on Gutiérrez's vote against the affirmative action amendment, the latter retained the support of most Puerto Ricans. The *Tribune* poll found 70 percent of Puerto Ricans favored Gutiérrez, even though 55 percent of them indicated disapproval of his anti-affirmative action vote. Because of the mayor's endorsement, which brought with it the support of one of the city's two Mexican American aldermen, Gutiérrez was also able to make some inroads into Soliz's base. Among Mexican Americans polled, 50 percent indicated they were for Soliz while 23 percent supported Gutiérrez. Gutiérrez solidified these advantages with extensive direct mailings and ads on Spanish TV, radio, and newspapers; Soliz was unable to match Gutiérrez's media campaign. In the end, Gutiérrez easily won the Democratic nomination, with 60 percent of the vote. Given the Democratic party's dominance in Chicago, the primary victory virtually assured his victory in the general election.

The election of the first Latino member of Congress is a notable boost to Latino political power in Illinois. However, it may be that the manner in which this was achieved is as significant for the development of Latino politics as the accomplishment itself. Apart from the implications of the decisive role of the Daley organization and the district's white electorate for future elections, the campaign leaves a legacy of strained relations between Mexican Americans and Puerto Ricans. The candidates' initial de-emphasis of an intra-Hispanic contest gave way in the closing days of the campaign to a depiction of the race as a contest between Mexican Americans and Puerto Ricans, as Soliz sought to shore up his support among Mexican American voters. Given the Mexican Americans' 2-to-1 edge among the district's Latino voters and their increased dominance as more become naturalized, there is a keen awareness in the Gutiérrez camp of the need to build bridges to the Mexican American community. The support that he received from more than one-fifth of Mexican American voters is an indication that national origin is not an absolute dividing line. Yet, if future contests continue to pit Mexican American against Puerto Rican candidates, the divisions that characterized this election might take on a more permanent character.

Other Local Elections

Although the new congressional district garnered the most attention, state legislative and judicial elections generated sharp competition and above-average local interest because of the newly created state senate, state house of representatives, and judicial districts.

In the race on the northwest side for the second state senate district, Miguel Del Valle, running as an incumbent, easily turned back a challenge from a white ethnic challenger as he received 72 percent of the votes cast. Del Valle, a Puerto Rican reform Democrat, has survived numerous challenges from the regular Democrats and appears secure in his post.

Independent alderman Jesús García, running in the newly created 1st Senate District on the predominantly Mexican American southwest side, faced stiffer competition. Although the district's population is over 80 percent Mexican American, their low share of the electorate provided a base for a strong challenge from a white candidate fielded by the regular Democrats. In a three-way race, García won with 51.4 percent of the vote, against 38.3 percent for his white opponent and 10.3 percent for another Hispanic also supported by the regular Democrats ("Election '92" 1992a). García had faced stiff competition from the regular Democrats in his past contests. This latest campaign exhibited similarities to those previous contests: a small majority against multiple opponents fielded by the regular Democrats, including one or more Latino names, in order to split the Hispanic vote. The presence of credible Anglo candidates in the two Hispanic majority senate districts spurred candidates' voter registration efforts and Latino civic and community group moves to forestall the possibility of a non-Hispanic victory.

Competition in the state house of representative districts was restricted to Latino candidates. As in the senate races, the main dividing line among aspirants in the two newly created districts was that between independent and regular Democratic candidates. In both new districts, the candidates associated with the regular Democrats edged out their reform opponents by very narrow margins—fewer than fifty votes out of more than ten thousand votes cast in the northside 4th District. In one of the two old districts, the incumbent regular Democrat ran unopposed, and the other featured a close contest between a regular Democrat and an ally of congressional candidate Juan Soliz. The latter took on the character of a grudge match, given the regular Democratic organization's endorsement of Soliz's opponent. Ten candidates ran in the three contested elections. The large field raised the level of interest in these local races.

Also enhancing the visibility and participation of Latinos at the local level were elections for judges in Hispanic majority judicial subdistricts. These judicial subdistricts were newly created for this election. They were seen as a means of increasing the number of minority judges and were created in response to the low number of minority candidates who had been slated by the Democratic party in past citywide elections. In this respect, the consequences of the reform were mixed. In the four Hispanic subdistricts the Latino candidates faced competition from a large field of white contenders. Latino candidates—one a regular Democrat, the other, an independent, won the two northside positions. The two southside slots went to white candidates supported by white ethnic ward bosses.

Significant Local Races with Non-Hispanic Candidates

Two other races involving non-Hispanics merit close examination, as they demonstrate the increased sophistication of the Latino electorate. The primary race between Carol Moseley-Braun and incumbent Senator Alan Dixon drew national attention as a referendum on the Senate's performance in the Clarence Thomas hearings. Women's anger at Dixon's vote for Thomas was a dominant factor, but his defeat also reflected a widespread disillusionment with the policies of the Reagan/Bush era and a perception of Dixon's acquiescence in them. Moseley-Braun's campaign received the enthusiastic support of independent Democrats such as State Senator Del Valle and Alderman García. These leaders were oriented toward developing a coalition with reform Democrats in the African American community. Regular Democrat Hispanic officials lined up behind Dixon. Close to 60 percent of Latinos voted for Moseley-Braun or the third candidate, Albert Hofeld—a wealthy lawyer whose lavish spending on ads attacking Dixon as a status quo candidate severely hurt the incumbent. Latino support for Moseley-Braun and Hofeld was higher than was support among white ethnics for those candidates and reflected the pervasive discontent with and desire for change in national policies.

To a large degree, Latino ticket splitting was also evident in the race for Cook County states attorney. Given its power to launch high-profile investigations of political corruption in Cook County, the office has served as a launching pad for Republicans aspiring to statewide office. Chicago's regular Democratic organization has a keen interest in who controls the office, as do good-government groups. The Republican incumbent ran as a reform good-government candidate and received the endorsement of numerous independent Democrats and good-government groups. Facing a potentially strong straight-ticket vote in the city fueled by the Clinton and Moseley-Braun candidacies, he ran an aggressive campaign to convince city Democrats to split their vote. He courted the Latino vote by putting a lot of money into Latino media advertisement, by showing up at numerous community events, and by addressing the issues of gangs and drugs. His support of a bill to reallocate a portion of drug forfeiture funds to local block watches and drug education (over the strong objections of law enforcement agencies) bought him considerable goodwill among community groups and approximately 42 percent of the vote in the four predominantly Latino wards.

Conclusion

In considering the potential influence of Latinos on the electoral process it is necessary to distinguish between the intensity of influence and the level (local, state, or national) at which it is exercised. The experience of Latinos in the 1992 Illinois elections reinforces previous analysis that the likelihood that Latino voters will exercise a decisive influence (as swing voters) at either the state or the national level is remote for the foreseeable future (i.e., for at least the next decade). Latinos' unswerving loyalty to the Democrats and the interrelated absence of party competition for their vote is a critical weakness. Their share of the electorate is insufficient, and as a voting bloc they lack financial, educational, or other resources to compensate for their lack in numbers. Moreover, as Valadez's (1994) study of the Mexican American Pilsen neighborhood in the 1990 elections demonstrates, Latino desire to participate in presidential elections is undermined by a view of local politics as more important than national politics. Valadez also found that residents of that Mexican American community see nonelectoral tactics as more efficacious because of the machine's continued, if diminished, dominance of the electoral sphere, its efforts to limit their access to the electoral process, and its unresponsiveness to their concerns. The current dominance of the electoral process by large blocs of dissatisfied white voters with no great allegiance to either party also works against special efforts on the part of the established parties to address Latino concerns. The Republicans' success over the past decade in framing minority issues in this light is a burdensome legacy for efforts to expand the influence of Latinos or other minorities.

In this context, any special effort by the Democrats to court the state's Hispanics or African Americans in order to forestall a defection to the Republicans at the national level is unnecessary. In the absence of party competition for their vote, special outreach toward minorities on the part of the Democrats would make sense only to increase turnout. Such efforts, however, have exposed the Democratic party to charges of catering to special interests and have contributed to the defection of Reagan Democrats. It is these disaffected white voters, not minorities, who have constituted the strategically decisive swing vote in the last three presidential elections. In 1992 they, not minorities, were the primary focus of the Democratic party's efforts in Illinois. Intent on courting disaffected white voters, the Illinois campaigns of Democratic presidential hopefuls and Clinton's general election effort invested few resources in mobilizing the Latino electorate and studiously avoided addressing special minority concerns that might alienate the Reagan Democrats. While not ignored by the Democrats, Latino voters and their concerns were a subsidiary element in Democrats' election strategies.

Although lacking the capacity to sway national- and state-level races regularly, Latinos were nonetheless able to exert some leverage. The Democratic party's presidential candidate folded Latino concerns into more general appeals, but did address those concerns. It was at the municipal and state levels that Illinois's Hispanics were able to exercise the greatest influence. In municipal races, as the conflict between reformers and machine Democrats *and* black versus white ethnics came to the fore, the salience of Reagan Democrats as the key swing vote faded. At the state and county levels, the rivalry between the two major parties provided opportunities not available in the national arena. These political factors and the specific demography of the Latino population made the Hispanic vote more crucial in local and state contests and the subject of more intense courting.

Latino success in the redistricting process is especially noteworthy. Intense competition between Democrats and Republicans for control of the legislature combined with negotiations and alliance formation backed by the threat of legal action resulted in a dramatic expansion of Latino elected officials at the municipal, state, and federal levels.

Finally, the Cook County state's attorney race was noteworthy as an illustration of the increased sophistication of the Latino electorate as reflected in split-ticket voting (as occurred in the Moseley-Braun/Dixon contest). The state's attorney race was also noteworthy as evidence of a trend on the part of state-level Illinois Republican candidates to court the Latino vote (Valadez 1994).

As alluded to earlier, the special characteristics of the state's Hispanic population confer on it advantages in municipal and state representative elections that vanish in statewide or national races. High percentages of noncitizens dilute Latino electoral impact in national and statewide elections and in most at-large electoral districts. The requirement that voting districts have roughly equal population (regardless of the citizenship status of that population) works to the advantage of Hispanics in areas of concentration where their *numbers* force the creation of aldermanic, state representative, and even congressional districts that can be controlled by their reduced *electorate* (de la Garza and DeSipio 1993). The noncitizens, who are irrelevant in larger contests, thus play a decisive if indirect role in local empowerment efforts through the process of redistricting.

The growth in Latino electoral representation in Illinois illustrates this link. Both the 1980 and the 1990 redistricting resulted in large qualitative increases in electoral representation. Even the gains made between the decennial redistrictings were based on the favorable opportunities created by these redistricting efforts. The growth of representation thus takes on the quality of a large leap every ten years followed by mop-up actions in between. Latino elected officials in Illinois are conscious of this relation. Their concentration on harvesting the opportunities offered by the redistricting reduced the importance they attached to and their involvement in the presidential races. Illinois's 1992 elections, then, point in the direction of local races and concentrated efforts to realize the potential created by redistricting as the most promising areas for the expansion of Hispanic electoral influence.

Notes

1. The map submitted by the mayor for the public referendum offered the African American community one majority ward and nineteen supermajority wards.

2. The shift from at-large judicial elections to subdistrict elections was not the consequence of the reapportionment process. It resulted from a suit and legislation introduced by State Senator Miguel Del Valle and several African American state legislators. They sued on the grounds that at-large elections were discriminatory.

3. A potential new source of Hispanic voters is the more than ninety thousand Mexican American area residents who became legal residents as a result of the 1986 immigration law and who began to be eligible for citizenship in 1993 (*Chicago Tribune* [June 9, 1991]). The impact of newly naturalized citizens, however, was negligible in the 1992 elections.

References

Bibby, John F.; Cornelius P. Cotter; James L. Gibson; and Robert Huckshorn. 1983. "Parties in State Politics." In Virginia Gray, Herbert Jacob, and Kenneth N. Vines, eds., *Politics in the American States: A Comparative Analysis*, 4th ed., pp. 59–96. Boston: Little Brown.

"Chicago Area a Melting Pot Where Hispanic Cultures Merge." 1991. *Chicago Tribune* (February 27).

Chicago Board of Election Commissioners. 1992. "Official Precinct Canvass March Primary Election."

City of Chicago. 1993. *Chicago Statistical Abstract: 1980 Community Area Profiles*.

Chicago Urban League, Latino Institute, and Northern Illinois University. 1992. "The Changing Economic Standing of Minorities in the Chicago Metropolitan Area." Interim Report.

de la Garza, Rodolfo O., and Louis DeSipio. 1993. "Save the Baby, Change the Bathwater, and Scrub the Tub: Latino Electoral Participation after Seventeen Years of Voting Rights Act Coverage." *Texas Law Review* 71 (7): 1479–1539.

Del Valle, Miguel. 1993. Interview with the author. February 1.

"Election '92." 1992a. *Chicago Tribune* (March 19).

———. 1992b. *Chicago Tribune* (November 5).

Fraga, Luis R. 1992. "Prototype from the Midwest: Latinos in Illinois." In Rodolfo O. de la Garza and Louis DeSipio, eds., *From Rhetoric to Reality: Latino Politics in the 1988 Elections*, pp. 111–126. Boulder, Colo.: Westview Press.

García, Jesús. 1992. Interview with the author. December 11.

Midwest Northeast Voter Registration and Education Project (MWNEVRP). 1992. *1992 Presidential Primary Hispanic Voter Exit Poll Chicago, Illinois, March 17, 1992*. Chicago.

———. 1991. *Hispanics in Illinois: Preliminary Population Database Based on the 1990 Census*. Chicago.

Padilla, Félix. 1985. *Latino Ethnic Consciousness: The Case of Mexican Americans and Puerto Ricans in Chicago*. Notre Dame, Ind.: University of Notre Dame Press.

Rivera, Roberto. 1992. Interview with the author. December 7.

U.S. Bureau of the Census. 1992. Unpublished data on Latino registration in 1990 (supplied by the Latino Institute).

———. 1991a. *Summary Tape File 1C.* 1990 Census of the Population and Housing.
———. 1991b. *Voting and Registration in the Election of November of 1990.* Current Population Reports. Population Characteristics Series P–20, No. 453. Washington, D.C.: U.S. Government Printing Office.
Valadez, John. 1994. "Latino Politics in Chicago: Pilsen in the 1990 General Election." In Rodolfo O. de la Garza, Martha Menchaca, and Louis DeSipio, eds., *Barrio Ballots: Latino Politics in the 1990 Elections*, pp. 115–136. Boulder, Colo.: Westview Press.
Wolfinger, Raymond, and Steven Rosenstone. 1980. *Who Votes?* New Haven: Yale University Press.

8

The Conservative Enclave Revisited: Cuban Americans in Florida

Dario Moreno and Christopher Warren

Ambiguity continues to characterize the debate about whether there is a Latino politics in the United States that is both identifiable and separable from the politics of other groups or from that of the nation as a whole (Vigil 1987; García 1988; Villareal, Hernández, and Neighbor 1988; de la Garza and DeSipio 1992; de la Garza et al. 1992; Hero 1992). For analysts of Latino politics, however, the 1992 elections provide the clearest and most revealing indicators to date of political patterns within at least some segments of the Latino population. The 1992 elections brought continued expansion of the conservative political base of Hispanics in Florida, especially Cuban Americans, and enhanced their political incorporation at the local, state, and even federal levels.

In metropolitan Miami-Dade County, Cuban Americans have consolidated their status as the core electoral constituency. They have strengthened their local political position in two ways. First, they continue to provide a significant share of the local vote and they vote cohesively. Second, because a recent federal court ruling overturned the county commission's at-large election system and replaced it with a single-member districting system, they are assured more offices for which Cuban Americans can elect their preferred candidates. With district elections and a larger commission, Hispanic representation rose from one seat out of nine (11 percent) to six seats out of thirteen (46 percent) in 1992. The Dade County School Board settled a similar suit out of court. Hispanic electoral successes in several of the county's more than two dozen municipal governments (i.e., Miami, Hialeah, West Miami, Sweetwater, and Coral Gables) also continue to demonstrate the breadth and depth of the Hispanic presence in local elected office.

In state politics, Cuban Republican legislators from Dade County have emerged as an important swing vote on matters ranging from the selection of state legislative leaders to the fate of major pieces of legislation. On the issue of reapportionment, for example, Cuban Republicans were nothing short of catalytic in dramatically modifying the Democratic majority's plans for congressional and state legislative district lines.

The statewide Latino influence is not felt just in the legislature. In statewide elections, South Florida's Latin (the preferred local usage) voters again demonstrated in 1992 that in close contests, their bloc voting could determine the outcome.

Nationally, the election of three Cuban Americans to the U.S. House (two from South Florida and one from New Jersey), combined with the ongoing lobbying efforts of such groups as the Cuban American National Foundation (CANF), has resulted in an expanded role in Washington. Although the latest changes in the Clinton administration's policy toward the treatment of Cuban refugees must be viewed as a setback for groups such as CANF, Cuban Americans have nonetheless emerged as a group whose support is actively courted by a growing number of officeholders from outside the state—from presidential candidates to members of Congress seeking campaign contributions.

Cuban American electoral victories in 1992, however, and the vigorous promotion of a broader political agenda that encompassed issues as diverse as trade with Cuba and legislative reapportionment, have not been the only gauges of political change. There are also some indications of a broadening of the partisan and ideological boundaries of the Cuban community, a broadening marked by an increase in the overtures made by political actors who previously would have had little expectation of attracting significant support from either Cuban elites or rank-and-file voters. The Clinton campaign's effort in 1992 to court Cuban support in Florida was only the most visible manifestation of such activity. Within the community itself, there are also more frequent challenges to the established conservative exile leadership that is represented by groups such as CANF. As discussed later, these challenges, while still limited in their scope and impact, suggest the emergence of a frequently younger, more moderate political leadership, and with it, a political agenda rooted more in domestic ethnic politics than in international exile politics.

Collectively, such developments have resulted in the emergence of a group that internally is increasingly complex, but that has found its niche in American politics, is still in the process of securing its base, and now has regular access to the corridors of power at all three levels of government.

A Demographic Profile

According to the 1990 census, Florida's Hispanic population has continued to grow, in both actual and proportional terms. It increased from approximately 860,000, or 8.9 percent of the total population, in 1980, to 1,574,000, or 12.1 percent of the total population, in 1990. Given the tendency for the census to underestimate urban, minority, and immigrant populations, these figures are likely conservative. In real terms, the population grew by over 83 percent from 1980 to 1990. Given the pace of growth, it seems likely that by the 2000 census, Hispanics will have overtaken blacks (who at present constitute 14 percent of the population) as the state's largest minority group.

Hispanic population growth outside of Dade County was also notable during the ten-year period, but not yet of political significance. Central Florida's Osceola County experienced a larger increase in its Hispanic population (in proportional terms) than any other county in the nation during the 1980s. These Hispanics in Osceola County, who are mostly of Puerto Rican origin, have followed the lead of Cubans in Dade and attempted to organize politically around that county's previously moribund Republican party. Moreover, Latins now make up from 7 to 12 percent of the population in the metropolitan areas of Fort Lauderdale, Palm Beach, Tampa, and Orlando. However, with more than one million Hispanics (by local estimates) representing almost two-thirds of the state's Latin population, Dade County remains the hub of Latin political and economic affairs in Florida. Thus, with Florida's Latin voting population being overwhelmingly Cuban and geographically clustered in the metropolitan Miami-Dade County area, we are best able to analyze the impact of the 1992 Latin vote in the state by examining predominantly Latin precincts (i.e., those with at least 60 percent Latin voter registration) within Dade County.

While Cubans constitute a clear majority of Florida's, and specifically Dade County's, Latin population, recent demographic patterns suggest the need to continue to observe how the growing national, economic, cultural, and political diversity of Florida's Latin community might affect what frequently has been viewed as a politically monolithic enclave. This perception of unity has generally bolstered the status of Cuban political leaders, who claim to speak for a united constituency. While Florida's Cuban population has continued to mushroom, however, the number of Hispanics from other countries has grown even faster. It is estimated that over three hundred thousand Latin Americans moved into Dade County during the 1980s. In 1980, slightly more than 70 percent of the Hispanics in Dade were of Cuban descent. The 1990 census shows that the proportion has dropped to just under 60 percent (see Table 8.1). Until the rate of citizenship increases and the active assertion of an alternative political agenda is evident, however, we do not expect the non-Cuban Latin population to have a discernible impact on political outcomes.

Although Hispanics now constitute a majority of the population of Dade County, and Dade is the most populated county with a Hispanic majority

TABLE 8.1 Dade County's Changing Hispanic Population

Latino National-Origin Group	1980 %	1990 %
Cuban	70.1	59.2
Puerto Rican	7.7	7.6
Mexican	2.3	2.4
Other	19.9	30.8

Source: U.S. Bureau of the Census.

in the nation, official county figures indicate that Hispanics constitute just 29.6 percent of the area's registered voters. Yet, while some significant portion of the discrepancy between population and registered voter figures obviously is related to noncitizenship, it is also important to realize that the county's estimate of Hispanic voters counts only those who are foreign-born. This method of identifying Hispanics stands in contrast to the self-identification method used in the census and by other levels of government in the reapportionment process. Based on an analysis of Dade County birth and death rates among Hispanics since 1960 (Metro-Dade Planning Department 1986), one may conclude that official county figures underestimate the number of Hispanic registrants by at least 10 percent, or some eighteen thousand or more registered voters.[1]

Cubans and Florida's Presidential Politics

Notwithstanding indications of growing political diversity and complexity within the ranks of Miami's Cuban voters, the 1992 elections once again underscored the phenomenon of strong Cuban loyalty to the Republican party (Warren, Corbett, and Stack 1990; Moreno and Rae 1992; Moreno and Warren 1992). Repeating a pattern especially evident in presidential elections since the Reagan victory of 1980, George Bush carried the Hispanic precincts of Dade County with approximately 70 percent of the vote, far surpassing his proportion of the vote either nationally or statewide (see Table 8.2).

Cuban Americans, from whom Bush anticipated strong support, were a particularly important element in his re-election strategy. Texas and Florida were vital to a Bush re-election. Initially, they were considered safe states for the Bush ticket, but they became increasingly competitive as the race drew to a close. The president's son Jeb Bush, chair of the Bush/Quayle campaign in Florida, expressed the importance of Florida in the GOP's electoral college strategy. "We can't win without winning Florida unless some new math gets invented between now and then [election day]" (Merzer 1992). However, as polls showed Clinton gaining ground in Florida, heavy Cuban

TABLE 8.2   Voting in Dade County, by Race and Ethnicity, 1992 Presidential Election

	Bush	Clinton	Perot
% of county vote	42	46	9
% of black vote	7	85	3
% of non-Latin white vote	31	55	13
% of Hispanic vote	70	22	6

Note: Estimates are based on homogeneous precinct analysis.
Source: Official election results, Metro-Dade Elections Department.

TABLE 8.3   Hispanic Support for Democratic Presidential Candidates, Dade County Precincts

Election	Candidate	% Received in Hispanic Precincts	% of County Vote
1980 president	Carter	20	44
1984 president	Mondale	12	41
1988 president	Dukakis	15	45
1992 president	Clinton	22	46

Note: Estimates are based on homogeneous precinct analysis.
Source: Official election results, Metro-Dade Elections Department, 1980, 1984, 1988, 1992.

support for the GOP was considered increasingly essential for victory in the state.

Even in the face of such bloc voting, it is important to note the subtler changes that mark contemporary Cuban American politics in Florida. The 1992 elections saw a broadening of the political space in Miami's Cuban American community, and the challenging of at least some previously held stereotypes regarding the political and ideological uniformity of Cuban voters. Indeed, as the campaign continued and Bush's standing in the polls fell, what was remarkable was that a point was reached at which overwhelming Cuban support for Bush could no longer be taken for granted.

Although Florida has demonstrated consistent Republican support in recent presidential elections, with the Republican nominee winning in nine of the last eleven presidential elections (he lost only in 1964 and 1976), Cuban Americans have been especially loyal to GOP candidates. Hispanic voters in Dade supported the Republican nominee for president in 1980, 1984, and 1988 by extraordinary margins, ranging from 4 to 1 to 7 to 1 (see Table 8.3). Only black voters have generally shown comparable solidarity in their support of Democratic candidates.

By 1992, however, there were some signs of Cuban disaffection with the Bush presidency. Like other regions in which Bush had lost political capital, South Florida was especially hard hit by the 1991-1992 recession. Two airlines with large operations in Miami, Eastern and Pan American, went into bankruptcy, costing the city thousands of high-paying jobs. Unemployment in Dade County was above the national average for the first time in many years. In addition, Bush directly alienated his more hard-line anti-Communist Cuban supporters by not enthusiastically backing a tougher policy toward Castro. The administration was slow to support the Cuban Democracy Act (popularly known as the Torricelli bill, after its House sponsor), which angered CANF and its chair, Jorge Más Canosa. The legislation tightened the decades-old U.S. economic embargo against Cuba while increasing phone and mail contacts. The Bush administration at first opposed key provisions of the bill that would deny U.S. aid to countries providing assistance to Cuba and bar U.S. subsidiaries abroad from trading with Cuba. Bush did not endorse the bill until mid-1992, well after Clinton had indicated his support for the proposed law while making a campaign swing through Little Havana in April.

Many Cuban Americans were also angered by revelations that the U.S. State Department was cooperating with Cuba to curb exile attacks on the island. Three ranking State Department officials told the *Miami Herald* that the United States was informing the Castro government of planned exile attacks against Cuba. Two of the unidentified officials said there had been cooperation with Cuba on three occasions during a six-month period. The official claimed that "anything that we knew about that would violate U.S. law we would have made known. We would inform the Cubans beforehand" (Whitefield 1992).

This policy was widely condemned in the Cuban community. The administration responded by having its top Latin America officials claim that staff members had overstated the degree to which the United States was cooperating with Cuba. Bernard Aronson, assistant secretary of state for inter-American affairs, told the *Miami Herald* that "our policy is to enforce the laws of the United States, including the neutrality law, but there's no ongoing policy of cooperating or collaborating with the Castro regime. There have been isolated incidents in the past when it was necessary to exchange information. But there is no ongoing or regular process of cooperating with Cuba as implied by an unnamed State Department official" (Whitefield 1992). Acting in both political and familial capacities, Jeb Bush went on Miami's Spanish-language radio to defend his father on the issue. He disputed the idea that the administration had been systematically involved in tipping Cuba off with regard to possible exile attacks.

The net impact of these incidents, combined with Bush's slide in the Florida polls, left the Clinton/Gore campaign with a political entree in Florida. Again, Cuban Americans played an important role in campaign strategy. As the first Democratic presidential nominee actively to court the Cuban community, Clinton in many respects went far beyond previous state and local Democratic party efforts in attempting to make inroads with Cuban constituents. On several campaign stops in Florida, Clinton attempted to assure Cuban American voters that he would maintain a hard-line policy toward the Castro regime. His early endorsement of the Torricelli bill became only his most visible overture.

With a real contest now taking shape in Florida, the role and significance of the Hispanic community was amplified as a potential swing vote. In 1984, Democratic candidate Walter Mondale made just one visit to Florida after his nomination, and that was to a safely Democratic condominium community in a predominantly Jewish section of North Miami. Dukakis made even less of an effort in the state, effectively conceding Florida to Bush by mid-September in the 1988 election. The Massachusetts governor withdrew all but a handful of campaign workers and lost the state by almost one million votes. However, the combination of Clinton and Gore's southern origins, and their relatively secure status in most of their must-win states, meant that there was a rare opportunity for a serious campaign and a possible Democratic victory in Florida.

The focus on Cuban Americans was but one important aspect of the Clinton/Gore campaign in Florida, albeit one that had many secondary objectives. The overall Clinton strategy for the state was to keep Bush pinned down trying to protect his own base. One pundit described it as "the political equivalent of a full-court press, of in your face campaigning, of going right after the other guy's strength" (Fiedler 1992). The overall strategy was then accentuated by focusing on important state constituencies. In North Florida, Clinton cited his "son of the south" roots, telling voters that the region felt like South Arkansas. Among Florida's Jewish voters, he criticized the Bush administration for its reluctance to back a ten billion dollar loan guarantee that would provide Israel with assistance in dealing with its refugee problems. However, the campaign's focus on the Cuban community was particularly intricate and, even given the lopsided vote against him, it can be considered a successful strategy from the standpoint of the campaign's broader objectives.

While not even the most optimistic Democrat believed that Clinton could win a majority of Cuban American voters, the strategy was aimed at cutting into the huge GOP margins of the last three elections. The Democrats believed they could win Florida if they could reduce Cuban support for Bush to 2 to 1, a margin that would translate into approximately two to three additional percentage points for the Democratic ticket in the statewide vote. State party leader Simón Ferro, himself Cuban American, described Clinton as "the candidate we have been waiting 20 years for. I think for once we're going to make a dent in this vote" (Fiedler 1992).

As the first highly publicized overture by a Democratic presidential candidate toward the Cuban community, Clinton's campaign promised to lay the groundwork for reversing some of the bitterness toward Democrats that still lingers among many Cuban Americans. Many conservative Cuban voters, and especially Cuban elites, have continued to routinely oppose the Democratic party's national candidates because of Kennedy's Bay of Pigs fiasco over thirty years ago and the Carter administration's controversial dialogue with the Castro regime in 1977. Clinton based his Miami strategy on addressing Cubans' fears that a Democratic administration would revisit U.S.-Cuban policy and lift the economic embargo against the Castro regime. Moreover, Bush's hesitancy in embracing the Torricelli bill combined with twelve years of unfulfilled Republican presidential rhetoric on the need to hasten Castro's demise actually seemed to at least temporarily place Clinton to Bush's right on the issue of Cuba. That Bush ceremoniously came to Miami to sign the Torricelli bill into law without inviting either the bill's author or its Senate sponsor, Florida Democrat Bob Graham, was widely viewed as petty partisanship—even during an election year. Few credited Bush's eventual support as having anything to do with the bill's passage.

Soon after his endorsement of Torricelli's legislation, Clinton raised $275,000 in one night at two Miami fund-raisers attended predominantly by Cuban Americans. Follow-up visits by both Hillary Rodham Clinton (whose sister-in-law María Victoria Arias, a Cuban Republican living in Miami, mobilized other Cuban Americans for the Clinton campaign) and Tipper Gore were also considered successes.

While formally endorsing Bush, Jorge Más Canosa had numerous contacts with the Clinton campaign and put in an appearance at the Little Havana fund-raiser. His appearance suggested a strong pragmatism even within an organization often inaccurately depicted as singularly tied to the Republicans.[2] Más Canosa himself stated, "Although I'm voting for Bush out of loyalty, Clinton's decisive support of the Cuban Democracy Act turned the Cuban American community around" (Falk 1992).

The overall Democratic strategy appeared to be paying off. The Hamilton poll taken in August showed that, while the Arkansan still trailed Bush 72-23 percent among Cuban voters, Clinton was doing twice as well as Dukakis had. Two months later, a Mason Dixon/Media Research poll showed a 55-36 percentage split between Bush and Clinton. Más Canosa, no doubt seeing the even more important national poll figures and wishing to assure continued access to the White House, issued a near-endorsement of Clinton, stating that "any fears that the Cuban American community may have of the Clinton administration with regard to Castro's Cuba have dissipated" (Merzer 1992).

Presidential Election Results

On election day, Bush's margin of victory in Florida was fewer than eighty-six thousand votes, a dramatic reduction of his almost one million-vote margin in 1988. Clearly, the Dade County Hispanic voters who cast 70 percent of their votes for Bush provided a critical edge in the state. Had Clinton and Perot, either individually or together, seriously split the Cuban vote, the state would have gone Democratic for the first time since 1976.

The importance as well as the distinctiveness of the Cuban American vote for Bush was illustrated by the fact that he lost to Clinton countywide and fared poorly among Dade's two other major ethnic groups. Non-Hispanic whites in Dade gave Clinton approximately 55 percent of their vote, while black precincts supported the Democratic candidate with nearly 85 percent of the vote (see Table 8.2).

Although Clinton had made the first concerted effort ever by a Democratic presidential candidate to court the Cuban vote, he still received only about 22 percent of the vote in Hispanic precincts. This weak showing must be measured against the fact that the Democratic candidates in the 1984 and 1988 elections had only 12 and 15 percent of the Hispanic vote, respectively. Moreover, Clinton, despite being in a three-person race, often ran ahead of local Democratic candidates in the Latin precincts, which reflected the weakness of the local Democratic party among Cuban American voters. Perot, who made virtually no direct appeal to Cuban voters in 1992, received less than 6 percent of the vote in the same Latin precincts, although he received 20 percent of the vote statewide (see Tables 8.2 and 8.3).

In sum, election day saw Cuban Americans voting Republican in numbers greater than some of the later polls had predicted. Although George Bush did not match his 1988 showing among Cuban Americans, he was still able to carry the Hispanic precincts by approximately a 7-to-3 margin. Cuban American voters were an important factor in Bush's Florida victory in a contest that proved to be closer than anyone expected.

While the Clinton campaign's hopes of cutting into Bush's margin of victory among Cuban voters fell considerably short of the 2-to-1 target, the inroads with the Cuban elite were unprecedented. Beyond opening lines of communication with CANF, in early September, 13 Cuban American members of Dade County's 120-member Republican Executive Committee endorsed Clinton and expressed their belief that the Democrat would do more than Bush had to rid Cuba of Castro.

Thus, while the Cuban vote can prove to be the decisive element in an otherwise close state election, the community's impact transcends the number of votes cast for any one candidate. Latins in Florida constitute 7 percent of the state's voters (NALEO 1992: 2) and 9.7 percent of Latino voters nationwide, but the state's Cuban community is responsible for 15 percent of all Hispanic campaign contributions nationwide. Cuban American influence within the Spanish-language media is also proportionately greater than population alone would indicate (Falk 1992).

That the Hispanic voters of Dade County figured heavily in the Florida strategy of both presidential candidates speaks to the enhanced political role of the community. Perhaps most important, the community's clout has shown itself to be significant when actively asserted at the polls or through lobbying and campaign support and is increasingly a status that is voluntarily recognized. Such voluntary recognition reduces the future costs of exercising influence over the political process.

Clearly, the new policy announced by President Clinton in May 1995 regarding the interception and return of new Cuban refugees attempting to enter the United States has not only altered long-standing policy, but has also preempted any future efforts by the administration to court Cuban American leaders or voters. It is still to early to calculate how serious a backlash was created by the change in policy. From the point of view of the president's political calculus, however, he decided that in both Florida and in the nation at large, a tougher stance on Cuban immigration was in his political interests, albeit at the expense of guaranteeing Cuban American enmity in 1996.

Congressional Races

In the U.S. Senate race, Cuban Americans overwhelmingly supported moderate incumbent Democrat Bob Graham over Bill Grant, a former North Florida congressmember who had little state or national party backing and who ran an underfunded skeleton campaign (Table 8.4). Graham's showing in the predominantly Hispanic precincts frequently approached Bush's 70 percent margin. Even measured against a weak opponent, the vote constituted a remarkable turnaround in Graham's fortunes among Cuban voters. Although he had received a much smaller majority of the votes in Hispanic precincts in his 1982 gubernatorial re-election (again, against comparatively weak opposition), in his 1986 Senate campaign against Republican incumbent Paula Hawkins, he received only 24 percent of the Hispanic vote (Moreno and Warren 1992: 134). While Graham's Senate sponsorship of the Cuban Democracy Act was praised by the Cuban leadership, in general it was only an extension of what has been his politically low-key service orientation toward his Hispanic constituents—a political strategy that seems to have turned very uneven support in the past into a more solid and predictable base, at least when not opposed by a prominent Republican candidate.

The fact that Democrats were able to reestablish a foothold with Cuban voters in the U.S. Senate by no means counterbalanced the more dramatic overall setback suffered by the Democratic party establishment in Dade County's delegation to the U.S. House. The Dade County delegation had always been dominated by non-Hispanic Democrats. In the late 1980s, Dade County's four-member U.S. House delegation (Claude Pepper, Dante Fascell,

TABLE 8.4 Hispanic Support for Democratic Candidates in Statewide Races, Dade County Precincts

Election	Candidate	% Received in Hispanic Precincts	% of County Vote
1982 governor	Graham	57	72
1982 senate	Chiles	58	71
1986 governor	Pajcic	21	49
1986 senate	Graham	24	56
1988 senate	McKay	20	53
1990 governor	Chiles	31	63
1992 senate	Graham	66	74

Note: Estimates are based on homogeneous precinct analysis.
Source: Official election results, Metro-Dade Elections Department, 1982, 1986, 1988, 1990, 1992.

William Lehman, and Larry Smith) had over one hundred years of U.S. House and Senate experience among them, with the seniority, clout, and committee assignments such longevity represents. However, as a result of the remarkable turnover of South Florida congressional seats in the 1992 election, Cuban Republican Ileana Ros-Lehtinen, who won Claude Pepper's seat after his death in 1989, is now the senior U.S. representative from Dade County. All of the others are newly elected. Of the three new members who have at least some substantial share of their district in Dade County, one is Hispanic and another is black. The previous incumbents in these three seats decided not to run for varying reasons, but reapportionment and the inevitable creation of more Hispanic-Republican and black-Democratic majority districts was a factor in two instances.

The election of Lincoln Díaz-Balart, the second Cuban American to serve in Dade's congressional delegation, was accomplished with little controversy or fanfare. In sharp contrast to the ethnically polarized election of Ros-Lehtinen in 1989, Díaz-Balart faced no opposition from non-Hispanic candidates in 1992. Although the former state senator did have Republican primary opposition from a state senate colleague who is also Cuban, he had no Democratic challenger in the general election—a rather startling state of affairs in a county that had not sent a Republican or a Cuban American to Congress prior to 1989.

Another race worthy of note for its symbolic indication of a new, broader dialogue within Florida's Cuban community was the challenge liberal Cuban American Democrat Magda Davis mounted against incumbent Ros-Lehtinen. Arguing for a more progressive U.S. policy toward the Cuban government and a liberal domestic agenda, Davis's candidacy augured against the perception of a monolithic Cuban American political bloc. While the re-election of Ros-Lehtinen was at no time in doubt, the Davis candidacy, along with the creation of organizations such as the mostly Democratic party-based Cuban Council for Democracy, illustrates the increased occurrence in Florida of Cubans running against Cubans, at times across partisan, generational, and even ideological lines. In the end, however, Davis's candidacy may have contributed in a marginal way to Clinton's poor showing in the Hispanic community. Her position on dialogue with Cuba and loosening of the embargo gave credence to those in the community who have generally distrusted the foreign policy of the Democratic party. Davis's positions proved extremely unpopular in the Cuban precincts, where she lost to Ros-Lehtinen by a margin of over 4 to 1. In the non-Latin white precincts, Davis ran much better, winning 47 percent of the vote.

Reapportionment and the State Legislature

Although the emphasis of the preceding analysis has been on the indicators of a broadening of the political dialogue within Florida's largely Cuban Hispanic community, one need only examine the ongoing state-level fight over reapportionment of U.S. House and state legislative seats to see what an effective political base the Republican party has become for Cubans. These fights also demonstrate how political cohesion remains the norm among both Cuban political leaders and rank-and-file voters.

As has been the case in several states, reapportionment has served as a primary catalyst in the creation of more Hispanic seats in both Congress and state legislatures. The 1992 election cycle was the first to feel the full impact of both the 1982 amendments to the federal Voting Rights Act and the recent federal court rulings that require the creation of minority districts where possible—essentially mandating "affirmative gerrymandering" (Derfner 1981; Dixon 1981; Wells 1981). Within the legislature's Dade delegation especially, incumbent non-Hispanic white Democrats confronted the triple whammy of a shrinking non-Hispanic white population, fewer legislative seats for the county, and the federal legal requirements for the creation of minority districts. Previously, incumbent lawmakers could secure safe partisan seats as long as some minority seats were established. Given that minorities got more seats than they had had, they were generally expected to be satisfied.

In 1992, however, Cuban Republicans were particularly assertive and, by any measure, successful in influencing the state's reapportionment. As significant as the winning of two seats out of four in the U.S. Congress was, it was the pressure exerted by Cuban Republicans in the state legislature concerning the redrawing of district lines that made it possible. At the same time, more Hispanic majority seats were secured in that body. Hispanic state legislators, having been instrumental in the reapportionment battles in both the state legislature and the courts, saw two additional Cuban Republicans elected to Dade's delegation to the state house and retained three seats in the state senate. As a result, Cuban Republicans now hold twelve of the twenty-five legislative seats (48 percent) that lie primarily in Dade, as opposed to the eight of twenty-eight state seats (29 percent) and zero of four congressional seats as recently as 1986. A Voting Rights Act suit brought by Hispanic legislators (*De Grandy v. Wetherell*) challenged state house district lines, but ultimately failed in the Supreme Court. There are now no non-Cuban Republicans in the Dade delegation to either Washington or Tallahassee, which reflects the extent to which the Republican party has been an effective vehicle for Cuban office seekers from South Florida.

Democratic attempts to appeal to Cuban American voters have been plagued by the inability or unwillingness of state and local party organizations to recruit attractive Hispanic candidates. In the 1992 contests, only two Hispanic Democrats ran for any of the combined twenty-nine seats in the congress, state house, and state senate. Instead, Dade Democrats nominated non-Latin whites to run against Cuban Republicans in districts that were designed to elect Latinos. This created ethnically polarized elections throughout Dade County, which may have also contributed to Clinton's poorer-than-hoped-for showing among Florida's Hispanic voters.

Indeed, the 1992 election reflected the degree to which the Dade County Republican party has almost become a front organization for the interests of the more conservative leadership of the Cuban community (Moreno and Rae 1992). While not always united on every issue, Cuban Republicans are now the most politically coherent and potent force in the Dade delegation to the state legislature. A Cuban, Eladio Armesto-García, defeated Bruce Hoffman, the only non-Hispanic Republican in the Dade delegation, in the Republican primary. Moreover, at least three otherwise very strong Anglo Democrats were defeated by Cuban Republican opponents on the strength of Latin bloc voting.

The strength of the Cuban vote was illustrated in the 34th State Senate District, where Cuban Republican Alberto Gutman faced prominent attorney and Democratic party activist Kendall Coffey. Gutman was well funded, but he ran on a very weak record as a state representative and was widely perceived as vulnerable in a district that had a slight Republican majority, but slightly under 50 percent Hispanic registration. However, Gutman easily defeated Coffey 59 to 41 percent, as he swept many Latin precincts by a 4-to-1 margin. Coffey lost despite being endorsed by the *Miami Herald* and carrying 55 percent of the district's Anglo vote. Significantly, Coffey ran well ahead of the Democratic presidential candidate in the Anglo precincts (in fact, George Bush won the district's non-Latin precincts), but Coffey ran behind Clinton in the Latin areas. Similarly, political newcomer Bruno Barriero narrowly defeated Democrat Steve Leifman in state House District 107 despite Leifman's endorsement by the Miami Beach political establishment. Leifman won the non-Latin areas 57-43 percent, but lost the Latin areas 77-23 percent.

Cuban Republican gains have not been evident only within the context of the Dade delegation to the state legislature, however. One could well imagine the Cuban legislators' influence being totally marginalized in the 120-member state house and 40-member state senate. But statewide Republican gains (after the election, they held half of the senate seats), combined with bloc voting by Cuban legislators and a willingness to vote with Democratic and urban coalitions when it serves their interests, have made the Cuban legislators a critical swing vote on many issues. With regard to the phenomenon, one longtime lobbyist was quoted as saying, "What you may find is the beginning of almost a third party. When you combine forces together they will be the swing vote. If you haven't had a relationship with them, you better start" (Branch 1992).

Conclusion

In his analysis of the Latino vote in California's 1988 election, Fernando Guerra identifies six conditions that are necessary if California's Latino voters are to play a significant role in a national election (Guerra 1992: 100): (1) unified Latino support for one candidate; (2) a close contest, with the state playing a critical role in the outcome; (3) a strategy for registration and mobilization of Latino voters; (4) visible participation in the nomination and subsequent campaign of the candidate; (5) the presence of other Latino candidates in other contests or of ballot issues relevant to the Latino community; and (6) the existence of a party or campaign organization to mobilize Latino voters without, in turn, alienating other groups in the more general electorate.

Our analysis shows that in terms of the six variables that most directly involve group cohesion and mobilization, Cuban Americans in Florida demonstrated cohesive support for their candidates of choice; were critical, and perhaps decisive, in a Bush victory in the state; demonstrated the ability to effectively mobilize other Cuban American voters; were broadly involved in a wide array of electoral contests and other issues, including reapportionment; and have been extremely successful in using the Republican party as a vehicle for lasting political incorporation. While the Florida Hispanic vote for Bush certainly did not alter the outcome of the presidential election in 1992, Latins in the state were nonetheless successful in attracting attention from the eventual winner. By virtue of their being actively courted by Clinton, expanding their role in campaign finance, gaining more of a voice in Washington, and further consolidating their leadership posture in state and local politics, Cuban Americans in Florida have demonstrated an ability to transcend their previous status as a cohesive group of voters courted by non-Hispanic candidates in elections and then downplayed afterward. Cuban Americans are making inroads in elite politics and are consistently building on their growing electoral clout to project themselves into those institutional processes that not only respond to narrow group interests, but more broadly shape political and policy agendas at all levels of government.

The only factors on the horizon that in any way promise to dilute the enhanced political status of Cuban Americans are the growing diversity of the state's Hispanic population and some initial indicators of slightly less cohesion along partisan, policy, and ideological lines. As suggested earlier, for the first factor to become politically significant, non-Cuban Hispanics would need to become citizens in much greater numbers than has been the case, would have to register and mobilize around alternative candidates, and would need to be in a position to push effectively for an alternative political agenda. There are virtually no indications at present of any of these things occurring. The second factor, while an interesting development in terms of undermining previously held stereotypes, is also not likely to jeopardize the basic solidarity of Cuban voters and their political leaders on issues that most directly concern the community. Cuban political elites and rank-and-file voters are demonstrating that they are not entirely knee-jerk in their support for the Republican party or in promoting a conservative line on all issues of public policy. Political maturation and enhanced effectiveness and clout are the likely outcomes, at least in the short term, of expanded political dialogue within Florida's Cuban community.

Notes

1. In analyzing 1992 election data, we chose Hispanic precincts that had at least 60 percent Hispanic registration. Hispanic registration was defined by the county as including only those who were foreign-born. On this basis, 107 Hispanic precincts were identified out of 516 in Dade County. We base our discussion of voting patterns among blacks and non-Latin whites on analysis of precincts estimated to have 85 percent black or non-Latin white registration.

2. The Free Cuba Political Action Committee, which is the foundation's vehicle for campaign contributions, contributed twice as much to Democratic candidates for office nationwide as to Republicans during the 1990-1992 election cycle.

References

Branch, Karen. 1992. "Ten Years of Cuban Caucus." *Miami Herald* (March 22).
de la Garza, Rodolfo O., and Louis DeSipio, eds. 1992. *From Rhetoric to Reality: Latino Politics in the 1988 Elections*. Boulder, Colo.: Westview Press.

de la Garza, Rodolfo O.; Louis DeSipio; F. Chris García; John A. García; and Angelo Falcón. 1992. *Latino Voices: Mexican, Puerto Rican, and Cuban Perspectives on American Politics.* Boulder, Colo.: Westview Press.

Derfner, Armand. 1981. "Pro-Affirmative Action in Districting," *Policy Studies Journal* 9 (6).

Dixon, Robert, Jr. 1981. "Fair Criteria and Procedures for Establishing Legislative Districts." *Policy Studies Journal* 9 (6).

Falk, Pamela S. 1992. "Exiles Set Policy Agenda on Cuba for Next Administration." *Wall Street Journal* (October 16).

Fiedler, Tom. 1992. "Clinton Clearly Fights for Florida's Voters." *Miami Herald* (September 13).

García, F. Chris, ed. 1988. *Latinos and the Political System.* Notre Dame, Ind.: University of Notre Dame Press.

Guerra, Fernando J. 1992. "Conditions Not Met: California Elections and the Latino Community." In Rodolfo O. de la Garza and Louis DeSipio, eds., *From Rhetoric to Reality: Latino Politics in the 1988 Elections,* pp 99–110. Boulder, Colo.: Westview Press.

Hero, Rodney E. 1992. *Latinos and the U.S. Political System: Two-tiered Pluralism.* Philadelphia: Temple University Press.

Merzer, Martin. 1992. "Bush, Clinton a Tossup in Florida." *Miami Herald* (October 29).

Metro-Dade Planning Department. 1986. *Hispanic Profile* (December).

Moreno, Dario, and Nicol Rae. 1992. "Ethnicity and Partisanship: The Eighteenth Congressional District in Miami." In Guillermo J. Grenier and Alex Stepik III, eds., *Miami Now: Immigration, Ethnicity, and Social Change,* pp. 186–204. Gainesville: University Presses of Florida.

Moreno, Dario, and Christopher L. Warren. 1992. "The Conservative Enclave: Cubans in Florida." In Rodolfo O. de la Garza and Louis DeSipio, eds., *From Rhetoric to Reality: Latino Politics in the 1988 Elections,* pp. 127–146. Boulder, Colo.: Westview Press.

National Association of Latino Elected and Appointed Officials (NALEO). 1992. *The Latino Vote in 1992.* Washington, D.C.: NALEO Educational Fund.

Vigil, Maurilio E. 1987. *Hispanics in American Politics: The Search for Political Power.* Lanham, Md.: University Press of America.

Villareal, Roberto E.; Norma Hernández; and Howard D. Neighbor, eds. 1988. *Latino Empowerment: Progress, Problems, and Prospects.* Westport, Conn.: Greenwood Press.

Warren, Christopher L.; John G. Corbett; and John F. Stack, Jr. 1990. "Hispanic Ascendancy and Tripartite Politics in Miami." In Rufus P. Browning, Dale Rogers Marshall, and David H. Tabb, eds., *Racial Politics in American Cities,* pp. 155–178. New York: Longman.

Wells, David. 1981. "On Affirmative Gerrymandering," *Policy Studies Journal* 9 (6).

Whitefield, Mimi. 1992. "Cuba Policy Was Overstated U.S. Says." *Miami Herald* (January 25).

9

Puerto Ricans in Postliberal New York: The 1992 Presidential Election

Angelo Falcón

Following the Democratic presidential primary in New York, an article in the *New York Times* raised the question of how Hispanic leaders planned to turn the raw numbers of a large and growing Latino population into political power. It discussed the mixed success of redistricting and the need to develop new strategies, especially naturalization campaigns, to increase the number of those eligible to vote (Suro 1992). The article made clear, however, that there was no consensus among Latino political leaders on how to do this.

While some have attempted to describe conditions under which the Latino vote would be a decisive factor in presidential and local elections (Guerra 1992), the absence of any overall effective strategy-setting by Latinos in the United States limits the effectiveness of this approach for understanding Latino politics and may cause us to ask the wrong questions. The narrowness of this bottom-line approach to Latino politics can, if not put in context, distort our knowledge of how Latinos participate in the American political system.

The ethnic and political diversity of the Latino population defies generalization and continually pushes researchers to deconstruct that population politically at the local level. As one study (Kosmin and Keysar 1992), highly flawed methodologically but widely covered nationally, found during the height of interest in the Latino vote in the 1992 elections, there is no single Latino electorate (Douglas 1992). Simply asking whether Latinos were pivotal to the outcome of this or that election is, of course, useful, but politics should represent more than just this.

The 1992 presidential year opened for Puerto Ricans with news of the candidacy of David Duke from Louisiana. The message they got from Duke's campaign was that "Hispanics and blacks are a threat to Anglo-

Saxon culture" (NOTIMEX 1992a). This was a dominant theme Puerto Ricans saw emerging from the more extreme wing of the Republican party, particularly in the campaign of Pat Buchanan. The country's Latino population, largely Democratic, was in the process being pushed even farther from a Republican alternative.

On the other hand, on February 12, Puerto Ricans in New York City were told that the Democratic candidates would be debating urban issues in the South Bronx (Arce 1992a). The attitude of many Puerto Rican political leaders at this early stage was perhaps best expressed by Dennis Rivera, president of Local 1199 in New York, when he projected just before the New York Democratic presidential primary in April that, "if the elections were tomorrow and the only candidates were Clinton, Brown and none of the above, I believe the last option would win by a large majority" (Pereira 1992a).

Twelve years of Reagan-Bush and the election of Bill Clinton in 1992 represented what could be characterized as a "postliberal" period in American politics. New York City was only two years away from electing a Republican mayor and rejecting a bid for a second term by the city's first African American mayor and three years away from electing a Republican governor over Democrat Mario Cuomo. Clinton's neoliberalism resonated with the traditional liberal Democratic coalition in part because of the stridency of the Republican Right during the campaign. Clinton established the conditions for a transitional phase in American politics whose ultimate character is yet to be determined. The implications of this changing ideological context for Puerto Ricans, who have been a major part of the liberal tradition in New York City since the 1960s, will be important to explore as the meaning of the Clinton presidency and other postliberal developments play themselves out.

One of these new developments includes the increased complexity of the country's racial and ethnic dynamics, particularly in large cities like New York. While in the 1988 electoral season much of this dynamic revolved around a black and Latino challenge to white political power, by 1992 it was the relationship between blacks and Latinos that had become a salient feature of the city's political landscape (Falcón 1992a). The 1992 presidential election clearly brought these growing fissures to light.

The outcome for the New York presidential election was not in doubt after Clinton, in effect, secured the party's nomination in the Illinois and Michigan primaries in March. Because New York is one of the largest solidly Democratic states, the Democrats can generally take it for granted and the Republicans generally concede it. There also was no Republican presidential primary in 1992. These conditions are magnified in overwhelmingly Democratic New York City.

The Puerto Rican vote is both a beneficiary and a victim of this political context. Most (80 percent) of the state's Latino population resides in New York City, making the city's Latinos the driving force for this community in presidential elections. The city's close to two million Latinos make up about a quarter of its total population, and Puerto Ricans make up about half of the Latino population. Because of such factors as U.S. citizenship by birth and higher levels of English language ability, Puerto Ricans represent close to 80 percent of the city's Latino vote. One consequence of this is that almost all of the city's Latino elected officials are of Puerto Rican background. The 1991 redistricting of the New York City Council was significant in making possible the election of the first Dominican to that body (*El Diario-La Prensa* [January 6, 1992]).

My approach in this chapter is to construct a narrative account of the key political events in this period. The lack of effective Adelante con Clinton! and Viva Bush! campaigns among the Puerto Rican and other Latino grassroots groups moves the focus of this analysis to the politics of Puerto Rican political elites. I particularly follow the activities of the three political figures who dominated Puerto Rican politics in New York in 1992. In a survey of Puerto Rican community activists, the most politically influential were (in decreasing order of influence) Bronx Borough President Fernando Ferrer; U.S. Representative José Serrano; and Dennis Rivera, president of Local 1199 of the National Health and Hospital Workers Union. While Ferrer and Serrano have been major players in Puerto Rican politics for some time, Rivera was a new player coming from a different base, the labor movement. Ferrer is the more machine-oriented of the three, Serrano is more of the liberal outsider, and Rivera is the progressive trade unionist. The roles they played and their interaction during the 1992 presidential election dominated what transpired politically throughout that year.

I also examine how the national political institution of a presidential campaign interacts with and influences local politics. This is an exercise in historical reconstruction, particularly when the politics of an upcoming mayoral election can be seen to permeate the entire process and define the relations between Puerto Rican politicians and with their black and white counterparts. Because the events I discuss here are so recent and because I focus on a community whose politics is usually not taken seriously by mainstream political analysts, this narrative relies heavily on accounts in both the English- and the Spanish-language press. It follows a chronological sequence from the April Democratic presidential primary to the Democratic National Convention in the summer to the local Democratic primaries in September to the November general election and its immediate aftermath.

The New York Democratic Presidential Primary

The Clinton Campaign

As the New York Democratic primary approached, Puerto Rican leaders reported that the Democratic candidates were taking them for granted. This was underscored by candidate Bill Clinton's pattern of canceling meetings with Puerto Rican political leaders in New York City. Two weeks before the New York primary, Clinton canceled appearances at a major statewide conference of Latinos in Albany and with the editorial board of one of the leading Spanish-language newspapers in New York City. New York State Assemblyperson Héctor Díaz, who organized the statewide conference, told the press that "it's offensive and Clinton has lost the biggest opportunity of his life" (Creste 1992a). When the Clinton campaign offered to send Hillary Rodham Clinton in the candidate's place, Díaz explained that "we didn't accept the offer. I think that as Hispanics we have to demand respect. If he committed himself to attend, he should attend." Another conference coordinator stated that "if he considers that Wisconsin is more important than New York and that the voters of Wisconsin are more important than the Hispanic voters of New York, so be it. What should be made known is that by insulting us in New York he is insulting us in California and other sections of the country" (R. García 1992a; Seifman 1992). According to another account, Clinton had pulled strings to get invited to the Somos el Futuro conference. Assemblyperson Díaz explained: "He called us and our union sponsor to get an invitation. Then he called on Monday to say he couldn't come, but his wife could. We went to a lot of trouble to make him the keynote speaker, at his request, and we don't want his wife" (*Daily News* [March 27, 1992]).

In the midst of this minicontroversy in the Latino community, Representative José Serrano publicly endorsed Clinton (Creste 1992a). Serrano, according to one reporter, was trying to present himself to the Clinton campaign as the major Hispanic political leader in New York, arguing that this entitled him to appear alone with Clinton at City Hall when he endorsed him. The Clinton camp did not, however, accept this, and Serrano gave his endorsement at a largely ignored press conference that included fellow Representatives Ted Weiss and Charles Schumer (Creste 1992b).

On March 29, Clinton, flanked by Representative Serrano and Dominican City Councilmember Guillermo Linares, held a press conference. There he pledged to invest in poor communities if elected president. He also expressed support for holding a plebiscite on the political future of Puerto Rico (Soria 1992a). This, however, was no substitute for the meetings with a broader groups of Puerto Rican and other Latino political leaders, and Clinton continued to receive criticism for ignoring Latinos (Arroyo 1992a).

The Brown Sleepover

Jerry Brown, on the other hand, was aggressively courting the Puerto Rican vote, largely under the direction of union leader Dennis Rivera. One Puerto Rican journalist observed that tensions between Mayor David Dinkins and Puerto Rican elected officials were being paralleled in the Democratic presidential primary. Dinkins endorsed Brown while the Puerto

Rican elected officials largely endorsed Clinton. On March 30, Rivera, a staunch Dinkins ally, announced that his union was supporting Brown over Clinton. Local 1199 has 117,000 members, mostly hospital and health workers in private hospitals.

A few days later, Brown made the front page of *El Diario-La Prensa* when he slept on the floor at Rivera's sparsely furnished Riverside Drive apartment. From the apartment, Brown spoke to reporters about this campaign and projected his populist style. Soon after, Brown also received the endorsement of several other New York unions.

The endorsement by Rivera's union brought some complications for the Brown campaign. Rivera was then having a major confrontation with Puerto Rican and black state legislators over their recent vote to cut Medicaid. He threatened to run candidates against those voting for the cuts, which generated a strong reaction from the minority politicians. Twenty-four of the twenty-nine minority state legislators from New York City signed a letter criticizing Rivera for his threats. Rivera told *New York Post* columnist Jack Newfield that "we will run primaries against any black or Latino legislator who votes for the Medicaid cuts. Most of them just go through the motions. They won't really fight for the poor. One of them told me not to resist the Medicaid cuts and just blame them on Cuomo. I can't accept that kind of cynical thinking" (Newfield 1992; C. Nieves 1992). Bronx Assemblyperson Roberto Ramírez later explained that "I feel frustration as well as annoyance at what I consider to be legislative blackmail" (Verhovek 1992a).

On April 2, on the advice of Rivera, Brown held a press conference in which he announced his support for self-determination for Puerto Rico and for lifting the trade embargo on Cuba. Appearing with Brown were Local 1199's Rivera, actor Raúl Julia, and Rubén Berrios, president of the Puerto Rican Independence party (PIP) (Creste 1992c; *El Vocero* [April 4, 1992]). Brown did not, however, gain maximum advantage from the event. He sat with one of the leaders of Puerto Rico's independence movement, but stated that he would support whatever status option the people of Puerto Rico agreed on. Since a very small percentage of the Puerto Rican electorate supports independence, this association was politically unhelpful.

A few days later, Clinton appeared to have locked up the support of the Democratic delegates from Puerto Rico with his endorsement by the island's two major political parties, the governing New Progressive party (NP) and the Popular Democratic party (PPD) (Creste 1992d). In New York, Brown blasted the results of the Puerto Rico vote by concluding that "there the party hierarchy controls the primary" (R. García 1992b). This statement created a stir among Puerto Ricans in New York, who are proud of the democratic nature of the political process on the island. State Assemblyperson David Rosado told *Noticias del Mundo*:

Brown apparently doesn't know anything about the history of Puerto Rico. To the contrary, history demonstrates that the Democratic presidential primaries in Puerto Rico have always been well-discussed and many times produce surprising results. In 1976, the prostatehooders beat the procommonwealthers with their set of delegates for Jimmy Carter. And in 1988 Jesse Jackson almost beat Michael Dukakis despite Dukakis having the support of Governor Hernández Colón. (R. García 1992b)

New York and the Urban Debates

The New York Democratic primary appeared to be the ideal setting for the candidates to discuss urban policy issues, and two forums for doing so were created. One was a Democratic candidates' debate at Lehman College in the Bronx, the other, known as the Urban Summit, was a meeting of big-city mayors convened by Mayor Dinkins at Gracie Mansion in Manhattan. "The Debate for Urban America," held on March 31 at Lehman College, was of particular interest to Puerto Ricans because it was being presided over by two prominent community figures, Bronx Borough President Fernando Ferrer and Lehman College President Ricardo Fernández.

Almost as soon as the debate was announced, organizers found themselves in a major controversy within the Latino community. Although Ferrer and Fernández would be moderating the debate, there were no Latinos invited to sit on the journalists' panel that would be questioning the candidates. Mayor Dinkins joined the fray by writing a letter to Ferrer, which he made public, criticizing Ferrer for excluding Latino journalists from the debate (Soria 1992b). *New York Newsday* columnist Sheryl McCarthy, who is black, found that "this seems like a very silly dispute, given that the debate is being moderated by two of the city's most prominent Latinos" (McCarthy 1992). Jorge Ramos, an anchor for one of the major Spanish-language television news programs, felt differently: "This is insulting to us. When we asked why there were no Hispanics on the panel, they said because Freddy Ferrer and Ricardo Fernández will be there as moderators. Well, Dr. Fernández is an educator, and Ferrer is a politician. They are not journalists" (Liff 1992). Dennis Rivera also criticized the debate organizers for this omission: "In my opinion, this contradicts the purpose for bringing this type of event to this city" (Creste 1992e).

In the end, the urban debate was generally a disappointment, with the highlights being the attempts of third-party candidates to be included. The title of Gail Collins's column in *New York Newsday* perhaps captured the debate well: "2 Country Boys Lost in the City" (Collins 1992a; Kasindorf and Kessler 1992). Collins found a certain irony in Clinton's embrace of urban issues in light of his position the previous summer that the party might be making a mistake holding the convention in New York.

Earlier that same day, Mayor Dinkins had convened his Urban Summit. It included a debate between Clinton and Brown before an audience of big-city mayors (Creste 1992f). Discussing how harried the preparation for the Urban Summit had become, despite its long lead time, one reporter observed that some observers believed that its timing on the same day as the Lehman debate was an attempt by Dinkins to avoid being upstaged by Ferrer, a potential rival for the mayoralty (Walt 1992).

Ethnic Politics in the New York Primary

In a statewide survey released on March 31, 57 percent of Puerto Rican community activists felt that the Puerto Rican Democratic primary vote would go to Clinton, with only 6 percent indicating Brown (Institute for Puerto Rican Policy 1992a). Over three-fourths of the activists gave Bush a "poor" job rating as president. The general feeling going into the primary, therefore, was that Clinton would be getting the lion's share of the Puerto Rican vote in New York State without any difficulty.

Clinton, who had been criticized for canceling meetings with Puerto Rican political leaders, found himself on the defensive again when the issue of his signing an English-only bill in Arkansas in 1987 came to light (de la Cruz 1992a). Explaining to a reporter why Arkansas felt it needed English as its official language, Clinton responded:

> We didn't. It was done without much thought by the legislature. Since we have a very small non-English-speaking population, my staff said: We've really got to protect bilingual education. If we write that out, you can let it go. I probably should have vetoed it and seen if they passed it over my veto, but at the time it didn't seem worth a big fight. (Collins 1992b)

Serrano jumped in to defend Clinton: "I think he's sincere when he says he is in favor of bilingual education." Clinton's national Hispanic coordinator, María Echaveste, added: "The Governor has always said that groups should maintain their own language and culture." She pointed out that only 1 percent of Arkansas's population was Hispanic and that the law had no negative impact on them (de la Cruz 1992a).

While Clinton's efforts to secure Latino support were tentative at best, he actively sought support from New York's Jewish voters. On the day of the Urban Summit and Lehman debate, in a repeat of a similar incident in Florida, Clinton accused the Bush administration, in "a hard-hitting speech" before the Jewish Community Relations Council in Manhattan, of "new stark rhetoric" against Israel and the Jewish community that has "so subtly ... broken down the taboo against overt anti-Semitism. That is very, very dangerous in any time" (Kasindorf and Kessler 1992). In response, William Kristol, Vice-President Quayle's chief of staff, charged Clinton with making an "irresponsible" pitch for Jewish voters, who represent a quarter of New York's primary vote (Lombardi 1992a).

Brown also found himself in a controversy with the Jewish community.

During the New York campaign, Brown stated that he had offered the vice-presidential spot on his ticket to the Reverend Jesse Jackson. Jewish opposition to Jackson had been a major factor in both the 1984 and the 1988 campaigns in New York and resurfaced when Jews protested Brown's embrace of Jackson. Brown was booed when he met with the Jewish Community Relations Council (Kasindorf 1992a).

Only days before the primary, Clinton got bad press in the Latino community because of canceling yet another meeting with Puerto Rican political leaders. He stood up a group of Latino politicians, including Bronx Borough President Ferrer, State Senator Olga Méndez, Herman Badillo and his wife, Councilmember Martín Malave-Dilan, and State Assemblyperson Vito López. This was the third meeting with Latino leaders that Clinton had canceled in one week. To try to patch things up, Clinton aide María Echaveste told Senator Méndez that she would do what she could to get Clinton to call her to apologize.

One explanation for this rash of cancellations, according to a political insider, was that

> the coordinator of the Clinton campaign here is Harold Ickes and the deputy coordinator is Hulbert James. Both are loyal to Dinkins, for whom they work. Their goal was to block the meetings between Clinton with the Hispanic officials in order to keep Fernando Ferrer marginal to the campaign. They are very scared of Ferrer and the possibilities of his launching a campaign for the mayoralty. They have no interest in helping Clinton with Hispanics. (R. García 1992b)

Puerto Ricans and the Clinton Victory

On April 7, primary day, Bill Clinton won the New York vote with 41 percent of the total. In the big surprise of the primary, Brown came in third, with 26 percent, trailing Paul Tsongas, who received 29 percent of the vote even though he had withdrawn his candidacy (Page 1992). One explanation for Brown's poor showing was his association with the Reverend Jesse Jackson and what this cost him in terms of the Jewish vote. Polls had Brown with 20 percent of the Jewish vote when he started campaigning in New York; but with his affiliation with Jackson, he wound up with only an estimated 9 percent of the Jewish primary vote (Siegel 1992). Brown acknowledged that his "alliance" with Jackson "was not accepted in some key communities" (Cooper and Rist 1992). Summing up his experience in the city, he characterized the New York primary as "the Lebanon of American politics, a war zone" (Kessler 1992). The strong Tsongas showing, despite his not being a candidate, was probably due to general dissatisfaction with the declared candidates (Nelson 1992; Purdum 1992).

One poll estimated that 63 percent of Latinos voted for Clinton, compared with 50 percent of blacks, 45 percent of Jews, 32 percent of Catholics, and 30 percent of Protestants (Richards 1992). It was interesting that, despite Latinos giving him a larger share of their vote than any other group did, as a group they were barely mentioned in the news coverage that followed the vote. One article in *New York Newsday* entitled "Classic Coalition Clings to Clinton" observed that Clinton did better in New York City than in the suburbs or upstate, largely because the black and Jewish vote was higher for him in the city. This article completely failed to mention the Latino vote (Richards 1992). The polls taken of the primary vote also largely ignored Latinos. The widely quoted independent Marist College poll estimated that Latinos made up 7 percent of New York State Democratic primary voters (Shaw 1992), while Voter Research and Surveys reported Latinos as only 3 percent of the vote and did not include them as a group in their breakdown because of the small size of the sample (Nelson 1992). Yet another poll, the *New York Times*/CBS News poll, found that Latinos made up 5 percent of the vote, but also did not present the Latino vote breakdown.

As most predicted, overall turnout for the New York primary was extremely low. The number of Democrats voting was 976,555, only 27 percent of those eligible and the lowest turnout since 1976 (*Daily News* [April 9, 1992]). The day of the election, the Spanish-language newspapers and media were predicting a low Latino turnout in the primary. *El Diario-La Prensa* cited Lee Miringoff of Marist College predicting a low overall turnout (Creste 1992g). *Noticias del Mundo* found little interest in the primary among Latino community activists and cited factors such as Clinton's snubbing of Latino leaders three times in one week and Brown's neglect of the Latino vote and his "insulting" remarks about the primary process in Puerto Rico (R. García 1992b).

Preparing for the Democratic National Convention

With the Democratic National Convention coming to New York City from July 13 to 16, political discussion turned more toward convention politics and the Bush versus Clinton race. The morning following the primary, Clinton finally met with the Puerto Rican politicians he had continually snubbed during the New York campaign. He met with Bronx Borough President Ferrer, State Senator Efraín González, Representative José Serrano, Assemblyperson Roberto Ramírez, attorney Herman Badillo, board of education member Ninfa Segarra, State Senator Olga Méndez, and *El Diario-La Prensa* publisher Carlos Ramírez, among others. Following the meeting, Ferrer told the press: "The truth is I was impressed with Clinton. We were able to express our concerns with the way he conducted his campaign in the Latino community until now. He led us to understand that he would initiate necessary changes to strengthen the Latino presence in the highest levels of his electoral campaign" (R. García 1992c). Clinton asked those present to prepare a plan for him for reaching Latino voters for the general election. Harold Ickes, Clinton's campaign coordinator in New York, whom some blamed for blocking past meetings with Latino leaders, was also present.

The Clinton meeting led to an early May meeting between Democratic party chair Ron Brown and local Puerto Rican leaders (R. García 1992d). Because the state legislature was in session in Albany, the New York delegation was led by Bronx Borough President Ferrer and included city councilmembers José Rivera, Adam Clayton Powell IV, Lucy Cruz, and Rafael Castañeira Colón.

In late April, a meeting was held in Manhattan to announce the formation of the Hispanic PAC-USA, which would raise funds to run Latino candidates. The PAC reportedly had fifty thousand dollars on hand and pledges for another two hundred thousand dollars. Its president was New Mexico Representative Bill Richardson, with Local 1199's Dennis Rivera as vice-president and the AFL-CIO's Jack Otero as treasurer (Creste 1992h). The event included the participation of Latino leaders from across the country, including New York City congressional candidate Nydia Velázquez, Democratic National Committee member Gloria Molina of Los Angeles, Representative Esteban Torres, Chicago Treasurer Miriam Santos, Frank Herrera of Texas, María E. Torano of Miami, Gabriel Herrera, Herman Badillo, and New York City Councilmembers José Rivera, Adam Clayton Powell IV, and Guillermo Linares, among others (Rodríguez 1992).

The Republicans also made use of this period between the primary and the party conventions. In May, a group of Latino Republicans held a press conference in New York City to present Bush's record of support for Hispanics. The group, the Republican National Hispanic Assembly, headed by George Ríos, gathered at the Roosevelt Hotel for what was to be a less-than-successful press conference. They received no coverage in the Anglo press, and in the Spanish-language press they were treated very critically. *El Diario-La Prensa*'s political reporter wrote that, after questioning, they admitted to having only four hundred members in the entire organization. Reacting to their rhetoric about Bush's Latino record and his connections to the community because of his son's marriage to a Mexican woman, de la Cruz sarcastically wrote: "I never would have imagined that someone would ever say that Bush is almost Hispanic. Does this mean that, from now on, we have to call him *Jorge*?" (1992a).

The Challenge from Labor

As the Democratic National Convention got closer, the role of at least one Puerto Rican, Dennis Rivera, appeared to be growing. Nervous about how New York City would play as the site of the convention, a major concern was what the labor unions would do, since a number of them were still negotiating their contracts with the city and other local institutions. There were reports that Local 1199 might stage some form of protest if its negotiations with fifty local nonprofit hospitals were not resolved by their end-of-June deadline. The union assured reporters that this was not true, that Rivera would never embarrass a mayor he helped elect, and that, in any case, negotiations were going well. In the meantime, Rivera was on television announcing the possibility of a major summit of minorities, women's groups, and unions in Washington, D.C. in mid-June that could result in "a massive demonstration in New York City" (Murphy 1992).

Accusing Clinton and the Democratic party leadership of not paying enough attention to what he called the party's core constituency of blacks, Latinos, labor, and poor people, Rivera called for an "emergency summit meeting." Invitations signed by Mayor Dinkins, Jesse Jackson, Rivera, and others went out for a summit to develop a plan for national health insurance, a progressive tax structure, and revised labor laws, all of which Rivera felt would be "the building blocks of a winning strategy" (Cohen 1992*a*). Also on the summit agenda would be the issue of the vice-presidential candidate. "Some of us do not rule out any options," Rivera said, specifying, "a minority or a woman or a trade unionist, for that matter."

Sister Souljah and the New Politics of Race

The "emergency summit meeting" Dennis Rivera called coincided with the annual conference of Jesse Jackson's National Rainbow Coalition in Washington, D.C. One purpose of Jackson's conference was to help propel his economic recovery plan, "Rebuild America," into the national spotlight. Jackson told reporters that he intended to push to have the delegates debate the plan at the Democratic National Convention. The plan's advocates would, he added, hold several demonstrations outside of Madison Square Garden (Cottman 1992).

Clinton dramatically used this National Rainbow Coalition conference to demonstrate his independence from "special interests" by attacking in his speech at the session what he considered racist statements by rap artist Sister Souljah (Ifill 1992*a*). This generated a major controversy that eclipsed whatever policy recommendations came out of conference. Black leaders across the country, including in New York, criticized Clinton for being "insensitive" to the black community (English 1992). Mayor Dinkins publicly cautioned Clinton to watch his style, while Sister Souljah, pointing out that she was "neither Murphy Brown nor Willie Horton," strongly criticized Clinton as a "white presidential candidate seeking the approval of white conservatives" (Cohen 1992*b*; Howard 1992). Clinton, despite widespread criticism from the black community, maintained his ground and repeated his criticism of Sister Souljah's statements (Clifford 1992). Even New York

Governor Mario M. Cuomo got involved, calling on Clinton to make peace with Jesse Jackson and the young rapper (Lombardi 1992b). The national discussion on race in the presidential election returned to its historical bipolar, white-black terms, leaving out other parts of the Rainbow, like Latinos.

The Perot Factor

The first phase of the Perot candidacy reached its peak in the period leading up to the Democratic convention. One Spanish-language radio talk show host conducted a call-in poll and found that 83 percent favored Perot's undeclared candidacy for the presidency (R. García 1992e). A *New York Newsday* poll conducted in late June found that 41 percent of Latinos supported Bush, 30 percent, Clinton, 21 percent, Perot, and 8 percent were undecided (Carroll 1992). The impact on the electorate as a whole was equally strong. *Newsday* found locally, with Perot in the picture, that Clinton's lead dropped from ten percentage points in a one-to-one with Bush to only five points in a three-way race. While the results of this poll were questionable, since it tapped much stronger support for Bush among Latinos locally than anyone else had found or than he had received in 1988, these were the numbers that were floated. According to them, Perot's candidacy would clearly increase the importance of the Latino vote in the general election. But as the Democratic National Convention was about to open, Perot withdrew from the race.

The Democratic Party Convention

As the Democratic National Convention approached, stories began to appear about the preparations. These included the role of minorities, such as the convention's African American executive director, Alexis M. Herman, and of minority companies contracted to provide goods and services to the convention. The *New York Times*, for example, highlighted the role of Cuban-born Marianios Molina's engineering firm, which was doing the electrical work for the convention. The *Daily News* published a profile of the New York Consortium of Minority Brokers, headed by Gwendolyn Gandy, which provided insurance for the convention, and included the participation of firms owned by Lydia Colón and Carmen Ortiz (Serant 1992). Word got around that Charles Uribe, a Puerto Rican, got the construction contract for the convention, while a Dominican, Fernando Mateo (later of "Guns-for-Toys" fame), got the carpeting contract. Despite these engagements, the prevailing feeling among Puerto Rican party activists was that the convention was dominated by blacks, with African Americans holding such key posts as party chair, executive director of the convention, and chair of the host committee.

Dominicans at the Gates

But while convention organizers and local officials worried about disruptions at the convention itself, Mayor Dinkins found himself defusing a major riot situation in the city's main Dominican neighborhood, Washington Heights. On July 5, twenty-four-year-old José "Kiko" García was shot in the hallway of 505 West 162nd Street by New York police officer Michael O'Keefe of the 34th Precinct under suspicious circumstances (Ben-Ali et al. 1992). This incident generated five days of rioting by a thousand residents, who set fire to buildings and cars and pelted police in riot gear with bottles and rocks, just seven miles north of convention headquarters at Madison Square Garden. Questioned about his motive for trying to bring peace to the neighborhood, Mayor Dinkins reported to the press: "Of course the convention is important to me. But my concern for Washington Heights has nothing to do with the convention. My concern is that we keep peace in our city" (Finder 1992).

Dinkins was able to keep the peace, and the Democratic National Convention was not marred by the disturbances in Washington Heights (Dao 1992a). The African American mayor, however, came under attack by the police union and Republicans such as Rudolph Giuliani for selling out the police and treating the real criminal as a martyr in order to court the Latino vote (Dao 1992b; Tumposky 1992).

The Puerto Rican Role in the Convention

Puerto Rican leaders had a marginal role in the Democratic National Convention. In one article about the major players, of the sixteen people mentioned, none were Puerto Rican; two were Mexican American—California Representative Edward Roybal and Los Angeles County Supervisor Gloria Molina (Kasindorf 1992b). The only Puerto Rican mentioned as having any formal role was Bronx Borough President Ferrer, who chaired the Democratic party's Hispanic Caucus, a post he would be forced to step down from after the convention because of new city charter restrictions on elected officials. The major Puerto Rican presence on the program was young William Figueroa, who led the convention in reciting the Pledge of Allegiance. Figueroa was the student for whom Vice-President Quayle misspelled the word "potato."

There were 550 Latino delegates to the convention out of a total of about 5,000 (Creste 1992i). The New York delegation of 331 delegates was 11 percent Latino, 22 percent black, 3 percent Asian, and 62 percent white (King 1992). On the day before the Convention was to open, July 12, Local 1199 sponsored a fund-raising dance at Roseland for the Hispanic PAC-USA, an event that featured New Mexico Representative Bill Richardson, Chicago Treasurer Miriam Santos, and singer-actor Rubén Blades, who cohosted it (EFE 1992a).

It was notable that at the same time as this event, Ferrer was holding a reception for Latino delegates. This was marred by an incident in which a mentally disturbed New Jersey woman was arrested for attempting to kidnap the seven-year-old daughter of José Renaldo Jarabo, president of the Assembly of Puerto Rico.

The next day, Ferrer was to preside over the meeting of the Hispanic Caucus to discuss the development of a Hispanic agenda. The meeting was postponed, however, because the air-conditioning in the hotel room was malfunctioning (R. García 1992*f*).

Around this time, word started to get out that there were tensions at the convention between various Puerto Rican political leaders, namely, Ferrer, Serrano, and Rivera. This came to a head with a controversy over Ferrer's last-minute replacement of Serrano as a convention speaker. About this incident, Ferrer observed: "It's sad that apparently there is room for only one Hispanic, one Puerto Rican leader. That's ridiculous and anti-Puerto Rican." He defended his speaking at the convention by pointing out: "I'm an official of the party, member of the Executive Committee. I have a role, a role to play in this convention. I am chair of the Hispanic Caucus. So why should I be jealous of my colleague, my friend, José Serrano?" As to why he was bumped from the convention program initially, Serrano pointed to three factors: he was the only Puerto Rican on the program; he supported nonintervention in Latin America; and his appearance would strengthen Dinkins politically. He explained that he was upset because he wasn't informed directly of the decision and by the fact that it was only two or three people who had protested his appearance on the program (Arce 1992*b*; R. García 1992*f*). Serrano was eventually given another spot—according to him, "at a better time"—on the convention program.

The role of Puerto Ricans from Puerto Rico at the convention reflected the shifting political regimes on the island. The lame duck governor of Puerto Rico, Rafael Hernández-Colón, did not attend the convention and offered no explanation (Marban 1992). While the commonwealth government was still in power and with the island's gubernatorial elections months away, it was Carlos Romero Barcelo of the prostatehood New Progressive party (PNP) who was playing a role at the convention as a Clinton supporter (R. García 1992*g*). Mayor Dinkins, for one, met with jubilant island officials during the convention and informed them that the Democratic party platform would support the continuation of the Section 936 tax credit for American corporations (Arroyo 1992*b*).

Redistricting and the Local Democratic Primaries

The local primaries in September provided the second test of the impact of the recent round of redistricting in New York. The year before, elections were held for the newly drawn fifty-one council districts (up from thirty-five before redistricting). The Latino community's representation on the city council doubled, from 9 percent to 18 percent, and the number of Latino councilmembers tripled, from three to nine (Santiago 1993).

In 1992, the number of Latinos nominated for the state senate doubled, from two to four; the number nominated for the U.S. Congress also doubled, from one to two. In the state assembly, however, Latinos increased their number of nominees only from five to six (Hanson and Falcón 1992: 19).

All Democratic party nominees were elected to office in the November general election, marking the first time Puerto Ricans and other Latinos in New York City had achieved parity in political representation and the community's first effective use of the provisions of the federal Voting Rights Act (Falcón 1992b). Latinos (about 15 percent of the city's electorate) wound up with 16 percent of the city's state senate seats, 18 percent of its assembly seats, and 15 percent of its congressional seats.

The redistricting process for the city's congressional seats generated the most controversy, particularly between African American and Latino politicians. New York Governor Mario M. Cuomo signed the two redistricting bills in protest. Cuomo's logic for signing the state legislative redistricting plan he disapproved of was as follows: "If I allow this apparently defective plan to stand, the objections I have will be reviewed by both the Department of Justice and the courts. On that basis alone, I am signing those bills" (Benenson 1992a). The Justice Department did not object to either plan; the bills' critics, particularly in minority communities, felt betrayed by the governor.

With both Governor Cuomo and Mayor David N. Dinkins publicly advocating the creation of three majority-Latino congressional districts in New York City, as opposed to only the two proposed by the state legislature, there appeared to be growing pressure in May to adopt a plan devised by a court-appointed master (Falcón 1992b). The master was a well known and highly regarded Republican judge from New Jersey. His plan was blasted by African American Representatives Major Owens, Charles Rangel, Edolphus Towns, and Floyd Flake as "a GOP plot" that was needlessly disruptive to black districts (Creste 1992j; Sisk and Lombardi 1992; Verhovek 1992b). If it was a GOP plot, it was one that had the support of the state's two top Democrats, Cuomo and Dinkins. Bowing largely to Representative Rangel, in July a congressional redistricting plan with only two majority-Latino districts was approved (Sack 1992a).

The seat of the incumbent Puerto Rican Representative from the Bronx, José Serrano, was protected. In addition, a new majority-Latino district, the 12th, stretches from the Lower East Side of Manhattan though parts of Brooklyn and into Queens. It was the most controversial on two counts

(Falcón 1992b). First was its "bizarre" shape, which joins Latino communities over three counties. Second was the decision of the well-heeled Jewish incumbent, Stephen J. Solarz, to run in what many considered a Hispanic district. Solarz competed in a field that included five Latino candidates in the Democratic primary. Nydia Velázquez emerged victorious in the primary. In November, she was elected, the first Puerto Rican woman to serve in the U.S. Congress and the city's second Latino congressional representative. As Serrano noted, "I am proud to have lost the title of being the only Puerto Rican Congressperson" (Arce 1992c; Arroyo 1992c; S. Nieves 1992; Powell 1992).

The General Election

Following his selection as the Democratic candidate for president on July 16, Clinton and running mate Al Gore almost immediately picked up a thirty-point lead in the polls. The Democrats' large lead and Clinton's rejection of traditional interest-group politics tended to manifest themselves in the exclusion of Puerto Rican and Latino concerns from the New York campaign. In an interesting exchange on the significance of the Clinton/Gore approach of appealing to the middle class, two of the party's longtime liberals disagreed. George McGovern felt that their approach would be more like a Trojan Horse. "I have a hunch," he said, "that they're much more liberal underneath and will prove it once they're elected." Former Vice President Walter Mondale, the unsuccessful 1984 presidential candidate, said he was under no illusion, feeling the party had changed in fundamental ways. "We kind of used up the old agenda," he concluded (Rosenbaum 1992).

Dennis Rivera argued that, if Clinton/Gore reached "out to the white suburban voters without activating and energizing the African American and Latino vote, you [wouldn't] get a winning combination." Jackson, for his part, felt that "there [was] a strategy of distancing from labor, from cities and from the Rainbow. Distance is an innovative way of building a coalition. For Clinton to win in a general election, the strategy must be inclusive. It must be expansive" (Sack 1992b).

These discussions of the appropriateness and utility of the Clinton strategy meant little in New York, where neither party actively sought presidential votes. This neglect was particularly evident in the Latino community. Despite having a Hispanic Caucus (chaired by Ferrer), the Democratic party platform, reflecting the new Clinton/Gore strategy of avoiding the impression of pandering to special interests, did not have a specific Latino agenda (Pereira 1992b). Apparently frustrated, Raúl Yzaguirre, president of the National Council of La Raza, told the press: "Clinton knows very little about the problems of our community and the Republicans will try to exploit this." Nonetheless, he concluded that Hispanics would support Clinton (NOTIMEX 1992b).

Meanwhile, in Washington, D.C., the National Association of Latino Elected and Appointed Officials (NALEO) issued a report that found Latinos extremely underrepresented in the Bush White House. According to the report, there were only 15 Latino staff members out of a total White House staff of 1,312, or only 1.1 percent. The report pointed out that this was a smaller percentage than under Reagan (1.7 percent) (EFE 1992b).

In New York, a poll taken after the Democratic National Convention found that 72 percent of New Yorkers supported Clinton, 17 percent, Bush. Among Latinos, Clinton support was higher, 82 percent, compared with only 12 percent for Bush (Ross 1992). Contrary to the desire of the Republicans (and the fears of Democrats like Clinton) that holding the Democratic National Convention in New York would be a disaster, it turned out to have been highly successful. In contrast with the exclusivity of the Republican National Convention, the visible presence of an African American mayor and the city's reputation as the "welfare capital of the nation" did not hurt the Democratic campaign.

The Democratic Black Mobilization

In contrast with what appeared to be minimal effort by the Democratic campaign to organize in the Latino communities, there was more of a focus on the black vote and particularly on black leaders. Clinton addressed the National Urban League annual meeting in San Diego on July 27. At the same time, Jackson was beginning a Democrat party-subsidized voter registration campaign tour of the South. David Bositis (1992) of the Joint Center for Political and Economic Studies, a black think tank, wrote in a *New York Times* op-ed piece: "Mr. Clinton cannot afford to assume he has the black vote sewed up. Outside the South, his black support in the primaries was not especially strong. His share of the black vote in four key states was 20 to 30 percent below his Southern share: California (61 percent), Maryland (49 percent), New Jersey (64 percent) and New York (52 percent)."

In New York, Representative Charles Rangel of Harlem observed of Clinton/Gore: "You don't see them picking up any black babies. Somewhere along the line, someone thought that this campaign was all about white middle-class people" (Moreno 1992). By early September, Democratic party officials had reached an agreement with Jesse Jackson that put him at the head of a black-voter recruitment drive for the Clinton/Gore ticket (*Los Angeles Times* [September 8, 1992]). On the stump, another reporter found, Jackson seemed "more passionate when criticizing President Bush than when he is praising Governor Clinton" (Egan 1992).

Despite this enlistment of Jackson for the campaign, Rangel was still saying weeks later that "it appears that at this point we are on the back burner. We are on an 'as needed' basis." As result, he told reporters, "I feel pretty damn hurt and embarrassed" (Ifill 1992b). A few weeks later, Rangel joined a group of black members of Congress on a get-out-the-vote bus tour of key southern cities, sponsored by the Democratic National Committee and the Congressional Black Caucus. At that point, he still felt that "we haven't gotten the attention that we should have. We don't know what Bill Clinton is going to do, but we know what we're going to do. We're going to beat George Bush" (G. Jordan 1992). In New York City's black neighborhoods in Brooklyn and Queens, the controversial Reverend Al Sharpton was conducting similar voter registration efforts. "We are," he told reporters, "going to have to have a program of accountability for Mr. Clinton." Reporters noticed that he minimized mention of the Clinton/Gore ticket during this voter registration campaign. According to the *Daily News*: "On the front seat of the bus, a fat roll of red, white and blue 'Clinton/Gore' stickers remained in a paper bag next to the doughnuts and a cooler full of sodas" (Sennott 1992).

Taking the Latino Vote for Granted

In contrast, it was early September and, as one reporter put it, Clinton and Bush had barely begun their campaigns in the Latino community. On September 2, Clinton held a private meeting with a corporately financed group called the National Hispanic Leadership Agenda in Washington to discuss its issues. This group was led by former San Antonio mayor Henry Cisneros and included Raúl Yzaguirre of the National Council of La Raza, Representative Solomon Ortiz of Texas, and others (NOTIMEX 1992c). Around the same time, a group of prominent Latino Republicans held a press conference at which Al Zapanta of the Veterans Coalition for Bush/Quayle pointed out that "Bush is the one who has appointed Latinos to more political posts. Clinton has not been a friend of the growing Latino community in the United States," this last in reference to Clinton's signing of a 1987 Arkansas English-only bill. Other Latino Republicans present were José Niño, president of the U.S. Hispanic Chamber of Commerce, and Antonio Villamil, an undersecretary at the U.S. Department of Commerce (NOTIMEX 1992c).

With the general election approaching, everyone expected record numbers to register and vote, in part because of voter registration campaigns by labor and good-government groups. But in the Puerto Rican community, interest in the election was not so high. In a "man on the street" poll, *El Diario-La Prensa* found that few Latinos were watching the televised presidential debates. Of twenty-eight Latinos surveyed, only seven said they bothered watching the debates. Interviews revealed great dissatisfaction with all three candidates for president (Soria 1992c).

In New York City, the Spanish-language press, basing its findings on anecdotal evidence, noted widespread, yet qualified, Latino support for Clinton (Soria 1992d; on Dominicans, see Lin 1992). In an editorial endorsing the Clinton/Gore ticket (October 22), *El Diario-La Prensa* wrote: "We are particularly worried by how little attention Clinton—to say nothing of Bush and Perot—has given to the preoccupations, the problems, the aspirations of Latinos in the United States.... Many Spanish-speaking voters, however, will [vote for Clinton] with great reservations due to the lack of attention paid them."

New York Latinos and the Clinton Victory

On November 3, Bill Clinton was elected president of the United States. At the national level, the Latino vote went 62 percent for Clinton, 25 percent for Bush, and 14 percent for Perot, and represented about 3 percent of the total vote (*New York Times* [November 5, 1992]). In New York State, one poll found that the Latino vote broke down as follows: 69 percent for Clinton, 23 percent for Bush, and 7 percent for Perot (*New York Newsday* [November 4, 1992]). Clinton outpolled Bush in New York by 15 to 1 among blacks and had a double-digit lead among whites (Benenson 1992b).

The national voter turnout rate was a record 55 percent, reversing a thirty-year decline, but in New York State it was only 48 percent, the same as in 1988. New York State was the only state not to register an increase in turnout since the last election and had a higher turnout rate than only three other states: Hawaii (42 percent), South Carolina (45 percent), and Georgia (46 percent) (Pear 1992). In New York City, on the other hand, at least one estimate of the voter turnout rate was much higher, 67 percent, with the Latino vote making up 14 percent of the total (Voter Assistance Commission 1993).

A recent analysis of the Latino vote in the 1992 presidential race in New York City provides a breakdown of Latino subgroup candidate preferences (Falcón and Hanson 1995). In New York City, Clinton had attracted 69 percent of the total vote. Using an ecological approach based on the election district as the unit of analysis, we found that his support among Latinos was significantly higher than among non-Latinos. Clinton received 77 percent of the Latino vote. Among Latinos, support for Clinton was highest in the Puerto Rican and Dominican election districts, with both giving him 77 percent. In South American election districts (largely Colombian and Ecuadorian), 59 percent voted for Clinton.

President Bush received 24 percent of the citywide vote and 20 percent of the Latino vote. In the South American election districts, he received 34 percent, while in Puerto Rican and Dominican election districts he received 19 percent. Ross Perot received 7 percent in the South American areas and 3 percent in Puerto Rican and Dominican districts.

Latinos made up 15 percent of the total vote received by Clinton in New

York City. They made up 10 percent of the Bush vote and 7 percent of the Perot vote. Given Clinton's margin of victory over Bush in New York City (45 percent), the Latino vote was not an important factor in the victory.

A few days after the election, Henry Cisneros announced that Clinton would appoint a Hispanic adviser and that he was assured there would be Latino representation in the president's cabinet (*Noticias del Mundo* [November 6, 1992]). A few weeks later, there was some speculation that Representative Serrano was being considered for the post of U.S. secretary of labor, which would have made him the highest-ranking Latino in the new administration. New Mexico Representative Bill Richardson, who led the Clinton Hispanic campaign, confirmed that he had been asked about Serrano and had recommended him enthusiastically for the post (C. García 1992*a*; Milligan 1992). In a few days, it became clear that Serrano was not really in the running for this appointment (C. García 1992*b*). Clinton's first year in office saw steadily increasing Puerto Rican complaints of being ignored, which fueled a movement for a Puerto Rican march on Washington called Boricua First! (H. Jordan 1994).

Conclusion

Bill Clinton won both the primary and the general election in New York City in 1992 on the strength of the city's traditional liberal electoral coalition, of which Puerto Ricans were an important part. Yet his message was not a traditionally liberal one. Puerto Ricans wound up supporting a candidate who consciously did not address their specific needs and who challenged the elements of a liberal program that Puerto Ricans have long come to expect from the Democratic standard-bearer. There was no special interest group politics anymore. It was, instead, replaced by a rhetorically more-inclusive "American agenda." As the Sister Souljah episode drove home, this was a president who would selectively challenge the liberal status quo. (Republican charges of his "pandering" to Jewish voters revealed what some might call a double standard.) Even New York City had been criticized by candidate Clinton as being too far out of the mainstream to be a good location for the party's convention. The much-anticipated showdown on urban issues in New York never materialized beyond two nonevents.

Clinton's was a postliberal message that should have alarmed traditional Puerto Rican leaders, yet it did not. This, it could be argued, was largely a function of what looked to many as an even more rightward movement by the Republican party, which made Clinton's neoliberalism palatable.

Puerto Ricans in New York found themselves being largely taken for granted by the Democrats in a political process that became little more than jockeying for position between Puerto Rican political elites within the Democratic party. While there was some concern about the presidential election, the stronger driving force appeared to be the 1993 mayoral elections, in which a black incumbent would be running for re-election. This created increased black-Puerto Rican political elite competition, which went as far, at times, as affecting Clinton's relationship with Puerto Rican politicians in potentially harmful ways.

This competition highlighted how relative the issue of political power between racial-ethnic minorities is. While much of the black leadership was lamenting a marginal role in the Clinton campaign, Puerto Rican politicians were so out of the loop that they were *envious* of this self-described black marginalization. What they saw was that the chair of the Democratic party was black, the executive director of the Democratic National Convention was black, the mayor of the City of New York was black, Jesse Jackson was black, and Puerto Ricans were totally on the outside. Even Clinton's Hispanic campaign coordinator, who had been based in New York, was not a Puerto Rican, but a Mexican American (a repeat, interestingly enough, of what Michael Dukakis had done four years earlier). Even though the Democratic National Convention was held in New York City, a Puerto Rican stronghold, Puerto Ricans fell to the status of outsiders in a party to which they had been very loyal.

The inability of Puerto Rican political leaders to coordinate an effective agenda throughout this process highlighted the damage that elite competition had engendered. The two top Puerto Rican elected officials, Ferrer and Serrano, got involved in an embarrassing competition for attention at the Democratic National Convention, while Dennis Rivera confusingly bounced between Democratic candidates, became absorbed in party politics, and blunted his progressive agenda. In the process, the needs and aspirations of one million Puerto Ricans, and another million Latinos, were not effectively represented.

In this sense, postliberalism and traditional liberalism seemed to merge in 1992 in their irrelevance to the politics of the poor and the working-class racial-ethnic communities like Puerto Ricans. As a result, the reliance on elected officials as the main vehicles for a community's political leadership and the overreliance on electoral politics over more direct forms of participation had become issues that need to be debated urgently in Puerto Rican and other similarly situated communities. The 1992 election revealed the limits and increasing poverty of American politics. For the vast majority of Puerto Ricans, it was just something they saw playing on television, no more significant than *The Love Connection* or *Tres Destinos*.

References

A complete list of newspaper references on the role of Latinos in the 1992 campaign in New York is available from the author at the Institute for Puerto Rican Policy, 286 Fifth Ave., New York, NY 10001.

Arce, Rose Marie. 1992a. "TV Debate Set in South Bronx." *New York Newsday* (February 12).
———. 1992b. "Schedule Change or Ferrer Fit?" *New York Newsday* (July 15).
———. 1992c. "Latino Cry: 'People Won.'" *New York Newsday* (September 17).
Arroyo, José. 1992a. "Clinton 'Ignoraba' Que Tenía Que Hablar con Hispanos." *Noticias del Mundo* (March 30).
———. 1992b. "Convención Demócrata Aprueba Apoyo a la que Incentiva Inversiones en PR." *Noticias del Mundo* (July 16).
———. 1992c. "Hispanos Vencen a Solarz: Nydia Velázquez Fue Consagrada Candidata al Congreso." *Noticias del Mundo* (September 16).
Ben-Ali, Russell; Michael H. Cottman; Alfred Lubrano; and Erik L. Smith. 1992. "Criminal or a Victim?" *New York Newsday* (July 6).
Benenson, Joel, 1992a. "Redistricting Plan Now Law: Reluctant Gov Signs Bill." *Daily News* (May 5).
———. 1992b. "In N.Y., They All Loved Bill: Best Margin Since '64." *Daily News* (November 4).
Bositis, David. 1992. "Clinton Has the Black Vote—or Does He?" *New York Times* (August 13).
Carroll, Maurice. 1992. "Unimpressed: Clinton's Leading, but Many City Dems Would Pick Perot." *New York Newsday* (July 5).
Clifford, Timothy. 1992. "Clinton Sticks to His Guns, Condemns Rap Star's Remarks Again." *New York Newsday* (June 17).
Cohen, Patricia. 1992a. "A Platform 'Summit': Liberal Planks Sought for Dems." *New York Newsday* (May 25).
———. 1992b. "Dave: Watch Your Style." *New York Newsday* (June 17).
Collins, Gail. 1992a. "2 Country Boys Lost in the City." *New York Newsday* (April 1).
———. 1992b. "The New York Newsday Interview with Bill Clinton: 'I've Been an Honorable Public Servant.'" *New York Newsday* (April 3).
Cooper, Alison, and Curtis Rist. 1992. "Time to Forgive? Jesse's Stigma Irks Dinkins." *New York Newsday* (April 9).
Cottman, Michael H. 1992. "Man with a Plan: Jackson Prods Dems to 'Rebuild America.'" *New York Newsday* (June 29).
Creste, Esteban. 1992a. "Políticos Hispanos Enojados con Clinton: El Candidato Canceló Abruptamente Varias Reuniones con los Latinos." *El Diario-La Prensa* (March 25).
———. 1992b. "Yo, Yo, Yo." *El Diario-La Prensa* (March 24).
———. 1992c. "Brown a Favor de la Autodeterminación de PR." *El Diario-La Prensa* (April 3)
———. 1992d. "Los Boricuas Votarán por Clinton." *El Diario-La Prensa* (April 5).
———. 1992e. "Desacuerdos sobre Debate Demócrata." *El Diario-La Prensa* (March 27).
———. 1992f. "Temas Urbanos sobre la Mesa." *El Diario-La Prensa* (April 1).
———. 1992g. "Después de Todo, NY Desinteresado en las Elecciones." *El Diario-La Prensa* (April 7).
———. 1992h. "Impulsar en Presencia Política Hispana." *El Diario-La Prensa* (April 28).

———. 1992i. "La Presencia Hispana en la Convención Demócrata." *El Diario-La Prensa* (July 13).
———. 1992j. "Congresistas Negros Se Oponen al Plan Federal de Redistribución." *El Diario-La Prensa* (June 14).
Dao, James. 1992a. "Washington Heights Calm Shattered by Disruptions." *New York Times* (July 10).
———. 1992b. "Police Union Says Dinkins Fueled Unrest: Slain Dominican Man Treated Like 'a Martyr.'" *New York Times* (July 14).
de la Cruz, Evido. 1992a. "Más Dolores de Cabeza para Clinton." *El Diario-La Prensa* (April 2).
———. 1992b. "Acaso Bush Es Hispano?" *El Diario-La Prensa* (May 6).
Douglas, William. 1992. "There's No 'Latin Vote.'" *New York Newsday* (October 15).
EFE. 1992a. "'Nosotros los Hispanos Somos el Futuro': Sueño de Ver a un Latino en la Casa Blanca." *Noticias del Mundo* (July 13).
———. 1992b. "La Casa Blanca Es el Organismo con Menos Hispanos." *El Diario-La Prensa* (July 27).
Egan, Timothy. 1992. "At Edge of Campaign, Jackson Labors for Democratic Victory." *New York Times* (October 20).
English, Merle. 1992. "Clinton Rapped: Called 'Insensitive' after Comments on Black Singer." *New York Newsday* (June 16).
Falcón, Angelo. 1992a. "Puerto Ricans and the 1988 Election in New York City." In Rodolfo O. de la Garza and Louis DeSipio, eds., *From Rhetoric to Reality: Latino Politics in the 1988 Elections*, pp. 147–170. Boulder, Colo.: Westview Press.
———. 1992b. "Time to Rethink the Voting Rights Act?" *Social Policy* 23 (2) (Fall-Winter): 17–22.
Falcón, Angelo, and Christopher Hanson. 1995. "Latino Immigrants and Political Participation: Puerto Ricans, Dominicans, and South Americans in the New York City Political System." Unpublished paper. New York: Institute for Puerto Rican Policy.
Finder, Alan. 1992. "Dinkins, Amid Crowd, Nurtures Fragile Peace." *New York Times* (July 9).
García, Carlos. 1992a. "Expectativa por versiones sobre futuro del congresista Serrano." *Noticias del Mundo* (November 16).
———. 1992b. "Serrano No Recibío Oferta de Secretario Pero es Orgulloso por Reacción ante Versiones." *Noticias del Mundo* (November 17).
García, Rudy. 1992a. "Hispanos de Nueva York Ofendidos con Clinton." *Noticias del Mundo* (March 25).
———. 1992b. "Poco Interés Hispano en Primaries de Hoy." *Noticias del Mundo* (April 7).
———. 1992c. "Por Fin Clinton Se Reune con Líderes Hispanos." *Noticias del Mundo* (April 9).
———. 1992d. "Políticos Hispanos Se Reunieron con el Presidente del Partido Demócrata." *Noticias del Mundo* (May 13).
———. 1992e. "Hispanos por Perot?" *Noticias del Mundo* (June 11).
———. 1992f. "Se Inicío Convención Demócrata en Nueva York: Caucus Hispano Discute Prioridades." *Noticias del Mundo* (July 14).

———. 1992g. "Puertorriqueños Pro Estadidad con Su Propia Agenda." *Noticias del Mundo* (July 16).
González, Juan. 1992. "City Voted to End an Era." *Daily News* (November 4).
Guerra, Fernando. 1992. "Conditions Not Met: California Elections and the Latino Community." In Rodolfo O. de la Garza and Louis DeSipio, eds., *From Rhetoric to Reality: Latino Politics in the 1988 Elections*, pp. 99–110. Boulder, Colo.: Westview Press.
Hanson, Christopher, and Angelo Falcón. 1992. *Latinos and the Redistricting Process in New York City: An Assessment and Profiles of the New Latino Assembly, State Senate and Congressional Districts*. New York: Institute for Puerto Rican Policy.
Howard, Susan. 1992. "Rapper: Big Mistake, Bill." *New York Newsday* (June 17).
Ifill, Gwen. 1992a. "Clinton at Jackson Meeting: Warmth, and Some Friction." *New York Times* (June 14).
———. 1992b. "Some Leaders Feel Ignored: Clinton Waves at Blacks As He Rushes By." *New York Times* (September 20).
Institute for Puerto Rican Policy. 1992a. "The 1992 Presidential Primaries: NPROS-92A Report #1." New York: Institute for Puerto Rican Policy.
———. 1992b. "Puerto Rican Politics in New York City, Part I: Most Politically Influential Puerto Ricans—NPROS-92A Report #2." New York: Institute for Puerto Rican Policy.
Jordan, George E. 1992. "Blacks Stump for Clinton." *New York Newsday* (October 13).
Jordan, Howard. 1994. "The Boricua First! Campaign." *Crítica: A Journal of Puerto Rican Policy & Politics* 3 (August).
Kasindorf, Martin. 1992a. "Brown Is Challenged on Choice of Jackson." *New York Newsday* (April 3).
———. 1992b. "Who Will Be the Stars?" *New York Newsday* (July 12).
Kasindorf, Martin, and Glenn Kessler. 1992. "Many Words, Few Sparks: Clinton, Brown Debate Focuses on Urban Issues." *New York Newsday* (April 12).
Kessler, Glenn. 1992. "Mauled by the Media?" *New York Newsday* (April 7).
King, Wayne. 1992. "Below the Podium, Democratic Nobodies Are a Kaleidoscope of Somebodies." *New York Times* (July 12).
Kosmin, Barry A., and Ariela Keysar. 1992. "Party Political Preferences of U.S. Hispanics: The Varying Impact of Religion, Social Class and Demographic Factors." Typescript. New York: CUNY Graduate School and University Center.
Liff, Bob. 1992. "Latinos Assail Ferrer over Debate." *New York Newsday* (March 26).
Lin, Wendy. 1992. "Immigrants Back Clinton." *New York Newsday* (November 3).
Lombardi, Frank. 1992a. "Quayle Aide: Clinton Not Kosher." *Daily News* (April 2).
———. 1992b. "Cuomo Pipes: Peace! Urges Bill to Reconcile with Jackson, Souljah." *Daily News* (June 18).
McCarthy, Sheryl. 1992. "Lehman Scores Debating Points." *New York Newsday* (March 30).
Marban, Pedro. 1992. "Gobernador de Puerto Rico No Asistirá a Convención: Se Desconoce Razones de la Ausencia de Hernández Colón." *Noticias del Mundo* (July 16).
Milligan, Susan. 1992. "Bronx Rep. Would Be Top-Ranking Hispanic in Gov't.: Serrano Up for U.S. Labor Boss." *Daily News* (November 14).

Moreno, Sylvia. 1992. "Invisible Citizens—Rangel: Clinton Snubs Blacks." *New York Newsday* (August 31).
Murphy, William. 1992. "Dems Jittery about Union Trouble." *New York Newsday* (May 25).
Nelson, Lars-Erik. 1992. "Reluctantly, N.Y. Goes for Bill." *Daily News* (April 8).
Newfield, Jack. 1992. "Who Fights Medicaid Cuts? A Lion Named Rivera." *New York Post* (March 24).
Nieves, Carmen S. 1992. "Legisladores Firman Carta contra Dennis Rivera." *El Diario-La Prensa* (March 31).
Nieves, Santiago. 1992. "Nydia Velázquez: 'We Have Been Disenfranchised Too Long.'" *New York Newsday* (September 21).
NOTIMEX. 1992a. "David Duke Arrmete: 'Los Hispanos y Negros Son una Amenaza para la Cultura Sajona." *El Diario-La Prensa* (January 19).
———. 1992b. "El Voto Latino Será Determinante." *El Diario-La Prensa* (July 22).
———. 1993c. "De Repente, Atención a los Latinos: Bush y Clinton Comienzan a Poner Sus Ojos Sobre la Comunidad." *El Diario-La Prensa* (September 3).
Page, Susan. 1992. "2nd Tsurprises: Non-Candidate Tsongas Comes In Ahead of Brown." *New York Newsday* (April 8).
Pear, Robert. 1992. "55 Percent Voting Rate Reverses." *New York Times* (November 5).
Pereira, Rodolfo. 1992a. "Dennis Rivera, Líder Sindical Puertorriqueño: 'Soy un Demócrata Descontento con Mi Partido.'" *El Diario-La Prensa* (March 30).
———. 1992b. "Urge Imponer una Agenda Latina." *El Diario-La Prensa* (July 27).
Powell, Michael. 1992. "Most Retain House Slots; Solarz Loses." *New York Newsday* (September 16).
Purdum, Todd S. 1992. "New Yorkers Cover All Bases, Saying They're Unhappy with the Players." *New York Times* (April 8).
Richards, Clay F. 1992. "Classic Coalition Clings to Clinton." *New York Newsday* (April 8).
Rodríguez, Lionel. 1992. "'Hispanic PAC: Chavos para candidatos." *El Vocero* (April 30).
Rosenbaum, David E. 1992. "Democratic Platform Shows Shift in Party's Focus." *New York Times* (July 14).
Ross, Barbara. 1992. "New York Loves Clinton." *Daily News* (July 28).
Sack, Kevin. 1992a. "Redistricting Plans Approved." *New York Times* (July 3).
———. 1992b. "Jesse Jackson: Waiting on Proposal from Clinton." *New York Times* (July 18).
Santiago, John, ed. 1993. *Redistricting, Race and Ethnicity in New York City: The Gartner Report and Its Critics*. New York: Institute for Puerto Rican Policy.
Seifman, David. 1992. "Sí Means No! Bill Backs Out of Hispanic Parley." *New York Post* (March 25).
Serant, Claire. 1992. "An Insure Thing for Dems: Minority Brokers Got Convention Covered." *Daily News* (July 6).
Shaw, Gaylord. 1992. "End's in Doubt: Vote Volatile after Candidates' Two-Week Slugfest." *New York Newsday* (April 7).
Siegel, Joel. 1992. "Dinkins to Jews: Forgive—Urges End to Anger Against Jesse." *Daily News* (April 9).

Sisk, Richard, and Frank Lombardi. 1992. "A GOP Plot, Dems Say of Fed Districting Plan." *Daily News* (May 28).

Soria, Enrique. 1992*a*. "Bill Clinton Promete Dar Énfasis a los Sectores Más Pobres: Las Comunidades Primero." *El Diario-La Prensa* (March 30).

———. 1992*b*. "Clinton Hace Campaña en Brooklyn." *El Diario-La Prensa* (March 31).

———. 1992*c*. "Hispanos: Debate?" *El Diario-La Prensa* (October 14).

———. 1992*d*. "Latinos de NY: Clinton." *El Diario-La Prensa* (October 21).

Suro, Robert. 1992. "Hispanic Politicians Seek a Recipe for Raw Numbers." *New York Times* (April 12).

Tumposky, Ellen. 1992. "PBA Big Socks Dave: Says He Sold Out Police to Court Latinos." *Daily News* (July 17).

Verhovek, Sam Howe. 1992*a*. "A Line in the Sand." *New York Times* (April 5).

———. 1992*b*. "Redistricting Plan Spurs Lawmakers' Criticism." *New York Times* (May 28).

Voter Assistance Commission. 1993. *Annual Report: January 1992–July 1993*. New York: City of New York.

Walt, Vivienne. 1992. "Plodding toward Mayors' Summit." *New York Newsday* (March 31).

About the Contributors

Manuel Avalos is assistant professor of political science in the Department of Social and Behavioral Sciences at Arizona State University, West, in Phoenix, Arizona. His current research focuses on the social, political, and economic inequalities of racial minorities in the Americas.

Bruce E. Cain is associate director of the Institute for Governmental Studies and professor of political science at the University of California, Berkeley. His writings include *The Reapportionment Puzzle* (1984); *The Personal Vote* (1987), with John Ferejohn and Morris Fiorina; and *Congressional Redistricting*, with David Butler.

Rodolfo O. de la Garza is Mike Hogg Professor of Community Affairs and professor in the Department of Government at the University of Texas at Austin and vice-president and director of research of the Tomás Rivera Center. He directed the Latino National Political Survey in 1989–1990, the first national study of Latino political values, attitudes, and behaviors. He is the author and editor of numerous books and articles on Latino politics, including *Latino Voices: Mexican, Puerto Rican, and Cuban Perspectives on American Politics* and *Barrio Ballots: Latino Politics in the 1990 Elections*.

Louis DeSipio is assistant professor of political science at the University of Illinois at Urbana-Champaign. His research focuses on ethnic politics, particularly Latino politics, and immigration and settlement policy. He is the author of *Counting on the Latino Vote: Latinos as a New Electorate* (University Press of Virginia, forthcoming) and an author and the editor of a five-volume series on Latino political attitudes and behaviors.

Angelo Falcón is president and founder of the Institute for Puerto Rican Policy, a nonprofit and nonpartisan policy center in New York City established in 1982. He is a political scientist who has written widely on Puerto Rican politics, urban politics, and public policy. Most recently, he has published "Puerto Ricans and the Politics of Racial Identity" in *Racial and Ethnic Identity*, ed. Herbert W. Harris et al. (Routledge, 1995).

Luis Ricardo Fraga is director of the Stanford Center for Chicano Research and associate professor of political science at Stanford University. He has published widely in scholarly journals and books on the topics of urban politics, politics of race and ethnicity, and educational policy. He is completing a book manuscript entitled "The Changing Urban Regime: Toward an Informed Public Interest."

F. Chris García is professor of political science at the University of New Mexico. His research and teaching interests include public opinion, political culture, and the electoral process in the United States, with emphasis on Latinos. His most recent works include collaboration on the volumes *Latino Voices: Mexican, Puerto Rican, and Cuban Perspectives on American Politics* and *New Mexico Government*, 3rd edition.

Fernando Guerra is assistant to the president for faculty resources at Loyola Marymount University. Dr. Guerra is also chair of the Department of Chicano Studies and associate professor of political science. His scholarly work focuses on state and local government and urban and ethnic politics. He currently serves as a mayoral appointee on the Los Angeles Board of Transportation Commissioners.

Rodney E. Hero is professor of political science at the University of Colorado at Boulder. He is the author of *Latinos in the U.S. Political System: Two Tiered Pluralism* (Temple University Press, 1992) and of numerous articles on Latino politics and on state and local politics.

Valerie J. Martínez is assistant professor of political science and a research associate in the Center for the Study of Educational Reform at the University of North Texas. Her major research interests focus on social welfare policies for children and the elderly. She is the principal investigator of a U.S. Department of Education project to examine the consequences of educational choice policy for low-income minority families in San Antonio, Texas.

Dario Moreno is associate professor of political science at Florida International University. His research focuses on the development of U.S. foreign policy and on the politics of Cuban Americans. He is the author of *The Struggle for Peace in Central America* (University Press of Florida, 1992).

Roberto Rey is in the Ph.D. program in the Department of Political Science at the University of Chicago. His research interests focus on minority politics in the United States and social movements in Latin America.

Christopher Warren is associate professor of political science at Florida International University, where he teaches urban and American politics. His research interests include the politics of ethnicity and class in urban areas, Miami politics, and the reform of local government structures.

About the Book

Ethnic Ironies describes the role of Latino electorates in national- and state-level politics during the 1992 elections. The book examines Latino Politics from the top down—looking at the efforts of candidates and campaigns to speak to Latino concerns and to mobilize Latino voters—and from the bottom up—reviewing the efforts of Latinos to win electoral office and to influence electoral outcomes.

Chronicling the campaigns and uncovering patterns of Latino influence, the core of the book consists of eight state-level analyses by experts who have observed firsthand the states with the most sizable Latino electorates. An overview chapter synthesizes and integrates the findings of these case studies, placing them in national perspective.

Ethnic Ironies is the third in a series of studies on Latino electoral behavior published by Westview Press, including *From Rhetoric to Reality: Latino Politics in the 1988 Elections* and *Barrio Ballots: Latino Politics in the 1990 Elections*. This latest study also serves as a companion volume to *Latino Voices: Mexican, Puerto Rican, and Cuban Perspectives on American Politics* and *New Americans by Choice: Political Perspectives of Latino Immigrants*.

Index

Adelante con Clinton!, 19–20, 65, 86, 118, 159
African Americans
   and Clinton campaign, 20
   in Florida, 177
   in Illinois, 150, 154, 158
   and New York politics, 186, 195–196, 199, 201–202, 203, 205
   and Perot, 18
Agenda setting
   and Cubans in Florida, 183
   and Latino organizations in 1992, 38–40, 44(n18)
   and Texas state legislators, 128
   See also Issues
Agran, Larry, 8, 63
Albuquerque Journal, 58
Albuquerque Tribune, 58, 59, 60, 61
Alonzo, Roberto, 116
Alta California Policy Center, 137
Anaya, Toney, 64
Antiabortion law, Arizona, 104
Apodaca, Jerry, 61
Apodaca, Patrick, 64
Aragón, Robert, 57, 62, 63, 69
Archuleta, David, 65, 67–68
Arias, María Victoria, 176
Arizona
   economy and demographics, 51, 96–98, 97(table)
   factors in Latino voting behavior, 98–104, 106–109
   Latino representation in, 104–105, 109(n2)
   1992 election in, 30, 33, 95–96, 105–106, 107(table)
   1992 presidential campaign in, 23, 25
Arizona Community Forum, 99, 100, 101
Arizona Hispanic Chamber of Commerce, 99, 101

Armesto-García, Eladio, 181
Aronson, Bernard, 174
Asian Americans, 67

Baca, Jim, 58
Baca, Polly, 86
Badillo, Herman, 192, 193, 194
Bañuelos, Robert John, 38
Barcelo, Carlos Romero, 198
Barrera, Roy, 26, 27
Barriero, Bruno, 182
Becerra, Xavier, 38, 141
Bemis, Gregg, 69
Benavides, Pete, 35, 121–123
Bentsen, Lloyd, 8
Bernalillo County (Albuquerque), New Mexico, 56–57
Berrios, Rubén, 189
Bilingual/bicultural education
   and Bush campaign, 28
   and Clinton, 191
   and Jerry Brown, 61
Blades, Rubén, 197
Block, Jerome, 57, 63
Bonilla, Henry, 34, 127
Boricua First!, 204
Bositis, David, 201
Brown, Jerry, 8, 9
   and Colorado primary, 78
   in Illinois, 10, 157
   and New Mexico primary, 57, 58, 60–61, 62, 63
   in New York, 10, 188–190, 191–192
   and Texas, 9, 43(n4), 116–117
Brown, Ron, 19, 194
Buchanan, Patrick, 8, 11, 12–13, 186
   and Colorado primary, 84
   and New Mexico primary, 62, 63
   and Proposition 187, xii
Bush, Barbara, 27, 118
Bush, Columba, 26, 27, 118

215

Bush, George
  and Arizona, 105, 106
  in California, 131, 138
  and Colorado, 85–87, 87–88, 91–93
  and Cuban Democracy Act, 21, 174, 176
  and Florida, 11, 43(n12), 172–174, 176–177
  in Illinois, 160
  Latinos for, 194, 202
  Latinos in administration, 201
  and New Mexico, 62, 63, 65, 67–68
  and New York, 196, 201, 203–204
  1992 general campaign strategy, x, 15–17, 25–28, 39, 42, 44(n14)
  and 1992 polls, 18, 68–69, 85–86, 105, 196, 201
  and 1992 primaries, 10–12, 13
  in Texas, 11, 118, 119
Bush, George P., 16–17, 26, 27, 118
Bush, Jeb, 172, 174
Bustamante, Albert, 34, 127

California
  demographics/noncitizenship rates, 5, 111, 131
  Latino organizations in, 137
  Latino political power in, 131–132, 134–135, 135–136, 143–144
  Latino representation in, xi, 132, 139–143
  1992 election in, 30, 38, 137–143, 138(table), 140(table), 142(table)
  1992 presidential campaign in, 23, 25, 27
  voter intimidation in, 43(n11)
Campaigns, 1992 presidential
  Bush general strategy, 15–17, 25–28, 42, 43(n12), 44(n14)
  California and Clinton, 139
  Clinton general strategy, 13–15, 18–24, 41–42
  Colorado and, 85–88
  Florida and, 172–176
  Illinois and, 158, 159–160, 165
  Latino influence/outreach during, x–xi, 3, 7, 38–41
  and minimizing white backlash, 133
  and New Mexico, 55, 65–68
  and New York, 193–196, 200–203
  Perot general strategy, 17–18, 28–29
  Texas and, 117, 118
  See also Primaries, 1992
Campbell, Ben Nighthorse, 84, 85, 87, 88
Campos, Marc, 126

Candidates
  California Latino, 140–143
  effect on Latino political participation of, 136
  and electoral opportunities for Latino, 133
  Florida Latino, 179–180, 181–182
  Illinois Latino, 161–162, 163–164
  New Mexico Latino, 57, 62–63, 69, 71
  1992 Latino, 34–38, 36–37(table)
  1992 presidential, 8
  Texas and Latino, 121–127, 128
  See also Campaigns, 1992 presidential
CANF. *See* Cuban American National Foundation
Canosa, Jorge Más, 12
Cardelle, Alberto José, 8
Carville, James, 23
Castro, Fidel, 21
Chávez, César, 116
Chávez, Linda, 4
Chávez, Martín, 57, 61
Chicago
  Latino influence in, 149, 150, 151–153, 151(table), 152(tables), 156, 165–166
  and 1992 election, 158, 158(table), 160–162, 161(table), 163–164
  redistricting in, 154
Chicago Tribune, 161–162
Cisneros, Henry
  and Clinton presidential appointments, 121, 204
  in Colorado, 86
  and National Hispanic Leadership Agenda, 202
  in New Mexico, 66
  and Republican National Convention, 17
  role in Clinton campaign, 22, 39
  in Texas, 116, 118
Citizenship
  and Arizona Latinos, 98
  and Colorado Latinos, 75
  and Illinois politics, 151, 166, 167(n3)
  and Latino political influence, 5, 38, 42, 135, 136
Civil rights law, Arkansas, 67
Clinton, Bill
  and Arizona, 105, 106
  in California, 131, 138, 139
  and Colorado, 78, 85–86, 87, 88, 91–93
  Cuban policy as president, 178

Index

and Florida, 170, 174–176, 177
in Illinois, 157, 158, 159–160, 165
and New Mexico, 57, 58–60, 61, 62, 63, 65–66
and New York, 187–188, 190, 191, 192–196, 200–203, 203–204
1992 general campaign strategy, x, 13–15, 18–24, 39, 41–42, 133
and 1992 polls, 18, 68–69, 85–86, 105, 192–193, 196, 201
and 1992 primaries, 8–10, 13, 43(n4)
presidential commitment to Latinos, xiii, 121
and Puerto Rico, 189
and Texas, 116, 117, 118, 119–121
Clinton, Hillary Rodham, 9, 58, 87, 176
Coffey, Kendall, 181
Collins, Gail, 190
Colón, Lydia, 196
Colón, Rafael Castañeira, 194
Colorado
demographic statistics, 51, 76–77, 76(table)
importance of Latino vote in, 75–76, 91–93, 92(table)
1992 election in, x, 30, 31–33, 41, 79–83(tables), 88–91
1992 presidential campaign in, 23, 24, 25, 27, 85–88
and 1992 primaries, 78–85
party affiliation in, 77–78
Competitiveness
and California Latino electoral networks, 143
as effecting Latino turnout, 106
and Illinois politics, 150, 160, 166
and New York ethnic politics, 205
and political power, xi, 132
Congress. *See* House of Representatives, U.S.; Senate, U.S.
Connecticut, 41
Considine, Terry, 88
Cruz, Lucy, 194
Cuba, 20–21, 174, 178
Cuban American National Foundation (CANF), 12, 21, 170, 174, 176, 177, 183(n2)
Cuban Americans
and Bush campaign, 27
and Clinton campaign, 20–21
elected officials, xi, 34

in Florida, 169–183
in Illinois, 153, 160
and 1992 campaigns, x, 12, 43(n12)
participation level, 43(n3)
Cuban Council for Democracy, 180
Cuban Democracy Act (Torricelli bill), 20–21, 27, 174, 175, 176, 178
Cuban Women for Clinton, 41
Cuomo, Mario M., 8, 196, 199

Daily News, 196, 202
Daley, Mayor Richard, Jr., 154, 161, 167(n1)
Dallas Morning News, 123
Davis, Magda, 179–180
"Debate for Urban America, The," 190
de la Cruz, Evido, 194
de la Garza, Kika, 15, 35, 118
de la Garza, Rodolfo, 6
Delegates, national conventions
from Arizona, 104–105
from Colorado, 84
at Democratic National Convention, 14–15, 43(nn 6, 7), 197
at Republican National Convention, 16, 65
from Texas, 117–118
Del Valle, Miguel, 156, 157, 163, 164, 167(n2)
Democratic National Convention, 14–15, 39, 43(nn 6, 7)
Arizona delegates to, 104
Colorado delegates to, 84
New York location of, 201
and New York politics, 196–198, 205
and Texas Latinos, 117–118
Democratic party
in Arizona, 100, 101, 102–103, 106, 108
in California, 140–141, 142
in Colorado, 78, 79–83(tables), 84–85
and controversial Latino issues, xii
in Florida, 173(Table 8.3), 177, 178–180, 179(table), 181
in Illinois, 150, 154–159, 161–166
in New Mexico, 56–57, 58–62, 63–64, 71
and New York politics, 186, 187–193, 196–203, 205
1992 platform, xi, 3, 39, 198, 200
and 1992 primaries, 8–10. *See also* Primaries, 1992
in Texas, 115, 116–117, 123, 124, 125–126
See also Clinton, Bill; Democratic National Convention

Demographics
  Arizona, 96, 98
  California, 131
  Colorado, 76–77, 76(table)
  effect on political power, 5
  Florida, 170–172, 172(table)
  Illinois, 149–150, 151–153, 152(tables)
  New York, 187
  population/voter statistics, 1, 51, 111, 147
  Texas, 114, 115(table)
Denver Post, 86
de Posada, Roberto, 25
DeSipio, Louis, 6
Díaz, Héctor, 188
Díaz-Balart, Lincoln, 36, 179
Dinkins, David N., 188, 190–191, 192, 195, 197, 198, 199
Dixon, Alan, 164
Domenici, Pete, 65, 67
Dominicans, 197, 203
Dukakis, Michael, xiii, 8, 14, 138, 138(table), 175
Duke, David, 8, 12, 185–186

Echaveste, María, 8, 9, 19, 191, 192
Economy
  Arizona, 96, 98
  Florida, 174
Education
  and Arizona Latinos, 97
  and Colorado, 89, 90–91
  and Illinois Latinos, 151
El Diario-La Prensa, 189, 193, 194, 202, 203
Election, 1988
  in California, 138, 138(table)
  in Illinois, 150
  Latino influence in, xiii
  in Texas, 119
Election, 1992
  in Arizona, 95–96, 104, 105–106, 107(table)
  in California, 131, 134, 137–143, 138(table), 140(table), 142(table)
  in Colorado, 75–76, 79–83(tables), 88–93, 92(table)
  in Florida, 172, 173(tables), 176–182
  in Illinois, 159(Table 7.7), 160–164, 161(table), 165–166
  Latino influence in presidential, x, xiii, 29–34, 30(table), 31(table), 32(table), 41, 42

Latino influence over campaign issues, x–xi, 38–41, 44(n18)
Latinos and congressional/state/local races, 34–38, 36–37(table)
and New Mexico, 55, 63, 69–72
New York presidential, 203–204
in Texas, 113, 119–121, 120(table), 121–123, 122(table), 124, 127, 128
See also Campaigns, 1992 presidential; Primaries, 1992
Electoral system
  and Arizona law, 103
  and Florida law, 169
  and minority political power, ix–x, xi, xii
  state differences in, 44(n17)
English-only laws
  and Bush campaign, 28
  Clinton and Arkansas, 191
  in Colorado, 84
  and Jerry Brown, 61
Ervin, Clark, 124–125
Ethnic identification, 77

Fernández, Ricardo, 190
Ferrer, Fernando, 39, 187, 190, 191, 192, 193–194, 197, 198, 205
Ferro, Simón, 175
Figueroa, William, 197
Flake, Floyd, 199
Florida
  demographic/socioeconomic factors, 147, 151–153, 151(table), 152(tables), 170–172, 172(table)
  Latino political power in, 169–170, 182–183
  Latino representation in, xi
  and 1992 election, x, 31, 33, 34, 172–178, 173(tables)
  1992 presidential campaign in, 21, 23, 25, 27, 43(n12)
  and 1992 primaries, 11
  1992 state races, 178–182
Fraga, Luis, 106, 150
Frost, Stanley, 57

Gandy, Gwendolyn, 196
García, Delano, 66
García, Jesús, 158, 163, 164
García, José "Kiko," 197
García, Sylvia, 126
Gay rights, Colorado, 89, 90
Giuliani, Rudolph, 197

Index

Gómez, Tomás, 59, 60
Gonzales, Emile, 59
Gonzales-Romer, Gloria, 16
González, Efraín, 193
González, Henry B., 35
Gore, Al, 8, 14, 18, 87, 200
Gore, Tipper, 87, 176
Government system. *See* Electoral system
Graham, Bob, 176, 178
Grant, Bill, 178
Green, Gene, 34, 124, 125–126, 127
Guatemalans, 153
Guerra, Fernando, 6, 106, 182
Guerrero, Lena, 15, 35, 118, 121, 123–124
Gutiérrez, Luis, 40, 161–162
Gutiérrez, Mary Sue, 61
Gutman, Alberto, 181

Harkin, Tom, 8, 61, 63, 78
Hawkins, Paula, 178
Heath, Josie, 84–85
Herman, Alexis M., 196
Hernández, Antonia, 39
Hernández, Tony, 78
Hernández-Colón, Rafael, 198
Hero, Rodney, 4
Herrera, Frank, 194
Herrera, Gabriel, 194
Herrera, Steve, 59–60
"Hispanic Community and the Republican Party: The *Real* Record, The," 11–12
Hispanic PAC-USA, xi–xii, 40, 194, 197
Hofeld, Albert, 164
Hoffman, Bruce, 181
House of Representatives, U.S.
    California Latinos in, 132, 139, 140–141, 140(table)
    and Florida, 170, 178–180
    Illinois election for, 160–162
    Latinos and, xi, 34–35, 36–37(table), 36–38
    New Mexico election for, 62–63, 69, 71
    New York Latinos in, 199–200
    Texas election for, 124–127
Houston, Texas, 116

Ickes, Harold, 192, 194
Ideology, political, 186, 204
Illinois
    demographics, 147
    Latino political power in, 149–150, 164–166, 167(n3)
    1992 presidential campaign in, 23, 25, 27
    1992 presidential election in, 30, 156–160, 157(table), 158(table), 159(tables), 161(table)
    and 1992 primary, 9–10
    1992 state and local elections, 160–164, 167(n2)
    redistricting, 153–155, 166, 167(n1)
    voter registration in, 156
Illinois Hispanic Democratic Council, 156
IMAGE, Inc., 59, 60, 61
Immigration
    and Colorado politics, 84
    effect on participation, 6
    Illinois politics and Mexican American, 152–153
    and presidential politics, 12–13, 17, 178
Integration, in New Mexico, 53–54
Intra-Hispanic alliances, 149, 153, 166
Issues
    anti-immigration, 12–13, 17, 84, 152–153, 178
    and Arizona initiatives, 104
    and Bush campaign, 87
    and Clinton campaign, 86
    and Colorado initiatives, 89–91
    and Cubans in Florida, 183
    Latino organizations and agenda-setting, 38–40, 44(n18)
    Latino political participation and, 7, 133, 136, 137
    and Latinos at 1992 Democratic National Convention, 43(n7)
    and New Mexico politics, 64
    and New York politics, 189, 190–191, 195–196
    and presidential race in Illinois, 157
    and Texas, 117, 128
    white backlash and Latino, xii–xiii, 41–42, 132–133, 139
    See also Campaigns, 1992 presidential

Jackson, Jesse, 8, 192, 195, 200, 201
James, Hulbert, 192
Jarabo, José Renaldo, 198
Jews, 191–192
Julia, Raúl, 189

Kennedy, Bobby, 56
Kennedy, John, 19

Kerrey, Robert, 8, 78
King, Alice, 58
King, Bruce, 56, 58
Kristol, William, 191

Labor unions, 195
Lamm, Richard, 84, 85
LaRouche, Lyndon, 63
Latino Institute, 155
Latino Issues Forum, 137
Latino National Political Survey (LNPS), 4
Latino organizations
  agenda setting in 1992 by, 38–40, 44(n18)
  and Arizona, 99, 100–101, 108
  effectiveness of, xi–xii, 3, 136–137
  in Florida, 180
  and Illinois politics, 149, 155, 156, 163
  in Texas, 118
  See also Leadership, Latino
Lattuzio, John, 65
Laurenzo, Ninfa, 16
Leadership, Latino
  California, 141, 142, 144
  and Clinton campaign strategy, 19
  Florida Cuban, 171, 177
  and Illinois politics, 155, 164
  and Latino political power, xi–xii, 3, 7, 108, 135–136
  New York and Puerto Rican, 187, 188, 193–194, 198, 204–205
  in Texas, 116
  See also Latino organizations
League of California Cities, Latino Caucus, 137
League of United Latin American Citizens (LULAC), 11, 14, 117, 137
Lehman College, 190
Leifman, Steve, 182
Linares, Guillermo, 188, 194
LNPS. *See* Latino National Political Survey
Lobato, Francesca, 57
Local/statewide elections
  Arizona initiatives, 104
  Colorado initiatives, 79–83(tables), 89–91, 93
  and Illinois, 162–164, 165–166
  and Latinos in 1992, 35
  in New Mexico, 63
  See also House of Representatives, U.S.; Senate, U.S.; State legislatures
López, Vito, 192

Los Angeles, 140, 141–143, 142(table)
  riots, 13, 18
Lucero, Carlos, 84–85
Luján, Edward, 64, 67
Luján, Manuel, Jr., 17, 26, 65
LULAC. *See* League of United Latin American Citizens
Luna, Al, 126
Luna, Casey, 58

MAD. *See* Mexican American Democrats
Madrid, Patricia, 58
Malave-Dilan, Martín, 192
MALDEF. *See* Mexican American Legal Defense and Education Fund
Marist College, 193
Márquez, Alfredo, 101
Martínez, Bob, 26, 78
Martínez, Matthew, 140
Martínez, Raymond, 59, 65–66, 67, 68
Martínez, Richard, 13
Martínez, Román, 127
Más Canosa, Jorge, 21, 174, 176
Massachusetts, 41
Mateo, Fernando, 196
McCarthy, Sheryl, 190
McGovern, George, 200
McNamee, Stephen, 101
Media
  Bush use of Spanish-language, 27, 44(n14), 87
  Clinton use of Spanish-language, 23, 86
  in Florida, 177
  in Illinois, 149, 162, 164
  in New Mexico, 59, 68, 71
  in New York, 187, 193, 194, 202
  and NHLA, 39
  Perot use of Spanish-language, 28
  role in maximizing Latino political power, 136
Menchaca, Martha, 6
Méndez, Olga, 192, 193
Menéndez, Robert, 34, 40
Mexican American Democrats (MAD), 9, 116, 118, 123
Mexican American Legal Defense and Education Fund (MALDEF), 24, 99, 137, 155
Mexican Americans
  and Clinton campaign, x, 9
  and Democratic National Convention, 197

Index

elected officials in 1992, xi, 34
  in Illinois, 152–153, 160, 162, 167(n3)
  in New Mexico, 53
  and 1988 election in Texas, 8
  participation and demographics of, 5
  Republican party affiliation, 7
Meyers, Larry, 121
Miami-Dade County, Florida
  congressional/state races, 178–180, 179(table), 181–182
  demographics of, 171–172, 172(table)
  political power of Cuban Americans in, 169, 172–173, 177–178
  and presidential politics, 12, 27
Miami Herald, 174
Miller, Bill, 123
Miringoff, Lee, 193
Mobilization, voter
  congressional campaigns and, 36
  importance in Texas of, 128
  and Latino vote in Arizona, 99, 108–109
  in maximizing Latino influence, 5–6, 7, 38, 42, 135, 136, 137
  See also Participation, political; Registration, voter; Turnout
Molina, Gloria, 14, 15, 22, 86, 139, 143, 194, 197
Mondale, Walter, 14, 175, 200
Montoya, Regina, 116, 121
Morales, Dan, 15, 118
Morales, Esai, 86
Moseley-Braun, Carol, 164
Muñoz, Chris, 78
Murray, Richard, 125
MWNEVRP (Midwest-Northeast Voter Registration Project), 155, 156

NAFTA. *See* North American Free Trade Agreement
NALEO. *See* National Association of Latino Elected Officials
Nance, James, 63
Naranjo, Emilio, 58
National Association of Hispanic Journalists, 14
National Association of Latino Elected Officials (NALEO), 4, 14, 24, 95, 119, 137, 201
National Council of La Raza (NCLR), 13, 40–41, 137, 200
National Hispanic Leadership Agenda (NHLA), xi–xii, 38–40, 41, 44(n18), 202
National Hispanic Leadership Conference, 38
National Rainbow Coalition, 195–196
National Urban League, 201
National Women's Political Caucus, 123
Native Americans, 100, 101–102
NCLR. *See* National Council of La Raza
Negative campaigning
  1992 Democratic, 191
  1992 Republican, 16, 17, 26, 27, 28, 67–68, 87
New Jersey
  and 1992 election, 31–33, 35, 41
  1992 presidential campaign in, 23, 24, 25, 27
New Mexico
  demographic statistics for, 51
  integration of Latinos in, 53–54
  Latino political participation in, 54–55, 54(table)
  and 1992 election, 31–33, 35, 41, 68–72
  1992 presidential campaign in, 23, 24, 25, 27, 65–68
  1992 primaries in, 55–63
  1992 state party conventions, 63–65
New Mexico AFL-CIO, 58
New Progressive party (NP), 189
New Progressive party (PNP), 198
Newton, Frank, 39
New York
  demographics, 147
  electoral law in, 44(n17)
  Latino political influence in, 185–187, 204–205
  and 1992 election, 30, 34, 203–204
  1992 presidential campaign in, 23, 25, 27, 193–203
  and 1992 primary, 10, 187–193
  redistricting and local representation, 198–200
New York Newsday, 190, 193, 196
New York Post, 189
New York Times, 10, 185, 196
New York Times/CBS News poll, 193
NHLA. *See* National Hispanic Leadership Agenda
Niño, José, 16, 202
North American Free Trade Agreement (NAFTA), 60
Noticias del Mundo, 189, 193

"Not Invited to the Party: Hispanics and the 1992 Presidential Campaign" (NCLR), 40
Novello, Antonia, 26
NP. *See* New Progressive party

Obledo, Mario, 60
O'Keefe, Michael, 197
Olivas, Ernest, Jr., 26
Ortega, Rubén, 100
Ortiz, Carmen, 196
Ortiz, Solomon, 39, 202
Otero, Jack, 15, 194
Owens, Major, 199

Pachon, Harry, 4, 119
Participation, political
    in Arizona, 98–99, 103, 108–109
    and Cuban Americans, 43(n3)
    factors influencing Latino, 5–6, 133, 135–137
    in Florida, 182
    and Illinois Latinos, 156, 157–158, 165
    Latino 1992 turnout, xii
    and Latinos in New Mexico, 54–55, 54(table)
    and New York Latinos, 202, 205
    See also Registration, voter; Turnout
Party affiliation
    in Arizona, 95, 98, 105
    in California, 134
    in Colorado, 77–78, 79–83(tables)
    in Florida, 172, 173–174
    in Illinois, 160, 165
    and Mexican Americans, 7
    in New Mexico, 54–55, 56
    in Texas, 43(n5), 114–115, 128
Pastor, Ed, 101, 102, 103
Peña, Federico, 86
Pérez, Carmen, 15
Pérez, Laree, 65
Perot, Ross
    and Arizona, 105, 106
    in California, 131, 138, 139
    and Colorado, 86, 88
    effect on 1992 election, xiii, 15
    in Florida, 177
    in Illinois, 159
    and New Mexico, 62, 71
    and New York, 196, 203–204
    1992 campaign, 17–18, 28–29, 39
    and 1992 polls, 18, 43(n8), 68–69, 86
    and Texas, 119

Political activism
    and Latinos in Arizona, 100–101
    role in Latino turnout, 106
    See also Latino organizations; Leadership, Latino
Political parties. *See* Democratic party; Party affiliation; Republican party
Political power
    Arizona and Latino, 95–96, 105–109
    California and Latino, 131–132, 143–144
    Colorado and Latino, 75–76, 78, 85, 88, 91–93, 92(table)
    factors influencing, ix–x, xi–xiii, 4–6, 6–7, 132–137, 182
    Florida and Latino, 169–170, 177–178, 181–183
    Illinois and Latino, 149–155, 164–166, 167(n3)
    New Mexico and Latino, 70, 72
    New York and Puerto Rican, 185–187, 204–205
    1992 Latino, ix, x–xi, xiii, 3, 29–34, 32(table), 40–42
    Texas and Latino, 119, 121, 122, 125, 128
Polls
    accuracy of, 144(n1)
    Arizona, 95, 105
    Colorado, 85–86
    Florida, 176
    Illinois, 161–162
    New Mexico, 61–62, 68–69
    New York, 192–193, 196, 200, 201
    during 1992 campaign, 18, 43(n8)
Popular Democratic party (PPD), 189
Population, 1, 51, 111, 147
    Arizona, 96, 98
    Florida, 170–171
    Illinois, 151, 152–153, 152(tables)
    Texas, 114
    See also Demographics
Powell, Adam Clayton, IV, 194
Powell, Ray, 56
PPD. *See* Popular Democratic party
Primaries, 1992, 3, 7, 8–13, 43(n4)
    in California, 140–141, 142
    in Colorado, 78–85, 93
    in Illinois, 156–159, 157(table), 158(table), 159(Table 7.6), 161–162, 163–164
    in New Mexico, 55–63
    in New York, 187–193, 198–200
    in Texas, 116–117, 123, 124–126, 127

Index

PRLDEF. *See* Puerto Rican Legal Defense and Education Fund
Projections, ix, 7
   and California, 131–132, 137
   in Texas, 114, 115
Proposition 187, xii
Puerto Rican Legal Defense and Education Fund (PRLDEF), 24
Puerto Ricans
   elected officials in 1992, 34
   in Florida, 171
   in Illinois, 153, 160, 162
   and 1992 presidential election, 187–193, 193–203, 203–204
   participation and demographics of, 5
   political influence in New York, 185–187, 204–205
   redistricting and representation, 198–200
Puerto Rico, 189, 198

Quayle, Dan, 57–58
Quayle, Marilyn, 67
Quezada, Leticia, 141

Race-based campaigning, 133, 195–196
Ramírez, Carlos, 193
Ramírez, Roberto, 189, 193
Ramos, Jorge, 190
Rangel, Charles, 199, 201–202
"Rebuild America," 195
Redistricting/reapportionment
   and Arizona, 99–103, 106–107
   and California, 140, 142, 143–144
   in creating electoral opportunities for Latinos, xi, 34, 133
   and Florida, 170, 179, 180–182
   and Illinois, 150, 153–155, 166, 167(nn 1, 2)
   and New Mexico, 62, 70
   in New York, 187, 198–200
   and Texas, 116, 128
   See also Representation, Latino
Registration, voter
   in Arizona, 99, 100–101, 103, 108
   Democratic efforts in, 201
   and Florida, 172
   and Illinois, 156, 157–158
   in maximizing Latino influence, 135–136
   in New York, 202
   in Texas, 114

Representation, Latino
   in Arizona legislature, 99–103, 109(n2)
   in Bush 1992 campaign, 26, 40
   in Bush administration, 201
   California elected officials, 132, 137, 139–143, 140(table), 142(table)
   in Clinton administration, 121, 204
   on Clinton campaign staff, 8–9, 14, 19, 22, 40, 86
   effect of redistricting on, 70, 99, 106–107, 116, 143–144, 154, 166, 180–181, 187. *See also* Redistricting/reapportionment
   in Florida, 169–170, 179, 180–181
   in Illinois, 154, 155, 162, 166
   New Mexico elected officials, 54, 63, 69, 70
   in New York, 187, 199–200
   in state legislatures, 35
   Texas elected officials, 121–124, 127, 128
   See also Delegates, national conventions; Candidates
Republican National Convention, 15, 16–17
   Arizona delegates to, 104–105
   Colorado delegates to, 84
Republican National Hispanic Assembly, 194
Republican party
   in Arizona, 101–102, 106
   in Colorado, 84
   in Florida, 179, 180, 181
   in Illinois, 150, 155, 164, 165, 166
   Latinos and the extreme right, 186, 204
   Mexican American affiliation, 7
   in New Mexico, 56, 64–65, 71
   1992 campaign rhetoric, xi
   and 1992 congressional/state races, 34
   1992 party platform, 3, 17, 43(n9), 104–105
   1992 primaries, 10–13
   in Texas, 114–115, 124–125
   See also Bush, George; Republican National Convention
Reyes, Ben, 34, 124, 125, 127
Reyna, John, 104–105
Reynoso, Cruz, 60
Richards, Ann, 123
Richardson, Bill
   and Clinton appointments, 204
   Clinton campaigning by, 58, 66, 86
   and Democratic National Convention, 15, 64

and Hispanic PAC-USA, 194, 197
1992 New Mexico reelection, 63, 69
Ríos, Freddy, 124–125
Ríos, George, 194
Rivera, Dennis, 186, 187, 188, 189, 190, 194–195, 198, 200, 205
Rivera, José, 194
Rivero, Felipe, 12
Rockefeller, Jay, 8
Rocky Mountain News, 85
Roemer, Gloria Gonzales, 84
Romer, Roy, 89
Romero, Ed, 61
Rosado, David, 189–190
Ros-Lehtinen, Ileana, 16, 26, 39, 179
Roybal, Edward, 15, 35, 140, 141, 143, 197
Roybal-Allard, Lucille, 38, 140

Sanabria, Herb, 60
Sánchez, Manuel, 57
Sánchez, Raymond, 15, 58
Sánchez, Shiree, 26
Sandoval, Marcella, 9, 22
Santos, Miriam, 194, 197
Schiff, Steve, 69
Schumer, Charles, 188
Segarra, Ninfa, 193
Senate, U.S.
    and Colorado, 79–83(tables), 84–85, 88
    and Florida, 178
    and Illinois, 164
Serna, Eric, 58
Serrano, José, 15, 187, 188, 191, 193, 198, 199, 200, 204, 205
Sharpton, Reverend Al, 202
Shaw v. Reno, xi
Shorris, Earl, 4
Sister Souljah, 195
Skeen, Joe, 69
Slatter, David, 124
Socioeconomic status
    and Illinois politics, 151, 151(table), 160
    and Latinos in Arizona, 96–97, 97(table), 98
    and Latinos in Colorado, 77
Solárez, José, 101
Solarz, Stephen J., 44(n17), 200
Soliz, Juan, 161–162
Sosa, Dan, Jr., 62–63, 69
Sosa, José, 16, 26

Sosa, Lionel, 26, 67
South Americans, 203
Southwest Voter Registration and Education Project (SVREP), 13, 99, 100, 108, 137
State legislatures
    Arizona, 99–101, 109(n1)
    California, 132, 137, 139, 141–143, 142(table)
    Florida, 169–170, 180–181
    Illinois, 154–155, 162–163
    and Latinos in 1992, xi, 35
    New Mexico, 70, 71
    New York, 199
    Texas, 127, 128
    See also Local/statewide elections
SVREP. *See* Southwest Voter Registration and Education Project

Tax limitations, 89–90
Tejeda, Frank, 36, 124
Term limitations, 104, 133
Texas
    demographics, 111, 114, 115(table)
    electoral law in, 43(n10), 44(n17)
    factors in Latino influence, 113, 114–116, 128
    Latino Republicans in, 43(5)
    and 1988 election, xiii, 8
    and 1992 election, xii, 33, 34–35, 119–121
    1992 presidential campaign in, 19–20, 23, 24, 25, 27, 117–118
    and 1992 primaries, 9, 10, 11, 43(n4), 116–117
    state and congressional offices, 121–124, 122(table), 124–127
Tomás Rivera Center, 137
Torano, María E., 194
Torres, Esteban, 15, 140, 194
Torricelli bill, 20–21, 27, 174, 175, 176, 178
Towns, Edolphus, 199
Treviño, Jesse, 9
Trujillo, Art, 56, 64
Trujillo, Frank, 59
Trujillo, Larry, 78
Tsongas, Paul, 8, 10
    and Colorado primary, 78
    in Illinois, 10, 157, 158
    and New Mexico primary, 57, 61, 62, 63
    and New York, 10, 192
    and Texas, 9, 43(n4), 117

Index

Turnout
  accuracy of statistics on, 44(nn 15, 16)
  in Arizona, 95-96, 99, 103, 104, 105–106, 107(table)
  Clinton campaign focus on, 23–24, 86, 118
  and Colorado, 85, 88, 93
  Latino 1992, 29–30, 31(table), 33–34, 42
  and Latino political power, xii, 135
  and New Mexico, 54, 54(table), 55, 63, 70
  and New York, 193, 203
  and 1992 congressional races, 36–37(table), 38
  in Texas, 117, 118–119, 120–121, 120(table), 121–123, 122(table), 126

Unity, Latino, 134, 182, 183
University of Colorado at Boulder, 86
Univisión, 15
Urban Summit, 190–191
Uribe, Charles, 196

Valenzuela, Edward, 100
Vásquez, Gaddi, 16, 26
Velázquez, Nydia, 194, 200
Veterans Coalition for Bush/Quayle, 202
Villalpando, Catalina, 16, 17, 26, 27, 43(n13)
Villamil, Antonio, 202
Villareal, José, 14, 19, 22
Viva Bush!, 25–28, 118
Voter Research and Surveys, Inc., 70, 193

Voting
  drop-off for Colorado initiatives, 91
  early, 103
  rights, 24, 43(n11)
  unified Latino, 134, 182, 183
  See also Registration, voter; Turnout
Voting Rights Act (VRA), xi, 6, 102, 133, 143–144, 155, 180, 199

Washington, Harold, 154
Washington Heights, New York, 197
Weiss, Ted, 188
White backlash, xii–xiii, 41–42, 132–133, 139
Whitmire, John, 127
Wiggins, Charles, 101
Wilder, Douglas, 8
Williamson, Barry, 123
Women
  California elected officials, 132
  Cuban Women for Clinton, 41
  and Illinois senatorial race, 164
  Latina candidates and elected officials, 35, 121, 123, 200
  turnout in Texas of, 117

Youth Development, Inc., 57
Yzaguirre, Raúl, 13, 39, 200–201, 202

Zapanta, Al, 202
Zia Research Associates, 61, 68